The Original 1913 Federal Income Tax Form

(Check those tax rates)

TO BE FILLED IN BY COLLECTOR.	**Form 1040.**	TO BE FILLED IN BY INTERNAL REVENUE BUREAU.
List No.	**INCOME TAX.**	File No. ....
.... District of	**THE PENALTY** FOR FAILURE TO HAVE THIS RETURN IN THE HANDS OF THE COLLECTOR OF INTERNAL REVENUE ON OR BEFORE MARCH 1 IS $20 TO $1,000.	Assessment List ....
Date received	(SEE INSTRUCTIONS ON PAGE 4.)	Page .... Line ....

UNITED STATES INTERNAL REVENUE.

RETURN OF ANNUAL NET INCOME OF INDIVIDUALS.

(As provided by Act of Congress, approved October 3, 1913.)

RETURN OF NET INCOME RECEIVED OR ACCRUED DURING THE YEAR ENDED DECEMBER 31, 191....

(FOR THE YEAR 1913, FROM MARCH 1, TO DECEMBER 31.)

Filed by (or for) .... of ....

(Full name of individual.) (Street and No.)

In the City, Town, or Post Office of .... State of ....

(Fill in pages 2 and 3 before making entries below.)

1. Gross Income (see page 2, line 12) .... $ _____

2. General Deductions (see page 3, line 7) .... $ _____

3. Net Income .... $ _____

Deductions and exemptions allowed in computing income subject to the normal tax of 1 per cent.

4. Dividends and net earnings received or accrued, of corporations, etc., subject to like tax. (See page 2, line 11).......... $ _____

5. Amount of income on which the normal tax has been deducted and withheld at the source. (See page 2, line 9, column A)..

6. Specific exemption of $3,000 or $4,000, as the case may be. (See Instructions 3 and 19) ....

Total deductions and exemptions. (Items 4, 5, and 6)........ $ _____

7. Taxable Income on which the normal tax of 1 per cent is to be calculated. (See Instruction 3). $ _____

8. When the net income shown above on line 3 exceeds $20,000, the additional tax thereon must be calculated as per schedule below:

	INCOME.	TAX.
1 per cent on amount over $20,000 and not exceeding $50,000....	$ _____	$ _____
2 " " 50,000 " " 75,000....		
3 " " 75,000 " " 100,000....		
4 " " 100,000 " " 250,000....		
5 " " 250,000 " " 500,000....		
6 " " 500,000....		
Total additional or super tax		$ _____
Total normal tax (1 per cent of amount entered on line 7)....		$ _____
Total tax liability....		$ _____

Other Books by the Author

Marx's Religion of Revolution
An Introduction to Christian Economics
Puritan Economic Experiments
None Dare Call It Witchcraft
Foundations of Christian Scholarship (editor)

How You Can Profit
From the Coming
PRICE CONTROLS

Gary North

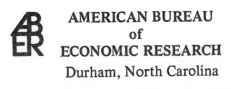

AMERICAN BUREAU
of
ECONOMIC RESEARCH
Durham, North Carolina

Copyright by Gary North, 1978

Printed in the United States of America

Library of Congress Cataloging in Publication Data

North, Gary
   How You Can Profit from the Coming Price Controls

Bibliography

1. Price regulation–United States. 2. Price regulation Germany. 3. Wage-price policy–United States. 4. Inflation United States.

Library of Congress Catalogue Number: 78-50896
ISBN number: 0-930462-01-7

To

Prof. Hans Sennholz

who saw first-hand what
this book predicts.

WILL THE SOCIAL SECURITY SYSTEM SURVIVE?

(This exchange between Sen. William Proxmire of Wisconsin and James Cardwell, Commissioner of the Social Security Administration, took place on May 26, 1976:)

PROXMIRE: " . . . There are 37 million people, is that right, that get social security benefits."

CARDWELL: "Today between 32 and 34 million."

PROXMIRE: "I am a little high; 32 to 34 million people. Almost all of them, or many of them, are voters. In my State, I figure there are 600,000 voters that receive social security. Can you imagine a Senator or Congressman under those circumstances saying, we are going to repudiate that high a proportion of the electorate? No.

"Furthermore, we have the capacity under the Constitution, the Congress does, to coin money, as well as to regulate the value thereof. And therefore we have the power to provide that money. And we are going to do it. It may not be worth anything when the recipient gets it, but he is going to get his benefits paid."

CARDWELL: "I tend to agree."

(The Social Security System, Hearings Before the Joint Economic Committee, Congress of the United States, 94th Cong., 2nd Session. May 26 and 27, 1976, pp. 27-28. Washington: Government Printing Office, 1977.)

TABLE OF CONTENTS

Senator John W. Bricker
The Senate
Washington, D.C.

Dear Senator Bricker:

   In my opinion I would suggest that if the Senate & Congress would
abolish that awful law of supply and demand it would increase production.
Stop hoarding for high prices as is now being done by the government and
others. Push all products for sale to the markets and start competition. The
law of supply & demand is a burden to the Consumer because they foot all
the bills.
   Trust you and your fellow senators and congressmen will act promptly.

Gerald V. _____

(Taken from *Dear Mr. Congressman*, by Juliet Lowell [New York: Duell,
Sloan and Pearce, 1948], p. 91.)

INTRODUCTION

A word of warning: some of you aren't going to believe what I have to say in this book. You won't believe that the events I am predicting could happen in America. Let me say from the start, some of the events have already happened in America, as recently as 1974.

Some of you won't be skeptical. Some may remember wartime price controls during World War II and Korea. Others may know how difficult it is to find a decent apartment on rent-controlled Manhattan Island. Some may be from Europe, in which case you know all too well that what I write about in this book can happen. For these people, this book will recall terrible memories. For this, I can only say, "I'm sorry." Not for the memories, but for the grim prediction that it can happen here, in America, in the land of the free. The partially free.

I am deadly serious about the possibilities described in this book. Most of the possibilities are unpleasant. Most of the people in this country will face painful decisions if the kinds of events I describe do take place. Yet for some—a tiny handful—the crises I outline in this report will be **bonanzas**—incredibly profitable opportunities the likes of which we have never seen in peacetime America.

Back in 1973 and 1974, price controls were in force. The chemical industry was hard hit by the controls, since they had been put on two years before, prior to the Arab oil embargo. Because of the shortages in the chemical industry a new profession grew up overnight: chemical brokering. *Business Week* (Feb. 9, 1976) describes what took place: "In the shortage years of 1973 and 1974, a special group of salesmen called chemical brokers thrived on the voracious demand for chemicals that were in short supply. They arranged barter deals and took markups ranging from 10% to 100% on an annual volume of business estimated at more than $600 million." The stories of overnight millionaries and multimillionaries of this period have become legendary within the industry. The significant fact, however, is that insiders within the petrochemical industry are now taking steps to take advantage of the next wave of price controls and shortages. One group is the American Chemical Exchange, a Chicago-based operation.

1

The directors know how important barter is during a time of controls-induced shortages; they know how crucial the middleman is.

There will be other opportunities, other industries, and other stories of instant millionaries during the next wave of price controls. What we saw in 1973 and 1974 was only a pale reflection of the possibilities for profit under a system of full-scale controls. There are risks, of course, but there are also profits.

Nevertheless, some people won't believe it. They won't **want** to believe it. Let me remind the skeptics of the reception of Harry Browne's 1969 book, *How You Can Profit from the Coming Devaluation.* The experts laughed. Then the experts howled. The experts said this amateur didn't know what he was talking about. How preposterous! He advised buying gold coins when gold was $35 per ounce and had been $35 for three decades. He advised buying Swiss francs, yet the dollar was the strongest currency in the world. The experts were wrong. Browne was right. Those who took Browne's advice made a killing.

I'm not saying that my track record is as good as Harry Browne's. Still, before Browne had taken his first seminar in free market economics, I was buying American silver coins. I started recommending the purchase of silver coins back in the summer of 1963, in the days when all American coins, from the dime to the silver dollar, were silver. They began going out of circulation in the fall of 1963. By 1967, they were completely out of circulation. Today a silver dime sells for 65 cents. I also told people to buy gold coins in 1965, when a double eagle ($20 gold piece) sold for $49.50. Today, they sell for over $425.

More to the point, in January of 1971, I specifically predicted that President Nixon would impose price and wage controls. I had warned that he probably would be forced to do this in an article which appeared in *The Commercial and Financial Chronicle* in the spring of 1969. But in 1971, I said he would, for sure. Seven months after that article was published (in *The Whole Earth Catalog),* Nixon imposed the price freeze. (To be honest, I had not thought that he would act that soon, but at least I warned people about it.)

Now I am predicting it again. **The U.S. government will be forced by public pressure to impose controls.**

He may deny it. He may say it won't be necessary. It doesn't matter what he says. It didn't matter what Nixon said. The decision will be made for him by public pressure. He will respond to that pressure. This book tells you **why** and **how** it will happen. It also gives you indicators that will help you to predict **when.**

Some people will make it big during the controls. Some people won't make it at all. Millions of Americans will see their hopes, plans, and savings wiped out if the controls are left on for over six years, and I think they will be. They will want to give up. But some people will get by rather well.

Not many, but some. They will come through the controls with their capital intact, or at least a good chunk of it intact. They will come through in a position to take leadership posts in their neighborhoods, communities, and even on a national level. I am writing primarily to this group. Yes, I think a few of my readers will hit the jackpot. (The trick then will be for them to look as though they hadn't hit the jackpot.) But the man I'm trying to reach is the middle class American who wants to protect his family, increase its assets in a time of crisis, and take a role of moral and economic leadership after the storm is over.

I am not a prophet. I have no crystal ball. But I do have a knowledge of the past. I have knowledge of economic theory. I have a knowledge of Washington politicians. After all, I worked on Capitol Hill in a congressional staff. I have seen the political beast at close range, and he is not a pleasant creature when he grows angry. Double-digit inflation will make him angry. The response of politicians to price inflation has been the same for 4500 years: impose price and wage controls. This will be the answer again.

No matter what you read in the newspapers, remember this: politicians are unable to repeal economic law. Economic law does not stop just outside the U.S. borders.

Not every event that I predict may happen will happen. There are no doubt hundreds of events that will happen that I have failed to mention. As I said, there are no crystal balls, or if there are, I don't own one. But I am confident that the types of events that I describe will take place, and the types of strategies that I outline will work, just as they have worked for 4500 years.

You will have to decide whether my logic makes sense. You will have to decide whether to take this book seriously. If you think it does make sense, then I implore you to keep my strategies in mind and begin to apply them. Do not put the book down and mutter, "very interesting, very persuasive," and then do nothing about it.

What I describe here could happen very soon. I don't know who you are, where you live, what kind of background you have, or when you are reading this book. All I know is this (as of early August of 1979): there are signs that the controls are coming.

Some of you may find parts of this book very confusing. I do my best to write clearly, but I realize that some of these facts and concepts will be very new. Not everything will be instantly clear. Never forget, something that confuses you may be "obvious" and even "elementary" to the next person. And what you find utterly clear may baffle him.

Take your time. Think about what you are reading. Mull it over in your mind. You don't have to absorb everything in one sitting. You don't have to understand every word. But you will be able to get the general picture if you finish the book. If something confuses you after three readings, go on to the next paragraph or the next page. If necessary, go on to the next chapter. You will get most of what I am saying. There is plenty of information here for everyone. Don't give up too soon.

These chapters were first published in my bi-weekly economic newsletter, *Remnant Review*. My regular subscribers pay $60 a year to get these reports. You're getting a bargain. Some people got the information before you did, but not many. My readers are a small, very special group. I hope that this book will get my main ideas before a larger audience. We need to get this information out to the public before it is too late.

Controls are coming. Not many people know this. Fewer still know what to do when they arrive. When you have finished this book, you will know more than most of the American public.

For businessmen, specialists, lawyers, and other serious researchers, I also recommend that you order a copy of a crucially important, though somewhat detailed study, *Historical Working Papers on the Economic Stabilization Program: August 15, 1971 to April 30, 1974*, published by the Government Printing Office, Washington, D.C., in 1974, a 2-volume set that sells for $14.40. It is almost unknown, even in official circles. It is the handbook for the preliminary price controllers. It will probably be the Bible of the next price control bureaucrats. It will not be available for inspection when businessmen and corporate planners really need it. (The book's order number is 0-564-606, 607.)

CHAPTER ONE
SIX DEADLY ASSUMPTIONS

Some of the facts and opinions in this survey will be familiar to some readers, but I suspect that there will be a lot of new information for everyone who reads it. I hope so, anyway. The economic issues that I treat here will be familiar in their basic outlines to most readers, but the implications for the long-run strength of the U.S. economy are not discussed very often. Ten years ago they were hardly discussed at all.

For those who haven't considered these facts, they may seem incredible. They just couldn't be true. All I can say to this kind of criticism is this: think it through. Check the facts out, and then make a decision. I am convinced that if present trends are not reversed—and politically, I don't think they can be reversed—then we are going to see massive bankruptcies. But these bankruptcies will not be declared openly. They will be concealed through a system of **repressed inflation**—the system of price and wage controls coupled with monetary expansion.

I am hitting at the very heart of men's hopes in these pages. I am not trying to scare people into action. I am doing my best to call people's attention to economic reality. Fear should not be our primary motivator in life. We should be willing to give fear its due, however. We should not take unnecessary chances. Any decision concerning the future which is not based on at least some of these facts is probably too risky.

It would be wonderful if a majority of Americans quit making any or all of the six economically disastrous assumptions that I deal with here. But they do make them, and they give little indication that they will cease making them in the near future. I would hope that none of my readers will continue to make any of them from now on. Forewarned is forearmed.

"My Pension Can Actually Be Paid Off"

If you are over 55, and if you don't live very long after your retirement, then this may be an accurate assumption. I doubt it, however. Problems with pension vesting will wipe out many dreams. So will the unwillingness of private pension funds' managers to keep bearing the risks of management. Thousands of small pension funds quit in 1975 and 1976, and the rate of drop-outs is accelerating.

The widespread use of pension funds in industry came during the Korean War. When the Federal government imposed price and wage controls, it left pensions out of the control system, so unions began making hard-nosed demands concerning pensions instead of wages. Corporations capitulated, sometimes knowingly, since they were aware of the vesting reality. Not many people stay with the same job for 30 years. They quit, or get fired, or leave for one reason or another, and they lose their pension rights. Union leaders knew this, too, but they needed "victories," so they allowed the corporations to give in on the pension question rather than wage settlements. It looked good, and it didn't cost much: the days of reckoning were (then) in the distant future. The future is rapidly approaching.

As of 1974, about 30 million workers were "covered"—a most misleading term—by some form of private pension program. This amounted to about 45% of the privately employed wage and salary labor force. The average pay-out per beneficiary (retired person) in 1974 was a paltry $2,000 per year, or under $170 per month. In recent years, these benefits have not kept pace with price inflation, and there is little reason to expect that they will keep up in the future. This is a grim prospect for anyone expecting a pension, let alone the risks of bankruptcy in the employer's program, or the other risks associated with all investment programs. The average financial reserve for each "covered" worker in 1974 was about $6,500. In short, each worker has "saved" about $6,500 for his entire retirement. Naturally, older workers have higher reserves, with the oldest having perhaps $13,000 in reserves, since they have contributed longer. How far will $13,000 go these days? (The figures appear in the *Social Security Bulletin* for June, 1976, p. 6.)

Benefits are rising to keep pace with price inflation, pressures from unions, and political pressures placed on businessmen to be socially responsible. Henry T. Blackstock of Goldman, Sachs & Co., has estimated that if pension fund assets are to keep up, by the year 2000, there will have to be literally trillions of dollars in assets. Where will pension fund managers invest the money? He concludes that "they're going to have to invest in government bonds and real estate to put that money to work" (*Business Week*, June 16, 1975). Government bonds? But where will the government get the money to pay the interest to keep the pension funds alive? There are only three choices: taxes, borrowing, or printing press money. The latter choice is always easiest for governments.

As for state and local pensions, they are in shambles. There is no single source of information on such plans, since no Federal agency supervises their management. They (unlike private pensions) are allowed to operate on a "pay as you go" system, meaning present taxes are used to pay off all retired beneficiaries, just like Social Security. There are about 2,300 public employee retirement programs, covering about 9 million employees and retired people, with total assets in the range of $90-95 billion. About 90% of this is invested in non-government securities, meaning stocks and bonds, and to a lesser extent, mortgages. This works out to about $10,000 of reserves for each potential and present beneficiary. But the major source of statistical data, the Social and Economic Statistics Administration of the Bureau of the Census (Department of Commerce), records only present assets and present payments of selected cities and states (*Finances of Employee-Retirement Systems of State and Local Governments*). These data do not include the really important figures, namely, the **expected future liabilities** of the various public pension programs. A 1975 survey of 44 Pennsylvania cities revealed that over 75% of them had pension programs that were not adequately funded. Cities tend to borrow money from pension funds to meet operating expenses, as New York City did so spectacularly in 1976. It cost taxpayers in Pittsburgh $10 million in 1974 to meet pension liabilities. The total unfunded pension liability was over $225 million. The Los Angeles police and firemen's fund had assets of $400 million in 1975 and liabilities of $1.6 billion (*Business Week,* Sept. 15, 1975). In 1975, the city of Oakland discovered that its police and firemen's retirement plan liabilities were accruing annually at a rate double the salary outlay, whereupon the benefits were lowered (*Business Week,* Sept. 13, 1976). Pension fund debt literally threatens the future survival of state and local finances. If cities go under, who will pick up the pension tab? If the Federal government does, how will it get the funds to make the massive pay-outs?

Speaking of Federal pay-outs, the National Taxpayers Union, a Washington-based research and lobbying organization, estimated in 1976 that the unfunded pension liabilities of the various Federal retirement programs stood at $500 billion. That's correct, **half a trillion dollars.** The only completely funded pension program in Washington is the one run for the employees of the Federal Reserve System, our nation's central bank. They must know something the rest of us are ignoring!

If you have a pension, ultimately, you have become a **long-term creditor** in a period of price inflation. You have given up present dollars for future dollars that will be worth far less in terms of purchasing power. You have made a mistake. The old rule of Shakespeare is a good one: neither a borrower nor a lender be; but he forgot to add, "especially a lender in a time of price inflation."

The fact is this: in a time of price inflation, no one but the very rich can afford to retire. Your best pension program is a second job into which you can someday "retire." **Forget your pension; start moonlighting.** And start investing in assets that do not get eaten up by price inflation.

What about a Keogh plan for the self-employed, or an IRA account, or a corporate pension program in a small, closely-held corporation (for example, one set up on paper in the state of Delaware for about $100)? Doesn't this allow a person a tax advantage of being able to avoid income taxes on funds invested in the program? True enough, you can postpone income taxes until you retire and (presumably) drop into a lower income bracket. This assumes that inflation, the worst tax of all, does not erode the value of your pension plan. It assumes that the government will not intervene "in order to help the small investor to manage his retirement funds" and compel you to put the whole fund, or most of it, into government bonds. This assumes that you can control the decisions concerning where your pension money will be invested. A Keogh plan or other retirement program that is administered by an insurance company or a bank trust department is going to be invested according to the "prudent investor rule," meaning it will be invested in those items that get wiped out by inflation: stocks, long-term bonds, mortgages. If you are not managing (strongly advising) your own fund, stay away from it. You are responsible for your retirement, not some trust fund employee. The prudent investor rule, as typically interpreted, is the most imprudent rule of all in time of inflation and price controls.

As you can see, when it comes to Federal "tax breaks" for the "little guy," I am almost a total skeptic. However, I recommend the following strategy for anyone who wants to risk later confiscation by the government in order to set up a retirement program with pre-tax dollars (Keogh, IRA, etc.). There are a few trust companies which allow you to select "hard money," inflation-hedging investment portfolios. If you are going to set up a retirement program, this is the only sensible way to do it. Here are my recommendations. Contact:

Lincoln Trust Co.
P.O. Box 5831 T.A.
Denver, CO 80217   or   First State Bank of Oregon
(303) 771-5100   1212 S.W. 6th
                                       Portland, OR 97201
                                       (503) 243-3525

Lincoln Trust is less expensive, but neither is excessive. I would set up an investment package like the following, after clearing it with the trust managers. Twenty per cent in short-term (91-day) Treasury bills, to provide you with liquidity. These are purchased in units of $10,000 initially, and additional units in the same transaction of $5,000. If you do not have this kind of money, then buy the T-bills indirectly in units of $1,000 by investing in a strictly T-bill mutual fund:

Capital Preservation Fund
459 Hamilton Ave.
Palo Alto, CA 95726
(800) 328-1550
(800) 982-5844 (Calif.)

Put at least another 30% in **numismatic** gold and silver coins, meaning those coins that command a collector's premium. You might try buying a complete set of the various United States gold coins, or sets of British gold sovereigns. For advice concerning a rare coin portfolio, call

Camino Coin Co.
P.O. Box 3131
San Mateo, CA 94403
(415) 341-7991

or

Numisco
175 W. Jackson
Chicago, IL 60604
(800) 621-5272

Another 30% could be in precious stones, such as diamonds, star saphires, or rubies, if you have the funds. Or if stones are not what you want, buy real estate, such as raw land on the fringes of safe small towns (under 25,000). (I do not generally recommend commercial property, since you get tied up in long-term leases—paper money-denominated fixed returns.) Finally, another 20% in other collector items, such as stamps, if you know something about the field. If not, then buy some pre-1965 "junk" silver coins, preferably dimes. My philosophy on coins is this: keep "bullion" coins—no numismatic premium, just the value of the metal—in your possession for emergencies, and go for the higher returns on rare coins in your tax-free investment portfolio. Since the return on investment is not taxed until you retire, you might as well go for the big capital gains. The collector's items will perform well in anything short of total breakdown, and if the monetary unit falls to zero, you will have your gold and silver "bullion" coins in reserve for survival. Jewels and numismatic coins perform well in a collapse, but you should try to save them for normal capital gains. Perhaps I am getting ahead of myself, since the rest of the book deals with problems and strategies, but I did want to offer some sort of possible alternative in the middle of a very pessimistic section on pensions. Convential pensions are in a great deal of trouble, or will be soon enough.

Another problem has only come to light since the spring of 1976, when Peter Drucker published his startling book, *The Unseen Revolution*, which deals with a phenomenon he calls "pension fund socialism." It seems that American pension fund managers have bought up about one-third of all shares of ownership of the 1,000 largest American corporations. Within 15 years, they will own a legally controlling interest in all American corporations listed on the New York Stock Exchange. There is tremendous significance in these facts for pensions. If the pension funds of the workers are invested heavily in American stocks, and the drift into corporate socialism (State capitalism, the corporate State, fascism, etc.) continues, then the equity of these pension funds will be destroyed. The productivity of the free enterprise system, on which all the pension hopes and dreams of American workers are based, cannot survive under socialism. It means either bankruptcy and the abolition of the pension obligations, or else it means the assumption of these liabilities by business' "partner," the Federal government.

Workers think they are going to beat the capitalist system. They think they can vote themselves benefits by expropriating the "capitalist exploiters" and the corporations. The trouble is, **they** are the owners. They are voting away their economic futures in the name of compassion, ethics, and kindness. They think they are doing it with other people's money. They aren't. When they find out, they will be outraged. Too late, of course. But stay out of their way.

"The Social Security System Is Solvent"

The Social Security system, if offered in its present form by a private insurance company, would be illegal in the U.S. It would be classified as a Ponzi scheme, named after an infamous swindler. Ponzi would offer people a high rate of return on their money, and then use the investments of future suckers to pay off the early investors. This is great, so long as there are new suckers available. Like any chain letter, the scheme breaks down when the majority of people who might be lured into the swindle are lured in. At best, it is a gambling operation in which everyone thinks he will be in early enough to reap the benefits. But the Federal government has never admitted that the Social Security system is, in fact, an enormous, compulsory chain letter.

Payments made into the Social Security program are used to cover existing obligations. It looked impressive at first, but since 1958 the birth rate has dropped, life expectancies have increased, and by the end of 1977, the **unfunded** liabilities of the system were approaching $17 **trillion**. This was the estimated deficit over the next 75 years, with the real crisis hitting around the year 2030.   At that time, there will be one retired person for every two people in the labor force. (We are not counting welfare recipients, you understand.) Since the Social Security system is tied to a cost-of-living escalator, any significant increase in price inflation could increase this deficit far more. The administrators assume 4% per year, a not very reasonable figure.

The estimate of up to $17 trillion was made by Dr. Rita Ricardo Campbell, a scholar employed by the prestigious Hoover Institution in Stanford, California. Her book, published by the Hoover Institution in 1977, provides the date: *Social Security: Promise and Reality*. What she concludes is that there is a lot of promise and a grim reality. Official estimates by actuaries with the Social Security Administration are much more optimistic than Dr. Campbell. They estimate the long-term deficit at about $4 trillion. (Does this make you feel better?) The biggest problems facing the program are these: double indexing of benefits (cost-of-living escalators) and the falling birth rate. The enacted revisions in the program which Congress voted and President Carter signed in late 1977 include a provision to "uncouple" **part** of the benefit structure from the Consumer Price Index (CPI), but not all of the benefits. Dr. Campbell's estimates of future fertility rates will probably be proven erroneous, since everyone's estimates of future fertility rates are invariably erroneous, but if she has guessed on the high side, then the deficit will be even larger, since fewer taxpaying workers will be entering the labor force to support the retired population.

The tax increases necessary to fund this deficit—whether $2 trillion, $7 trillion, or the possible "uncoupled" $8-$10 trillion—are enormous, as the bill signed into law in 1977 indicates. It may well be the largest long-term tax increase that any single piece of legislation has proposed in this nation's history. The President immediately proposed a $25 billion tax cut to make up for the increase in Social Security taxes, since these taxes could quite easily trigger a major recession. But if tax cuts are voted, then the whole Federal deficit, which includes Social Security, is right back where Dr. Campbell says it is. The deficit will have been transferred out of Social Security and into the general fund. The only way a government can fund such massive deficits is through the creation of fiat money. If that happens, pensions will not amount to much anyway. The purchasing power of the monetary unit will be reduced to a fraction of its present value—and its present value is not much to brag about.

If you are unconvinced by now that the Social Security "debate" sounds like something out of *Alice in Wonderland*, consider this fact. The *Washington Star* (April 4, 1977) reported that the Carter Administration was seriously considering the possibility of a **reduction** in the Social Security taxes. Supposedly, the tax revenues generated from Carter's proposed **energy** program were going to be allocated to finance a growing part of the bankrupt Social Security system. But when the energy program ran out of gas, Carter decided that he was ready to sign the largest single increase ever proposed in Social Security taxes. However, he assured the American people that this increase would not slow down the economy, since he intended to ask for general tax cuts to compensate for the Social Security increase. If any of this makes economic sense to you, there is a well-paid job waiting for you on the White House staff if you can convince others that it makes economic sense—"others" meaning those who are not on the payroll of the Federal government and who therefore cannot escape paying Social Security taxes.

By keeping the deficit out of the Social Security system and lowering taxes generally, the deficit is simply transferred to the general fund. What is the economic meaning of this? (The **political** meaning should be clear: no one is willing to take a stand against Social Security, and the public has to be made to believe that the program is in good shape financially, a true retirement program, in other words. It is not that politicians are somehow afraid of Federal deficits; they are afraid of deficits inside a program which is supposed to be sound by private insurance fund standards—or at least provide the illusion of being sound.) The general fund runs annual deficits of $50 to $70 billion. An increasing portion of this deficit will have to be funded by the creation of money through the Federal Reserve System. No one objects to deficits in the general fund, so increasing oceans of fiat money are therefore close to inevitable. To compensate for the astronomical increase in Social Security taxes scheduled over the next decade, the annual Federal deficits will begin to approach $100 billion a year. I believe that a $200 billion deficit is a realistic projection for fiscal 1984.

But what about the famous Social Security trust fund? Sorry about that. It is a $40 billion pile of government bonds. The administrators buy Federal bonds, the government spends the money, and the pieces of paper are called the trust fund. We pay taxes to pay the interest into the trust fund. Prior to the 1977 Social Security tax revision, the trust fund was expected to be depleted by the early 1980's. So Congress passed the huge tax increases. Guess what? The trust fund is now expected to be depleted by 1985. *The New York Times* buried the following story on page D9 (August 6, 1979). The director of the Congressional Budget Office, Alice Rivlin, wrote a letter in July of 1979 to Congressman Robert Gaimo, who heads the House Budget Committee, warning him that "there could be a significant deterioration in the financial soundness of the Social Security system during the next five years." She predicted that by 1984 (good old 1984!) the trust fund could be down to 5% of annual benefit outlays. Inflation is driving up benefits too fast, she warned — far faster than Congress had anticipated. Surprise, surprise!

Back in 1937, when this fiasco began, the maximum annual payment made by each worker was $30. His employer also paid in $30. By 1965, the total payment by both had risen from $60 to $336. (I am referring here only to the old age pension portion of the Social Security tax, not to the smaller disability portion.) In 1976, the total maximum payment climbed to $1338, employer and employee contributing half. (The total figure for old age plus disability was $1,790.) Is it any wonder that the Social Security tax is the Federal government's second largest revenue producer, ranking above the corporate income tax? The increase has been frightful in the last decade. Yet the real crisis is not expected to hit until 2000. Will anyone be solvent by then if taxes continue upward at this pace?

It shouldn't take a degree in accounting to figure out where the system is headed. It is certifiably bankrupt. When voters figure out what this program has cost them, they will quit. Only they will quit in a special way: print the money to pay off the old people, and declare price controls to turn off the cost-of-living escalator. That will get them out of a bind gracefully. Of course, it will wipe out all those who are dependent upon their Social Security payments for survival.

The Federal government plans to steal many trillions of dollars from us while we work in order to pay us a pittance when we become disabled or old. Consider a worker in 1977 who makes the maximum salary which is subject to the Social Security tax, $16,500. The employer "contributes" 5.85%, or $965, and the wage earner "contributes" an equal amount. The total "contribution" is $1930. Now the whole idea of the employer "contributing" anything is ridiculous. The employer simply hires labor services. He pays the tax collector $965. It would make no difference to him if he paid this money directly to the worker. So the worker could in fact get a raise of $965 and not hurt the employer one whit. (The worker does get a tax break when the employer "contributes" the $965, since the worker does not have to pay any income taxes on this money.) A married man with two children might pay, say, 15% of this extra $965 to the tax collector, depending on his available deductions. So take $145 (15%) away from him, for a net income of $820. Adding the two "contributions," we get $1,785 as his "savings liability." Assume that he begins his career at age 21 receiving $16,500, and assume also that the Social Security tax base remains at a $16,500 maximum. The man works for 44 years until he retires at age 65. He saves $1,785 per year, or $148.75 per month. If he receives 6% on his money and reinvests all of this interest, tax-free (which the new retirement tax laws allow for people not covered by some form of corporate retirement system), at age 65 he will have total savings of $384,409. At 6%, he can live off his capital with a $23,065 annual income and never touch his principal. He can then will the $384,409 to his heirs when he dies.

Obviously, I am making the strongest argument I can. Not everyone starts out in life earning $16,500, although if inflation rates continue as they have over the last decade, it will not be long before everyone does start out this high. Furthermore, not everyone can discipline himself to save $1,785 per year, even if the extra money were made available in the form of a Social Security tax cut. Part of the $1,785 is "disability insurance," not strictly retirement "savings." But the numbers are accurate. He could save almost $385,000 over his lifetime if he chose to. The Social Security system has in fact confiscated his right to choose.

There is an advertisement which appears from time to time in the *New York Times*. It pictures a smiling young woman who announces, "When I'm 59½, I can retire on more than $290,000 with my IRA." The IRA is a retirement program which allows people who are not covered by a corporate retirement program to set aside up to $1,500 per year in a tax-free savings account. The Dollar Savings Bank of New York is encouraging people to put their money in long-term (4 year) accounts paying 7.75% per annum. In short, the numbers are there. Compound interest works for you. Now I am not naive enough to believe in inevitable compound interest. Interest rates can change. Economic conditions change. Our economy is not experiencing 6% real growth, meaning growth without price inflation, so we should not expect to get 6% for three or four decades unless the government is pumping up the money supply (as it is doing) in order to make us **think** that we can get 6% per annum, compounded. But there is no doubt that if we were to eliminate Social Security and allow people to save the money they would otherwise have paid in taxes, the economy would benefit. The saved capital would make it easier for the economy to approach that 6% real growth figure.

The proposed revisions of Social Security do not retain that $16,500 maximum base for computing the tax. It is being raised drastically over the next decade. The *New York Times* (Nov. 28, 1977) reports that in the House version, maximum contributions—"contributions" sounds so voluntary—will hit $3,025 per worker in 1987, or 7.1% on a maximum base of $42,600. Remember, the employer is supposed to match this "contribution." This means that the average worker will be shelling out $3,000 from his own pocket. (He also pays Federal income tax on this $3,000, and he is fairly close to the 33% tax bracket, so subtract another $1,000 from his pre-tax income.) His employer will be paying $3,000. What if he were allowed to keep all $6,000 and invest it for his retirement? At the end of 44 working years, he would have a nest egg of $1,292,132. He could live fairly well on his interest at 6%, since it would amount to $77,528 per year. And he would have a nice legacy to leave his heirs, too. Instead, the House and Senate offer him a promise of $20,000 per year when he retires, and he cannot pass along his "savings" to his children.

By now you may be saying to yourself, "These figures are crazy. Nobody earns $42,000 a year for 44 years. The example is ridiculous." You are absolutely correct; **in a non-inflationary period**, almost nobody earns as much as $42,000 in even one year of his or her career, let alone 44 years. As you know, however, we are not living in a non-inflationary period. If the government stabilizes the money supply, we are almost sure to have a major economic recession, and possibly a depression. Therefore, the government is not going to stabilize the money supply, so we are going to have more price inflation pressures. Assume, though, that the government could painlessly stop price inflation. Since only about 2% of American families have incomes in the range of $42,000, there will be very little Social Security revenue generated by raising the "contribution" base to $42,000. A cynic might conclude that this proposal is based on **envy**, not on any serious hope of balancing the Social Security budget. If price inflation were to stop tomorrow, the big revenue gains would have to come from the proposed increases in the "contribution" **rate**, not the base. In other words, the middle class is so large that the middle class cannot support itself, now or in the future, by raising taxes on the rich. (I wonder when the middle class voters will finally figure this out? They haven't in 50 years.)

Nevertheless, even today average family income is higher than most people think. Women constitute over 40% of the U.S. work force. Working wives have increased family incomes considerably. In 1974, in families where the head of the household was a full-time employee, average family income exceeded $16,000, according to the *Statistical Abstract of the United States, 1975*, a government publication. Since 1974, price inflation and incomes have risen at over 6% per year. Therefore, although the 1977 figures are not yet available, it would be safe to estimate that family income approached $19,000. Remember, both wage earners are subject to the Social Security tax, so it cost them and their employers over $2,200 in "contributions."

What if price inflation continues? We return to the laws of compound interest. An annual increase of 7.3% will double the original base in a decade. (A 10% per year increase will double the original base in 7.3 years.) A 7.3% increase of prices is hardly out of the question, assuming that government refuses to impose price controls. (Naturally, I never assume this.) With 7.3% price inflation per year, the average family today will double its **monetary** income by 1987. It will bring in $38,000 in that year. Two years later, in 1989, it will earn $43,750. Since most families in this income level will have to have both adults working, the $42,000 maximum taxable base for Social Security will not be a limit at all, since that base only applies to an individual worker, not a family's total income. Where both adults are employed, and if both earn $42,000 apiece, the maximum tax base will actually be $84,000 in 1987.

If the familiar 7.3% price inflation rate continues, then by 1998 the average family will be bringing in close to $84,000. This sounds incredible, but this is what the mathematics of compounding tells us. At that time, if husband and wife earn about the same, and if the Social Security tax rate is not increased (dreamer!), the average American family will be paying $6,000 in "contributions," the employers will be paying $6,000, and each family will owe an additional $3,000 in Federal income taxes to pay for the $6,000 earned that went to Social Security. Total burden: $15,000. If you think people are grumbling about taxes today, stick around. Of course, we are only discussing Social Security. The average family will also be paying about $33,000 or so in Federal income taxes, plus state income taxes, plus property taxes. Well over half of the average family's income will go to governments.

Do you see why governments like price inflation? Year by year, everyone gets kicked into a higher tax bracket. The graduated ("progressive") income tax is first imposed in the name of soaking the rich, and then governments print up so much fiat money that prices and incomes rise so high that the middle class is forced into the same tax brackets that their parents and grandparents tried to impose on the rich. Envy catches up, eventually.

In short, it will not be very long before most families will be earning **monetary** income in the "unrealistic" $42,000 range, unless the government freezes wages. The price level will be rising, too. Most important, the **government's proportional share will be rising** because of graduated income taxes.

One of the assumptions underlying the economic analysis in this book is that monetary inflation does not stand still. To stimulate the economy, the government needs to increase the rate of monetary inflation. To "keep the boom alive," the government has to pour proportionately more and more fiat money into the economy.* We have seen the results of this fiat money-induced boom: price inflation in 1979 of well over 12% per annum, as of the middle of the year. This is worse than I predicted in the 1978 edition of this book, since I said it might go to 10% in 1979. Never forget: a 10% rate of price inflation, if it continues, will double prices in 7.3 years. As I wrote in the 1978 edition, "then we go to 12% or more." The ink was hardly dry on the pages before we did. Only a recession can slow this disastrous rate, but then the government will reinflate again, but from today's higher level of inflation.

It is the thesis of this book that price inflation will **not** continue upward at 10% per annum **in the legal, visible markets.** (It will probably exceed 10% in the black markets, but these markets are not used to calculate the government's official price indices.) The government will impose price and wage controls, probably in less than a year after prices in the Consumer Price Index exceed a 10% per annum rate of increase. Therefore, the average family will not wind up with the high monetary income necessary to fund the Social Security deficit successfully. This means that some of the government's hoped-for increase in revenues will not appear, but it also means that Social Security pay-outs will be frozen, too. Meanwhile, real prices (black-market prices) will be skyrocketing, and the retired person who is dependent on Social Security for survival will not be able to survive. His real income—purchasing power in the true markets, namely, the black markets—will shrink. The government will print up paper money to pay off its bills, and the cost-of-living escalator in the Social Security program will be frozen solid. The "beneficiaries" will be wiped out.

By now you may have concluded, as I have, that the proposed reforms in the Social Security system do not represent a long-term solution, even if the estimated $227 **billion** in additional revenues that the higher taxes should bring in over the next decade actually do materialize. The deficit over the life of the program is too large. Never forget, however, that politicians are not that concerned about salvaging the program economically. They are worried about salvaging it politically. Inflation of the money supply will allow the government to pay off the program; price and wage controls will allow the government to freeze the level of benefits per recipient; black markets will allow the politicians to blame somebody else for the awful plight of the "beneficiaries" of the Social Security program. To salvage the program politically, the politicians have to find a scapegoat. Price and wage controls will create one: the black market.

---

*For a further explanation of this theory of the economic boom, see my essay, "Repressed Depression," *The Freeman* (April, 1969); reprinted in my book, *An Introduction to Christian Economics* (Nutley, New Jersey: Craig Press, 1973), chapter 6. See also Ludwig von Mises, *Human Action* (3rd ed.; Chicago: Regnery, 1966), chapter 20.

Can the Social Security program be saved? Not without drastically reducing almost everyone's real (non-inflationary) income. Here are the only possibilities open to the government. First, raise the taxes of every worker who is covered by Social Security, meaning every worker who hopes someday to receive something from the program. This is what the **preliminary** reform program is supposed to do, although it will have to be revised again to fund the deficits that will appear in the 1990's. Yet the late 1977 reform already constitutes the largest single tax increase ever imposed in one piece of Congressional legislation. The taxes will be so great that the average worker will be heavily burdened, probably on the level of the Scandinavian worker or a British worker. This means the creation of a socialist economy in this nation. Second, the government can print up money and allow everyone's monetary income to increase. This will push workers into higher tax brackets, eventually approaching 50% of total income. This, too, is socialism. Furthermore, inflation increases the level of pay-outs for Social Security beneficiaries, so this may not salvage the program after all. Third, the government can print up the money, mail out the checks each month, and freeze prices and wages in order to freeze the pay-out per "beneficiary." This will destroy the free market, or at least the **legal** free market. The result will be shortages, declining real income for almost everyone, and the creation of black markets everywhere. It will require government rationing of goods and services. This, of course, is one form of socialism. Conclusion: **to salvage Social Security, the government will be forced to create some form of socialist economy**. This means a falling level of production and a falling standard of living. As the wise man once remarked, "You can't redistribute it if there ain't any."

I realize that some of my readers, especially older ones who have "contributed" to Social Security over the years, will probably think that I am heartless in suggesting that we should abandon the whole program. I am not heartless. I am an economic realist. I am not saying that we should abandon a wise, honest, morally sound retirement program. I am saying that the Social Security tax system is not a retirement program, that it is not financially sound, and that the whole idea is not moral. In any case, the numbers are not there. I am not proposing that we should abandon the elderly poor in this country. I am saying that **we are about to abandon them anyway**. I am saying that the Social Security system is not only morally bankrupt, but it is statistically bankrupt. I am saying that people who are more than a decade away from retirement would be absolutely foolish to plan in terms of any benefits from Social Security when they retire. I am not arguing that we ought to abandon a good program; I am arguing that we have never had a good program. Either the Social Security system will collapse, or else there will be a collapse of the monetary system which finances the Social Security system. It is a question only of **which** of the two systems will collapse, Social Security or money. Or, more ominous,

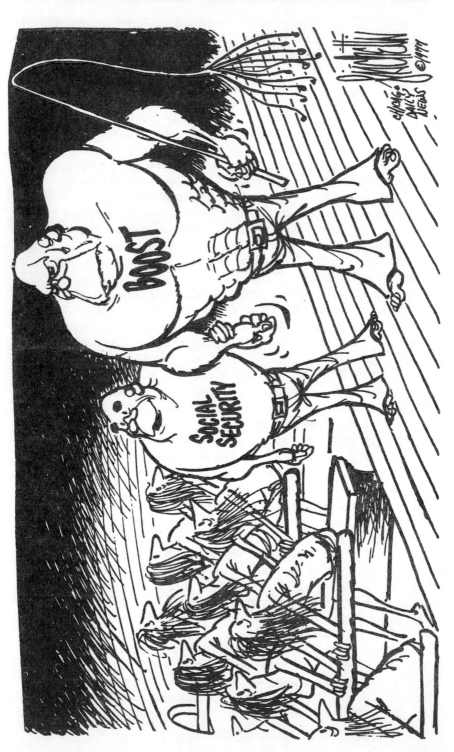

'Folks, I want you to meet my replacement'

the possibility that **both** will collapse, which I think is very likely, given the politics of Social Security.

It is estimated that by the year 2000, two workers will be supporting one retired worker. That means a tax revolt is politically inevitable. The only way that a **visible** tax revolt could be avoided would be for the two workers to be working on the side in the so-called black market, pocketing money or bartering, refusing to report the income, and putting up with the Social Security bite out of their **declared** incomes. The money will be next to worthless, so they will be only mildly upset with the fact that a large chunk of this fiat money is taken from them and paid to Social Security "beneficiaries." The word "beneficiary" will then be about as accurate as the word "contribution" is today.

A person's retirement should be planned by the person himself. Each man must save for retirement, or refuse to retire. (The whole concept of mandatory retirement grew out of the original Social Security Act, which specified age 65 as the year in which benefits would begin.) If a person is feeble, then his family should take care of him or her, not the imitation family of the Federal government, with its imitation (paper) money. If the family cannot afford it, then local churches or other voluntary agencies must come to the rescue. When we trust governments to provide for our retirement, we are in effect throwing away our futures. Governments cannot be trusted. Government money cannot be trusted. We are facing a political, economic, and social crisis, or long series of crises, precisely because we have convinced several generations of Americans that they can trust the government and the government's money. The American public has believed a lie, and the American public is about to pay very dearly for its error.

No politician dares to declare the obvious. He cannot say the system is totally bankrupt. So he will vote in the short run to solve the problem by stopping the drain of funds. He will print money, declare price controls, freeze the cost of living index, and pay off the government's debts mercilessly. It will destroy the economy, but he can always blame the capitalists. He can raise corporate taxes, thereby endangering all private pension funds, and when they go bankrupt, he can have the Federal government assume their obligations. Print money, print money: the politicians know no other answer.

Is it any wonder that Congress has exempted Federal employees from the Social Security system? Is it any wonder that Sen. Frank Church has told all those in municipal government not to pull out of Social Security (thereby reducing its income)? They would lose so many wonderful benefits, Church has pointed out—like the biggest benefit of all: participating in the great American taxpayer shearing contest. Stand still, little sheep, and get sheared.

You must not rely on Social Security. You must understand that it is finished. You must take evasive action. There is a wave of paper money coming, and you don't need it for anything other than paying off existing debt and paying the tax collector. Move fast, little sheep, or get sheared.

"The Federal Government Guarantees the Future Value of My Bank Account"

This is what most investors want to believe. It is what the bureaucrats in the Federal Deposit Insurance Corporation (FDIC) probably want investors to believe. This is the Federal agency which insures deposits up to $40,000. I suspect that this is what most citizens do believe. It isn't true.

The FDIC is an independent agency of the Federal government. Congress does not appropriate funds to run it. It is supported by insurance payments made to it by the insured banks. But these premiums are low because the Treasury is understood to be the ultimate insurer of all deposits that come under FDIC supervision. In a major monetary crisis, the Treasury would have to bail out the FDIC. Everyone knows this.

The FDIC has practically no reserves. It is clearly not a true insurance program. Consider the following statistics. As of 1975, the FDIC insured 65% of all banking deposits in the U.S., 569 billion dollars' worth out of a total of $876 billion. To back up this massive quantity of deposits, the FDIC's fund stood at a paltry $6.7 billion. This means that of the officially insured deposits, the available fund would actually be about 1.2% of the actual deposits. But in a major financial crisis, the Federal government could hardly permit 35% of all deposits to be threatened with total contraction; the money supply would shrink, and the depression would be aggravated. Therefore, the FDIC really is (politically is) responsible for the whole structure of bank deposits during a major crisis. For this, the fund constitutes .77%, that is, three-quarters of one percent.

The bad news doesn't stop here. The fund is not much of a fund. Like the so-called "trust fund" of the Social Security system, the FDIC fund is almost entirely composed of Federal debt certificates. It owns $6.5 billion of U.S. Government securities. The total assets of FDIC are about $8.3 billion, including its buildings. By now the grim reality should be apparent: FDIC isn't much of an insurance scheme.

Why does it work? Because people think it can work. It can work, too, so long as there is no major panic. It can fulfil its obligations. But in a crisis, it would have to sell its U.S. debt certificates, and who would buy them if all the banks were going bankrupt? What would people use for money if their checking accounts were being wiped out by the bankruptcy of the banking system? Obviously, there would be one major buyer: **the Federal Reserve System**. The FED would create the money to repurchase the bonds. In other words, all bank accounts will be paid off, in full, up to $40,000—paid off in paper money.

This is the point. Yes, your bank account is insured. Yes, the FDIC is strong enough to back up your bank. But in a crisis, it can survive the test only by tapping the U.S. Treasury and the Federal Reserve System. It taps the one asset available to the Federal government during a crisis: fiat money.

This means that your bank account or accounts are insured, **nominally** insured. The dollars in your bank account are safe, if it is a Federally insured bank. In a major economic crisis, all accounts are effectively insured, meaning politically insured. But the **purchasing power** of those dollars is **not** insured. In other words, the **future value** of the **present** purchasing power of your bank accounts is not insured.

The problem goes even deeper than this. Because of the implied contractual obligation of the U.S. government to stand behind the independent agency known as the FDIC, the Treasury is an engine of inflation. The **threat of depression,** in other words, is reduced primarily by the **promise of monetary inflation.** But if monetary inflation is the answer to contraction, then the value—present value—of your bank account is not only not guaranteed, it is positively denied.

Once the Federal Reserve System begins to buy Federal government debt certificates in order to provide the funds necessary to give depositors their money, the process of fractional reserve banking takes over. The Treasury bills in the FED's vault do not remain inactive. They serve as a reserve asset, and this asset then becomes the base for a new wave of credit—fiat credit—produced by the commercial banking system. There will be certain factors retarding this expansion. One of them might be the public's preference for holding cash, which shrinks the total money supply (M-1) because it substitutes cash for fractionally reserved checking accounts. Another is the unwillingness of businessmen to borrow money if they expect depression. But once people understand that the Treasury has entered the markets to bail out the banking system, and people put money back into the banks and businessmen borrow in confidence, the fractional reserve process will accelerate, for the FED may be sitting on top of billions and billions of new Treasury debt, all ready and waiting for the commercial banking system to multiply at 2.5 to one or 3 to one for every dollar's worth of new debt in the FED's vault. The money supply will soar.

This will create a wave of monetary inflation to compensate for the previous threat of contraction. Thus, the only answer that the Federal government has for deflation and depression is monetary inflation. This leads to price inflation and ultimately to the breakdown of markets under price controls. Under these conditions, the present value of men's bank accounts is worth a lot more than the discounted value of their bank accounts' future purchasing power. The present interest rates are too low to compensate for this loss of future purchasing power. The public and the bankers have not caught on yet. They will, and there goes the value of your bank account.

This is why I recommend that people convert the present value of their bank accounts to hard goods. Store that present value in something safer than paper money. Buy a home, equipment, durable goods, land outside the urban riot zones, or whatever. But don't hold on dearly to your paper money-denominated bank account simply because the account is insured by an agency of the Federal government. The number of dollars is undoubtedly insured; this fact almost insures that the future purchasing power of those dollars is not insured.

"A Depression Is Impossible Today"

Back in 1931, the Viking Book Company published a delightful, humorous little book, *Oh Yeah?* It was filled with quotes from the late 1920's by famous economists, political leaders, industrialists, and investing "experts" that assured everyone that prosperity was here to stay. It wasn't. Page after page of optimism, yet for all the optimism, one quarter of the work force in the United States was unemployed in 1933. It didn't matter how many Ph.D's had said that depression was impossible in 1929. It came anyway. Irving Fisher, Yale's prestigious economist, had predicted continued prosperity in early September, 1929; three years later, he had lost his whole fortune which had been in the millions. It sounded great in mid-1929; it was a joke by 1931.

These days, there is just as much optimism among economists, political leaders, and industrialists as there was in 1929. There can't be another depression, we are reassured; the Federal government has the means available to prevent one. All the top experts at all the top universities are agreed: the economic policies of John Maynard Keynes and his followers will prevent any future depression. These men assure us that they know how to use Federal power and Federal coercion to redistribute other people's money—**your** money—to benefit the unemployed poor. These poor people, as well as the Federal bureaucrats, will spend us into prosperity if a depression should begin. Spend ourselves rich: this is the new magic of socialist planning. This means that people on the dole will use your money to spend themselves rich, and if all goes well, you may be allowed to go along for the ride.

The government never spends a dollar unless it has first confiscated a dollar from a productive member of the society. It can get funds from only three sources: 1) direct taxation (meaning from the wallets of the middle classes); 2) borrowing (meaning that the interest payments must be paid for from taxes collected from the middle classes); and 3) the creation of money. In the third case, the government spends the money into circulation, yet nobody else has reduced his spending (by paying taxes or by loaning the government money). Therefore, prices will tend to rise as goods and services are chased by the new dollars and the old dollars. There is no new production. There is no new wealth.

The experts tell us that the new Federal spending will encourage businessmen to invest more money and create new output and new jobs. This may be true, but someone has to pay for these investments. Who pays? Those on fixed incomes who cannot spend more money as prices rise in response to the newly created inflationary dollars. It is a form of forced saving. Furthermore, the old boom-bust cycle begins once again. Businessmen invest because they think that rising demand for their goods will continue. But this requires ever-increasing quantities of **unexpected** and **unforecasted** new money; once begun, the Federal government cannot "kick the habit" of inflated money. There may be a renewed economic boom, but only because a new boom has been created by the inflated dollars. A new wave of inflation begins. The only way to stop this new wave of inflation is to stop the creation of new, fiat money. This, of course, brings back the depression.

What do we mean by depression? Usually, we mean those features of economic life that appeared in the 1930's. These included the following: falling production of goods and services, falling prices and even more rapidly falling wages, unemployed resources including unemployed people, an unwillingness of businessmen to borrow money for capital expansion, and pessimism. Another sign of depression is a falling stock market. Naturally, bankruptcies are common, as people fail to meet their debt obligations. When all of these features are visible in an economy, we say that it's experiencing a depression.

The problem with this analysis is that some of these features are present during periods of repressed inflation (price controls): reduced output of goods and services, bankruptcies, unemployment in some areas of the economy, and pessimism. What we do not see is a rising price level (illegal markets excluded, of course). We see unemployed people and unemployed resources, such as in Germany in 1946. But we do not see anyone who is unable to borrow money; nobody **wants** money, however, simply because in a totally controlled market, money won't buy anything. In a **partially** controlled market in which price controls are not enforced vigorously, borrowed funds can be used for black market purchases, and people **are** willing to borrow. But the really bad features of a depression are present in a truly repressed inflation—the price control economy. One big **difference**, however, in a controlled economy, is that **those who know how to buy and sell in the alternative (black) markets can prosper**. In a depression, it takes very different skills to prosper. **Barter**, however, can be found in both systems. During a depression, people often don't have enough money to buy goods; in a repressed inflation, people are not willing to accept money in exchange for goods.

By inflating the money supply, the Federal government can temporarily **postpone** a depression. Once the fiat money has lured businessmen, investors, and savers into making poor economic decisions concerning the future condition of the economy, the nation's capital structure becomes radically distorted. The depression is simply the market's response to this government-induced distortion, or better, series of distortions. The government can postpone the readjustment of the economy for a time, even decades, but only at the expense of more distortions, more fiat money, and more wiped-out pensions, annuities, and other long-term credit instruments. Then, when the government finally stops producing fiat money, the banking system collapses, the money supply shrinks, prices fall, and unemployment skyrockets.

There is one way, and only one way, to avoid the traditional deflationary depression at the end of mass inflation. That way is the ration-card economy. Price controls can create an economy so prostrate, so broken, so unproductive that the traditional depression never occurs. In June of 1948, Dr. Ludwig Earhard, the finance minister of Germany, announced that all bank accounts would be reduced by 90%, the reduced money supply would then be stabilized at the new level, and all price controls would be removed—the next day! He went on the radio on a Sunday night to announce this, and Monday morning millions of unemployed workers went back to work. The German economy began its 30-year economic miracle. This policy of freeing up the economy, of making men responsible for their own actions, was incredibly successful. Thus, the deflation of the money supply did not bring with it the traditional deflationary depression. Why not? Because Germany's economy was in such shambles that there was nowhere to go but up, once personal freedom to make voluntary contracts was restored. In short, repressed inflation had been so devastating that Germany avoided a traditional depression. Repressed inflation was far worse. Sadly, our own government will be forced to take this repression road as the alternative to a traditional depression such as we experienced in the 1930's. To avoid something terrible, the politicians are going to impose something far worse. If they leave the controls on long enough, if they see to it that serious attempts are made to enforce the controls, if they ration goods and services, if they continue to inflate the money supply, and if they do not allow the market to operate, yes, we may escape a so-called depression. We may find our economic system in such chaos that the ultimate deflation (or conversion to a totally new currency and credit system) will not produce a deflationary depression.

Does this comfort you?

"My Guaranteed Annuity Is Safe"

What is an annuity? Basically, it is a contract between an individual and an institution. The individual turns over to the institution a fixed amount of money, and the institution guarantees to repay the individual a fixed quantity of money, month by month, over the remainder of his lifetime.

Very often, the individual pays a nominal sum over the first 20 years of his working days, or perhaps a lump sum when he is about 40 years of age, and the institution agrees to begin paying him his monthly checks when he turns 65. The interest on his money is used by the institution to build up sufficient equity to allow the steady repayment of its obligation at the specified time. Obviously, the earlier a person turns over his money, the longer the interest can accumulate, and the smaller the lump sum has to be to assure a stated monthly income after age 65. Those who live long lives, of course, can benefit greatly. People whose parents died at age 55 would be wise not to purchase an annuity, however, if their parents died from natural causes.

What is the weak link in the annuity contract? Everyone should see it instantly, yet few people do. **The contract is denominated in paper money**. In the twentieth century, except in Switzerland, all annuities have been unsound economic bargains for the vast majority of individuals who have purchased them, and an excellent investment for institutions selling them. Back in the 1930's, companies that sold annuity contracts would feature advertisements of smiling elderly couples, sailing on lovely ships, with the caption: "We retired happily on $200 a month." Indeed they did; a person investing in an annuity in the United States in 1921 probably made a smart decision, assuming the company or institution didn't go bankrupt in the 1930's. But those making annuity contracts since then have watched those ads change over the years: $300 a month, $400 a month, $500 a month, and these days, the monthly income is left unstated. Why advertise failure?

Inflation does not create wealth. It destroys wealth by redistributing wealth and creating an unwillingness of people to invest in money-denominated, long-range capital projects. Eventually, though very late in the "game," most people catch on. But for millions of unsuspecting families, the information comes too late. The modern annuity looks good to investors, especially those who were **scarred by the depression** and still think of economic crisis in terms of falling income, falling prices, and unemployment. They remember how tough it was back in the 1930's. They remember how well people did who had guaranteed paper money incomes during an era of falling prices. They never forget the losses of their youth, almost like generals who never forget the strategies of the last (lost) war. They prepare for a crisis that will not come, or at least will be preceded by another kind of crisis that wipes out the strategies aimed at solving the crisis of the 1930's.

When a person asks the question, "Will my annuity be safe?" he really means something very different: "Will my **real income** be safe?" The salesman of an annuity can point to long years of fulfilled contracts—money-denominated contracts—and boast with pride of the certainty of payment. Too few Americans think through the implications of long-run contracts. They forget that their joy in getting a mortgage which they will pay off with "depreciated dollars" will be matched by their sorrow in being repaid in those same depreciated dollars. Yet people are optimists in America, and they want to look at the positive side. Skinning their creditors with fiat money is the bright side of long-term contracts; being skinned by their debtors is forgotten. For some reason which I cannot explain, people refuse to understand that huge corporations like insurance companies are debtors to those who buy annuities from them, and that middle-class individuals are, economically speaking, creditors to these huge firms. "How could I be a creditor to Prudential? After all, I'm just a little guy, and it's huge." So they become creditors, just like the savings and loan company that loaned them the money to build their homes. To be a creditor in times of inflation is to be foolish.

There is one possible way around this problem, the one recommended for many years by the conservative American Institute for Economic Research. Buy a Swiss annuity payable in Swiss francs. Those who took their advice in the 1950's and 1960's, and who are now receiving their monthly checks, have seen their investment appreciate by about 40%. The Swiss franc has remained stable in purchasing power, while the U.S. dollar has dropped in relation to the Swiss franc. But how many people will call a Swiss bank's branch in New York, and ask about the possibility of buying a Swiss annuity through a Swiss firm using the bank as an intermediary? Only the very wise, very informed, and very suspicious (unpatriotic, so-called) investors who do not want to be skinned alive by inflation during their retirement years. Who knows the name of the major Swiss banks, like Union Bank of Switzerland, Swiss Credit Bank, or Swiss Bank Corporation? Not the average buyer of an annuity, certainly. (If you are interested in purchasing a Swiss annuity, you might want to contact Assurex, S.A., Obstgartenstrasse 7, 8006 Zurich, Switzerland.)

In the final analysis, no one can guarantee the value of an annuity. At best, you can have the dollar income guaranteed, but in a time of inflation, this guarantee is not very meaningful. In a time of depression, meaning falling prices, or in a time of stable money, higher production, and falling prices, the annuity is a good deal. But companies tend to go bankrupt, leaving the owner of the annuity out in the cold. If you expect inflation, stay away from annuities. If you already own one, you had better not rely on it to provide you with security in your retirement years.

"The Government Will Control Inflation"

This is the heart of the problem. The government, meaning the Federal government, can control inflation. By this, I mean that the government can control the supply of money coming into use in the economy. It can regulate the banks to prohibit new deposits (checking accounts) that serve as money, prohibit the central bank (Federal Reserve System) from buying

Federal debt to be used as reserves for new money, demonetize gold or permanently freeze its official price, and refuse to create money directly by printing it. That will stop the process of monetary inflation. By stopping the process of monetary expansion, the Federal government can undoubtedly put a stop to price inflation. But as investors ought to have learned by now, this decision will lead to a severe recession and finally a depression. Politically, no existing political party can afford to take such a necessary and drastic step.

The best the government can do is to control official prices. This really ruins those who are afraid or otherwise hesitant to participate in the unofficial markets. But the government can achieve an absolutely crucial political goal, without getting blamed (for a while) for the painful and often disastrous consequences associated with the achievement of this goal. The goal is simply the reduction and outright abolition of government indebtedness. It pays off with worthless paper money. That the government can and will do. If that's what you mean when you say, "The government can control and will control inflation," then I guess you're right.

Controlling official prices means controlling the voluntary transactions of individuals who want to trade at prices above the officially decreed maximum. This is the heart of the meaning of price controls. The result, inevitably, is to reduce productivity. It is free men who produce most effectively. The price control system is almost the worst thing that can happen to a free economy. It is not as bad, perhaps, as outright confiscation by government officials, but it is close.

The free market is like a giant auction. In fact, it is a giant auction. What the government says is that the auction is not allowed to go as high as some of the participants are willing to take it. It is as if the bureaucrats came to every auction in the country and product by product, sale by sale, stepped in and decreed a maximum price on the bidders. Worse, the price controllers do it when they know that the maximum market (voluntary) bids will be above their officially permitted prices. So what happens when half a dozen bidders in a bidding battle hit a maximum price, and the auctioneer says, "That's it, gentlemen; no more bids?" What happens in an economy as complex as ours when the bureaucrats announce to 20 million bidders, "That's it, Americans; no further bids?"

Everyone knows that the auctioneer (seller) tries to get the highest possible price for his goods. We know that he can get no higher price than the final buyer is willing to pay. We don't pass laws—officially, anyway—that single out auctioneers as Price Gougers or Exploiters of the People. Yet we single out sellers (producers) as monopolists and exploiters for raising their prices to a level that other buyers are willing and able to pay. **Buyers set prices.** Or more specifically, the final buyers who are still willing and able to make the purchase set prices when they buy from the seller who is offering the lowest bid available. Prices climb because there are effective bidders left in the Great American Auction (or even the Great World Auction).

This auction has made us the richest people in the world. It has led to the incomparable growth of the American economy. The Great American Auction has enabled the poor people of this nation to live better than kings of the middle ages, better than most of the people on earth. And now we face the prospect of a controlled auction. Nevertheless, the basic problem still remains: **How are the scarce economic resources going to be allocated if the price controllers set maximum prices on the legal bids?**

This book is an attempt to answer this question. The man who finds the answer first has an enormous advantage over the other potential bidders in the Great American Auction (controlled).

CHAPTER TWO
SHUTTING OFF THE COST OF LIVING ESCALATORS

Again and again I'm asked why I think that the Federal government is going to reimpose price and wage controls. "Haven't they learned that controls don't work?" A variation on this question is, "Hasn't the American public learned that controls don't work?" These questions betray a fundamental lack of knowledge about the learning process of men who live in an era totally skeptical of permanent principles, especially economic principles. Every President is praised—Nixon excepted—for surrounding himself with "pragmatic" advisors who will not seek to impose any ideology on the public. Nixon alone is supposed to have been lax in not surrounding himself with "moral" men, i.e., economic and political Liberals who are smart enough not to get caught. The press once whooped it up for Jimmy Carter's advisors by using the same old pitch: Carter is not an ideological Southerner or an ideological Christian, just as Jack Kennedy was not an ideological Roman Catholic. All was supposedly well. In fact, the main worry among the "pragmatic" members of the press was that he kept asking us to "trust me," and no one in his right mind ever trusts a pragmatist.

The pragmatism of modern Liberals is viciously ideological. It tells us that principled action over the long run cannot "work." It tells us that we must try anything and everything in crisis situations. It tells us that basic economic laws do not and cannot exist, for that would imply a fundamental stability of nature, including human nature. Everything is up for grabs in the pragmatist's universe. And everyone is grabbing.

In the Midwestern summer school sponsored by the Intercollegiate Studies Institute back in 1972, Russell Kirk was brought in to give a speech about American conservatism. He began his lecture by relating a discussion he had with President Nixon. "Dr. Kirk," Nixon told him, "the American people are not interested in a President who serves as some kind of moral leader." Indeed they weren't, and they got just exactly what they wanted. Now they want the trappings of moral leadership, but with sufficient pragmatism attached (say, about 95%) to insure that the economic cornucopia doesn't run dry. That's what men believe today: pragmatic economic policies can and must produce a world of abundance.

This leads me to the topic at hand. In early August of 1971, Nixon and his top economic advisors discussed the possibility of imposing price and wage controls. Paul McCracken was against it—so against it that he wrote a widely distributed essay for an eastern banking publication demonstrating why controls cannot work. (It was delivered during the week of August 15—after the controls had been imposed—and McCracken then went out for the next few months to barnstorm for the controls. Then he resigned from his post as chairman of the Council of Economic Advisors. Too late.)* Prof. Sam Peltzman, who was then serving in a research spot in the Council's staff, told me later that not a single man on the council favored controls. Most of them were good economic empiricists, especially University of Chicago empiricists (pragmatists with graphs), and they all knew that controls "don't work." But Arthur Burns, chairman of the Federal Reserve System, wanted controls, and Nixon felt that he had to Do Something. So he did. He was greeted with huzzahs from every political group except big labor, i.e., unions. The National Association of Manufacturers cheered, the National Chamber of Commerce cheered, and when surveyed, 75% of randomly selected citizens cheered. The July, 1972 issue of *Nation's Business* reported that the overwhelming majority of top-level American businessmen supported Nixon. The only argument concerned the length of time Nixon should leave on the controls: forever vs. a few years. The result was predictable: the shortage economy. In short, the conservative (anti-controls) pragmatists did not carry the field against the political (Do Something) pragmatists.

Pragmatists, meaning political pragmatists, do not learn **from** history because they do not believe **in** history. They do not believe that there are lessons to be found in history, they say, because each era creates its own tentative rules. Look at American foreign policy. Intellectuals were generally isolationists at the turn of the century, but their support of domestic economic intervention (Progressivism) led them into the arms of Woodrow Wilson and "Col." E.M. House. After the debacle of World War I, they returned to isolationism, especially after 1925. By 1939 they were being dragged by Roosevelt back into internationalism. The "Munich Syndrome" dominated American foreign policy until Vietnam's losses began to affect voting behavior. Now American intellectuals are divided; they don't know whether to speak softly and carry a big stick, speak loudly and carry a big stick, or speak loudly and sell the big stick to the U.S.S.R. (on long-term, below-market loans) or the Arabs, or give the big stick to Israel. History teaches them nothing because pragmatism is at bottom the rule of chaos, the abandonment of any principles that might be used to sort out the facts of history and create meaningful, instructive patterns. They laugh at Henry

*United States Steel got McCracken to front a two-page advertisement against controls in 1976: *Reader's Digest* (July, 1976).

Ford's dictum, "history is bunk," but they believe it.

The Astronomical Federal Debt

One of the most worthy organizations deserving of your financial support is the *National Taxpayers Union* (NTU), 325 Pennsylvania Ave., S.E., Washington, D.C. 20003. The NTU publishes a monthly newsletter, *Dollars and Sense* ($15), and it provides Sen. Proxmire with most of his ammunition, e.g., Congressional junkets, obscure research projects, etc. The NTU digs up these choice tidbits as media devices; they make such good copy. But NTU also digs up important facts that the public would otherwise ignore—crucially important facts. They rummage through obscure Treasury Department reports and find out what the real level of Federal indebtedness is.

The United States government operates on a "cash" basis of accounting. Normally, even moderately large businesses use the accrual system, i.e., future income and future outlays. John N. Myer, in his useful little paperback book, *Understanding Financial Statements* (New American Library, $1.50), writes: "The cash basis is so simple as hardly to require any knowledge of accounting ... As will be shown, this method of measuring income does not produce a useful estimate of performance and, therefore, its use is more or less limited to small retail businesses where the owner is in such close contact with all phases of the operation that he does not require a better measure of performance." Or, he might have added, in cases of multi-trillion dollar economies in which no one in government wants to let the voters know what is going on "in all phases of the operation." NTU has let the accrual cat out of the accounting bag. The organization ran a full-page ad in the *Wall St. Journal* (May 14, 1976).

"The one trillion dollar misunderstanding could be the basis of national bankruptcy. One trillion dollars is the amount that the total financial obligations of the federal government grew last year.

"The so-called 'national debt' represents a small fraction of the total future financial obligations of the government. It is like the tip of an iceberg floating in a sea of red ink. Consider these Treasury Department figures:

National Debt	$ 595,000,000,000
Other Fiscal Liabilities	69,000,000,000
Undelivered Orders	130,000,000,000
Long-term Contracts	12,000,000,000
Government Guarantees	175,000,000,000
Insurance Commitments	1,481,000,000,000
Social Security Obligations	2,710,000,000,000*

*Vastly underestimated; see Chapter One.

Unadjudicated Claims	10,000,000,000
International Commitments	10,000,000,000
Miscellaneous Commitments	31,000,000,000

"This isn't even a full list of the federal government's debts. NTU recently completed a computation of the unfunded liabilities of 21 of the federal government's 60 employee retirements plans. This computation shows that taxpayers will pay out $499.155 billion in pensions, even if there is no inflation for the rest of the century. A small inflation rate for a few years would astronomically increase these pension obligations.

"Last year alone, $12 in unfunded financial obligations were created for every dollar of deficit spending. While the 'national debt' increased by $84 billion in 1975, the inflation created by deficits raised the future obligations of government at a rate of about $83 **billion per month**. In all, more than $1 trillion in future obligations were created.

"Unchecked, this can mean nothing but disaster. A vicious cycle of deficit spending and inflation is underway. Each new deficit causes greater inflation, which causes greater deficits, which cause still greater inflation.

"The longer the situation is allowed to continue, the smaller the likelihood it can be corrected. The Office of Management and Budget has predicted that a continuation of current trends (with no new programs added to the books) would lead to an annual deficit of **$700 billion** by the end of the century."

This isn't possible, right? No one could possibly have permitted such a state of affairs to have arisen, right? Some watchdog in the Congress would have blown the whistle, right? Well, the watchdog has now blown the whistle, only the dogs don't come when they're called. They are too busy passing new, unfunded legislation on the assumption that where money is concerned, there's always more where that came from. And there always is. It comes from the Federal Reserve System. The problem with money, however, is that it, unlike other economic goods, does not confer additional social utility when more of it is produced.

"STOP
THE
PRESSES!"

The cartoon conveys an important economic fact, the one made famous by Prof. Ludwig von Mises: "Only the government can take something valuable, like paper and ink, and convert it into something worthless." But an underlying presupposition of the cartoon is more specific than the cartoonist suspected (unless he is very sharp): **private** counterfeiters would stop at this point, **but only if they were out of debt.** If they could still pay off obligations denominated in paper money, they would not stop the presses. And this is the terrible fact of modern economic life in every Western, industrial nation: the governments have amassed inconceivably large debts. Furthermore, governments are not constrained by the graph in the cartoon. They will continue to print money in response to the demand of the public, for the public sees the problem in terms of rising prices—rising prices which outrun the ability of each individual or family to keep pace with. The problem is seen as a **shortage of money** in the final stages of mass inflation, as buyers and sellers anticipate the next round of monetary expansion and hike their bids (prices) in advance. The public cries out for more money. The government responds, and prices go up even faster. The bureaucrats are helpless. The government literally can't spew the paper and credit out fast enough to keep up with rising prices, as the German government learned to its dismay and confusion in 1922-23.

But if the government is the primary debtor in the economy, this fact may not disturb the bureaucracy, at least not until their salaries lag behind the salary level of those in the private sector (and eventually, this is exactly what takes place). If the government owes anything near the $5.7 **trillion** indicated by the NTU figures, the bureaucracy will be less hesitant to pay off its obligations in fiat paper money—what we would call **nominal solvency** but **actual bankruptcy.** This is perhaps the greatest curse of long-term debt: everyone thinks of himself as a debtor, rather than a creditor (i.e., future pensioner, future annuity recipient, etc.), and therefore men are less willing to resist fiat money. The bureaucracy and the politicians need to find a way to pay off their nominal obligations, but there is no way that future productivity will permit repayment or fulfillment in terms of money with stable purchasing power. There is only one politically acceptable way to default: fiat money. **What the Federal government needs is money with real purchasing weakness.** What the government wants, the government surely can get. All it has to do is sell its debt to the Federal Reserve System.

The Indexation Dilemma

On the one hand, the Federal government has a vested interest in greater **monetary** inflation, namely, its ability to pay off existing Federal debt. This is why the favorite Federal statistic among politicians, bureaucrats, and Keynesians, is the ratio between Federal debt and GNP. As nominal GNP rises—fiat-money-induced GNP—the ratio tends to drop, since the denominator (nominal GNP) is rising faster than the numerator (Federal debt, i.e., the **cash-balance** Federal debt, not the accrual system debt estimate). Thus, things look wonderful. The Federal government really isn't doing too badly after all. Indeed it isn't; but the **creditors** of the Federal government—pension funds, insurance companies, savings bonds owners—are getting destroyed. As Milton Friedman so aptly put it, the U.S. Treasury Department is the biggest bucket shop in the world. (A "bucket shop" is a company which sells commodities on margin but does not cover these purchases in the cash or futures market. This is illegal if run privately.) Friedman might have added that Social Security is the biggest Ponzi scheme in the world, i.e., a system that promises to pay high returns, but which pays off to earlier investors with funds collected from new investors. It, too, is illegal if operated privately. But the Federal Reserve System stands behind the Federal Ponzi scheme, guaranteeing that there will never be a day when new sources of pay-out funds are not available for distribution.

On the other hand, the Federal government is presently imperiled by greater **price** inflation. This is because Social Security payments are tied to a cost of living clause. As the consumer price index (CPI) rises (and with monetary inflation, it won't fall), the Federal debt, especially the accrual system debt, necessarily rises. Increasing benefits are literally bankrupting the Social Security system. They are selling off the Federal debt certificates in the Social Security "trust" fund. They have no choice. This is why the huge increase in Social Security "contributions" became necessary.

But it is not simply the Federal pensioners and Social Security recipients who are "indexed." It also includes millions of union members whose firms have obligated themselves to meet cost of living increases. There will be thousands of bankruptcies if the government does not make available sufficient fiat funds to allow businesses to meet their nominal obligations. Yet this is not going to answer the long-term problem. We now face this crisis: there is the looming problem of "declining real money balances." As inflationary expectations take over, the public bids for goods and services wildly, and prices rise proportionately faster than the money supply increases. On the other hand, as we saw in 1975, the policy of monetary stabilization   **also** leads to the "real money" crisis—prices rising faster proportionately than the money supply. The policy of monetary inflation, once it produces high inflationary expectations among the consumers, cannot be stopped without a period of so-called declining real money balances, whether the government adopts mass inflation policies or stable money policies. With millions of laborers tied to a cost of living escalator clause, bankruptcies are guaranteed, for neither .the various governments nor private firms will be able to meet their contractual obligations once inflation expectations take the price level to new levels. They cannot print the money fast enough to keep up. In short, fiat money is only an interim solution to the problem of default. Fiat money can only mask the default in the early and middle stages of mass inflation, **if the prices are allowed to rise freely**.

The Politically Inevitable Solution: Controls

The final clause is the tip-off. There is no other politically acceptable solution. The bureaucrats must mask the effects of the masked default. They have to escape from the burdensome Federal liabilities that are tied to the cost of living index. Without the stabilization of the **official** price indices, the Federal government, not to mention private industry, cannot escape the debt burden, for at the end of every mass inflation, prices outrun the expansion of the money supply. The existence of price indices helps to tear off the mask of nominal solvency, revealing actual default. But where there is an official price index there is also the possibility of an official solution. The solution is a price freeze.

I first offered this thesis on the cost of living escalators in the middle of 1976. It appeared in *Remnant Review* (June 2). *Remnant Review* is conservative in ideology, and its readers are presumably believers in the free market economy. It was therefore of considerable interest to me to read that Prof. Lester Thurow of the Massachusetts Institute of Technology, the most radical economist who was an advisor to candidate Jimmy Carter (though not, apparently, to President Jimmy Carter), offered a very similar analysis in an essay which appeared on the editorial page of the *Wall Street Journal* some 15 months later (Sept. 12, 1977). He writes:

> The U.S. economy is not 100% legally indexed, but it has rapidly become heavily indexed since 1974 with the introduction of *de jure* and *de facto* escalators by government, industry, and labor. Cost of living escalators are increasingly being built into government programs and wages. . . .
> Basically there are three policy options. Policymakers could attempt to crack the current system of private indexation by creating truly enormous quantities of idle resources. If policymakers were willing to recreate the Great Depression they might be able to destroy the current system of private indexing, but this would require an enormous price in terms of lost output and private suffering. The second option is simply to sit back and admit that there is nothing that can be done about the inflation rate. Since the economy is almost completely indexed informally, the indexing might as well be made formal to cover those small parts of the economy that are not now protected by cost of living clauses. After all, with indexing inflation does not hurt anyone—or so the argument goes.
> If neither of these solutions is acceptable, the only remaining solution is "incomes policies." What the incomes policies have to do is clear. How to do it is much less clear. . . . Converting the current system into a legally indexed system would give the government a

handle to reduce the allowable index adjustment below the previous year's rate of inflation, but enforcing such a reduced escalator would be equivalent to wage and price controls.

When Prof. Thurow says that practically everyone is formally indexed, he is not exaggerating. But it is very interesting to learn just how many Federal workers and former Federal workers are indexed, along with other beneficiaries of Federal welfare programs. The following statistics appeared in *U.S. News and World Report* (Aug. 18, 1975), and these figures are somewhat out of date, so they underestimate the extent of indexing in America. Also not included were state and local workers.

Social Security beneficiaries 31,300,000
Food-stamp recipients 19,200,000
Union members in private industry 7,000,000
Aged, blind, disabled on Federal aid 4,100,000
Retired Federal workers or their survivors 1,400,000
Retired military personnel or their survivors 1,047,000
Railroad-retirement beneficiaries [Federally funded] .1,000,000
Postal workers 600,000
Disabled coal miners, widows, and dependents 507,000

The *Wall Street Journal* (March 10, 1976) reported that indexation is spreading quite rapidly. The writer made an important point: indexation in the United States always has come in periods of price inflation, and has leveled off or waned in periods of price stability. The implication seems to be that as price inflation accelerates, more and more people will become covered by some sort of indexation clause protection, thereby compounding the problem of price inflation. Equally important are other kinds of contracts besides labor contracts. One purchasing agent—the profession above all others that is alert to price increases—made this comment: "Suppliers these days are cranking just about every cost factor imaginable into escalator clauses, from environmental costs and taxes to the wages of janitors in their New York headquarters. They have the equivalent of cost-plus contracts and thus have little incentive to keep down costs." For those of you who do not remember "cost-plus," these were the government contracts of World War II in which war production manufacturers were guaranteed a specified profit on their operations, meaning a fixed profit percentage on total costs expended. This led to guaranteed waste in every line of production: the more waste, the higher the cost; the higher the cost, the larger the total number of dollars received as profit. The cost of living escalator is not quite so bad (since your buyer may go bankrupt if you, the seller, overdo it), but escalators unquestionably lead to a reduced concern about forecasting the future state of the economy as far as prices are concerned. This reduces efficiency.

However, it is my contention that the reason why price controls are coming has very little to do with the public's comprehension of the reduced efficiency of American business. Controls are coming because of two primary reasons. First, the recipients of the new fiat money expect prices to stay low, thereby enabling them to buy at yesterday's prices with today's new money. But everyone cannot do this if the majority of the population gets access to the newly created fiat money. The auction has to raise prices, and the beneficiaries will cry for controls—to stop the **effects** of their competitors, who also have access to the new fiat funds. Second, governments in general, and the Federal government in particular, are the nation's largest debtors. They have to shut off the cost of living escalators to prevent fiscal bloodletting. Once everyone has his own cost of living escalator to protect him, the Federal government will freeze him by freezing all prices. When most of the economy is on the escalator, it will be shut off. There is no escape in private contracts, at least not in the long run (the 1980's).

By now, you should be getting the picture. Each new economic crisis comes as as a result of the most recent "solution" by the Federal government. The bureaucrats in Washington cannot grasp the fact that **legislation today is the cause of tomorrow's economic problems**, not the cure. The old-timers simply do not learn from experience. Arthur Burns, the former chairman of the Federal Reserve System, was calling for wage and price controls in March of 1976 *(Los Angeles Times,* March 23, 1976) just as he called for them in the spring of 1971. Nixon listened to him in 1971, imposed the controls—against the advice of his own Council of Economic Advisors—and the disruptions of 1971-74 began.

The price freeze will be welcomed by many American businesses and all state and local governments that are being steadily bankrupted by the cost of living escalator clauses. It will appear obvious to any corporate treasurer or bureaucratic budget director that the continual escalation of prices is **the** threat to his company or his branch of civil government. This drum and bugle corps will join with the pensioners (who worry about rising costs) and consumers whose incomes are not keeping pace with price inflation—a growing segment of the population during an inflationary panic. It will seem so simple: freeze prices by arbitrary dictate and thereby turn off the cost of living escalators.

Of course, there will be black markets ("alternative zones of supply"). Prices on these thin, risky markets will be even higher than would have prevailed in an open market. But this is politically irrelevant. Politicians can then blame hoarders, speculators, and other hedgers for "profiteering," which will get many men elected to high public office. But far more important is the **unofficial** character of the alternative markets. They are not part of the official cost of living escalator clauses. **The mask of solvency is cemented onto the face of actual default.** Men will pay their higher prices by standing in line, or by paying under the table, or by actually reducing consumption. Ration coupons will replace fiat money in the market, and unless some special-interest group is very clever and very powerful, no one will have his income in ration coupons indexed to a cost-of-living-in-coupons escalator.

A great default is coming, you must recognize the form in which this massive default is coming. Be prepared.

CHAPTER THREE
INFLATION AND UNEMPLOYMENT

Back in the 1950's, an English economist, A.W. Phillips, investigated the relationship between wage rates and unemployment during several periods of British history. He found that as wage rates rose, unemployment dropped; conversely, when wage rates subsequently stabilized, unemployment increased. Businessmen bid up the price of labor during times of price inflation, competing against one another for the services of working men and women. But when price inflation was reduced, these same businessmen preferred to reduce the number of employees. This empirical relationship between wage rates and unemployment was broadened by enthusiastic Keynesian economists to describe the relationship between "inflation" (meaning price inflation) and unemployment. The graph which describes this relationship has generally become known as the Phillips Curve. When price increases are at a high level, unemployment is low. As the rate of price increases is reduced, unemployment increases steadily. This trade-off between price increases and unemployment has become one of the most popular concepts among professional economists, both inside the Federal government and "outside" it, so to speak, in the universities.

It should not be too difficult to understand why this little graph should have become a touchstone for contemporary economists. The Employment Act of 1946—probably the classic piece of Keynesian legislation—requires the Federal government to maintain high levels of employment. This is to

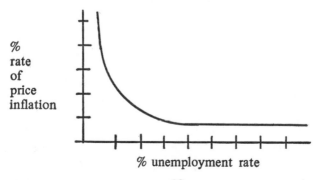

% unemployment rate

be accomplished by the proper fiscal measures. The Federal government is supposed to intervene in the marketplace whenever "effective demand" drops as a result of the individual preferences of those who would trade (or refrain from trading) voluntarily. The state is to increase "effective demand" by buying up strategic items, such as airplanes that do not fly, or even worse, that fly for a little while and then come down very, very fast. Apparently, there is not enough "effective demand" for these items on the free market, and those who produce them often find themselves unemployed when they continue to manufacture them.

The Federal government gets the funds to make these purchases by taxation (direct and indirect) and borrowing. But doesn't this pull money out of the economy that would have been spent anyway, you ask. No sir; it pulls money out of the economy that might have been saved, but saved money is not always invested, and uninvested money isn't being spent, and this reduces "effective demand," so the government spends the money (neither saves nor invests), thus putting people back to work. (You don't understand this because, frankly, you're a bit of a dummy and have never received a Ph.D in economics from Harvard.) There would appear to be two important laws associated with Keynesian policies of full employment: 1) the government which taxes invisibly, taxes best; 2) try to stay off of Air Force jets.

The policy makers believe that when unemployment increases, they can simply crank up Federal spending, and unemployment figures will inevitably tumble. This is an act of faith. Thus, when they confront certain unpleasant facts, such as 1975's unemployment rate of 9% and price inflation at 8%, they prefer to avoid the implications. They say, for example, "All things considered, I think the calendar year 1975 needs a deficit larger than we have ever had in peacetime. A deficit of 6 per cent of GNP would be about $84 billion—frightening to the layman but still 6 per cent. The price level in 1980 will be a bit higher with such a deficit than otherwise. But singlemindedly seeking to minimize that price level would logically lead to your favoring continuation of the recession, and even a wish to let it slide into a depression." These words come from Paul Samuelson, the World's Most Distinguished Economist *(Newsweek*, May 5, 1975). "All things considered," the guy ought to be locked up.

Ratcheting Disaster

What we are witnessing is a series of escalations between price inflation and unemployment. The government intervenes each time with baskets full of new money—the invisible tax—in order to increase "effective demand." What it accomplishes, of course, is the redistribution of wealth **from** those who have late access to the newly created money **to** those who have early access. Those who enter the markets with the new money buy at yesterday's prices. They leave fewer goods and services for those who have not yet been the beneficiaries of the "trickle-down" credit. Prices go up in response to reduced supplies and more money in circulation. But each time government intervenes, those on the tail end of the Federal milk cow start scrambling for the remaining teat. Prices get bid up faster in response to injections of new money, since the public gets smarter about the way to hedge against price increases. The better the public's knowledge, the more rapidly prices respond, and the less effective the "effective demand." Instead of "effective demand," the planners get price increases. This is not what they want.

When the economy is depressed, the planners want to increase spending but lower taxes. This means a larger deficit. But then they face a new problem: rising short-term interest rates. They compete for the public's savings-which-are-not-actually-invested (to coin—or print—a phrase). One thing is for certain: when the Federal government gets access to these "uninvested savings," they stay uninvested. But this debt competition results in higher short-term interest rates, which reduces private spending and/or saving-investment. This is not a good way to beat a depression. So the deficit gets partially funded by the Federal Reserve System's fiat money.

The new money races through the fractional reserve banking system, multiplying happily. Up goes "effective demand," up go the airplanes, and then up go prices. Business "booms," wages go up, everyone is kicked into a higher tax bracket, revenues exceed the forecasts by the planners, and next year's budget deficit is reduced. At this point, the FED generally reduces its purchases of Federal debt. The money supply stabilizes, but the public still continues to bid up prices for a while. Businesses compete to build more plants and build up inventories. Short-term interest rates continue to soar, thus reducing some private entrepreneurial plans to ruins. Finally, investment ceases, laborers are fired, orders are cancelled, and the boom turns into a bust. Down go profits, down go wages, down goes GNP, down go expected Federal revenues, and down go the political incumbents. (What about the airplanes, you ask. Actually, they were grounded—one way or another—six months earlier!) We are back where we started. Only we aren't. We are at a higher plateau.

Former Secretary of the Treasury, William Simon (or, if you prefer, Secretary of the Deficit), has put it very well: "This is the third time in ten years that we have been presented with bills for past Government failures due to irresponsible economic policies. Each time we refused to accept them, and the next time the bills were higher. Just go back and use this simple comparison: Into 1970, inflation was over five percent, interest rates at nine and a quarter; last year, interest rates and inflation peaked at about 12 percent. I suggest that if we refuse to pay the bill this time, it will become unacceptably high in the future. I must admit that on occasion, I really question the ability of democracy to beat inflation." *(Playboy* interview, May, 1975.) Each time, the ratchet goes higher. Each time, the recession is greater and the monetary expansion necessary temporarily to correct it is greater.

When Samuelson blandly dismisses higher prices in 1980, he apparently assumes that all we need is one more dose of the Keynesian magic. Just one more staggering increase of the money supply, and then we may be able to get back on an even keel. He makes no guarantees, however. What we—we?—need to do is to target for annual real GNP growth at 6%. This should be the target "for some time." Admittedly, there are risks. Nevertheless, "The rewards justify the risks." When I think of Samuelson and his ideological colleagues "targeting" a real growth rate of 6%, compounded annually, I visualize an eight year old holding a Ruger .44 magnum in both hands, shouting: "Watch this, Dad!" Yes, indeed, Dad; just watch. From behind that wall.

Hayek's Predictions

The greatest living economist is F.A. Hayek, Mises' former pupil. He has devoted his life to a study of the components that make possible a free society. In 1974, in the words of a noted Indianapolis leprechaun, John Ryan, Prof. Hayek honored the Nobel Prize Committee by accepting its award; as a result, he has received far more attention by the press, both in this country and in Europe. As the scholar who first introduced Prof. Mises' monetary theory of the trade cycle to the English-speaking world, Hayek has not deviated significantly from the basic outlines of that theory in the last 40 years. He wrote a pair of splendid articles for the London *Daily Telegraph* (late '74), and his opening statements lay it on the line: "The responsibility for current world-wide inflation, I am sorry to say, rests wholly and squarely with the economists, or at least with the great majority who have embraced the teachings of Lord Keynes. What we are experiencing are simply economic consequences of Lord Keynes." (Oct. 15, 1974)

What aspect of Keynes' theory does Hayek have in mind? His defense of **deficits financed by fiat money.** Every reputable economist prior to Keynes would have predicted that these policies would lead inevitably to price inflation, Hayek argues. Naturally, the politicians readily adopted a supposed theoretical justification for reducing unemployment by increased government expenditures. But the theory was supposed to apply only when there was unemployment of a very special kind: unemployment without rising prices. "And now, when the steadily accelerating rise of prices has rather discredited this view, the general excuse is still that a moderate inflation is a small price to pay for full employment: 'rather five per cent inflation than five per cent unemployment,' as it has recently been put by the German Chancellor."

The chief harm, argues Hayek (following Mises) that the inflation of the money supply brings is the disruption of **relative** prices. Monetary inflation "gives the whole structure of the economy a distorted, lopsided character which sooner or later makes a more extensive unemployment inevitable than that which the policy was intended to prevent. It does so by drawing more and more workers into kinds of jobs which depend on continuing or even accelerating inflation. The result is a situation of rising instability in which an ever-increasing part of current employment is dependent on continuing and perhaps accelerating inflation and in which every attempt to slow down inflation will at once lead to so much unemployment that the authorities will rapidly abandon it and restore inflation." He might also have added that what is true for labor—a nonspecific resource—is even more true about highly specialized capital goods. Unemployed machines, when financed with 6% or 8% or 12% loans, can produce bankruptcy quite rapidly if they are no longer profitable to operate because of a slowing down or outright abolition of monetary growth. Take a look at a capital intensive industry like the auto industry; consider the electrical utilities, while you're at it. A disrupted capital market will misallocate capital on a massive scale—a fact revealed when the expansion of the money supply does not keep pace with the public's expectations of further price increases, and a recession appears.

Thus, writes Hayek, "We have been led into a frightful position. All politicians promise that they will stop inflation **and** preserve full employment. But they **cannot** do this. And the longer they succeed in keeping up employment by continuing inflation, the greater will be the unemployment when the inflation finally comes to an end. There is no magic trick by which we can extricate ourselves from this position which we have created." In short, unemployment can no longer be avoided. "The only alternative we have, and which, unfortunately, is not an unlikely outcome, is a command economy in which everyone is assigned his job; and though such an economy might avoid outright worklessness, the position of the great majority of workers in it would certainly be much worse than it would be even during a period of unemployment."

The key, as stated before, is **relative** prices. The attention focused on aggregate prices and wages by statistical indicators has unfortunately blinded the public, the politicians, and the economists to the crucial nature of relative prices and wages. As he writes in the October 16 issue: "The sort of unemployment which we temporarily 'cure' by inflation, but in the long run are making worse by it, is due to the misdirection of resources which inflation causes. It can be prevented only by a movement of workers from the jobs where there is an excess supply to those where there is a shortage. In other words, a continuous adjustment of the various kinds of labour to the changing demand requires a real labour market in which the wages of the different kinds of labour are determined by demand and supply." Again, his logic would apply equally well to **all** factors of production. "Without a functioning labour market there can be no meaningful cost calculation and no efficient use of resources." Yet it is the attempt of the state to control the movement of **aggregate** prices, by means of fiscal and monetary policies, which disrupts the very **mechanism of adjustment**: the flexible price system.

He thinks that people will learn that inflation-generated increased wages always lead to increased prices. There is little in economic history to support his confidence at this point. Even in the final months of the 1923 German inflation, everyone was calling for more money to catch up to runaway prices. Hayek is far more fearful of the politicians, however. "What is likely to drive us further on the perilous road will be the panicky reactions of politicians every time a slowing down of inflation leads to a substantial rise of unemployment. They are likely to react to it by resuming inflation and will find that every time it needs a larger dose of inflation to restore employment until in the end this medicine will altogether fail to work. It is this process which we must avoid at any price."

Hayek's final sentence indicates the crux of the conflict between Keynesian and conservative economists. Samuelson wishes to avoid unemployment at any price—and the price keeps going up, compounded annually. Hayek wishes to avoid price inflation because he grasps a fundamental truth: it first destroys the capital and labor markets by disrupting prices; it then destroys people on fixed incomes when the public races to outbid each other with the newly created money; and finally it destroys almost everyone else when the inevitable contraction and readjustment follow. Depressions are the product of government-induced monetary inflations. In the immortal words of Prof. Mises, when asked by a student what the government should have done in 1930, he replied: "The government should have done nothing . . . earlier."

Hayek calls the shots without hesitation—without adding, as Leonard Cassidy has put it, a string of "unless we's." We have run out of "unless we's" on this side of the catastrophe. An interview with Hayek in *Reason* magazine (Feb., 1975) reveals his present thinking: "What I expect is that inflation will drive all the Western countries into a planned economy via price controls. Nobody will dare to stop inflation in an ordinary manner because as things are at present, to discontinue inflation will inevitably cause extensive unemployment. So assuming inflation stops it will quickly be resumed. People will find they can't live with constantly rising prices and will try to control it (inflation) by price controls, and that of course is the end of the market system and the end of the free political order. So I think it will be via the attempt to regress [repress?] the effects of a continued inflation that the free market and free institutions will disappear. It may still take ten years, but it doesn't matter much for me because in ten years I hope I shall be dead." (Box 6151, Santa Barbara, CA 93111: $12 per year.) In the long run, even the Austrians are all dead. But if Hayek lives as long as Mises did, he will not escape. Nevertheless, Hayek seems to believe that as far as an individual is concerned, Prof. Mises' remark is correct: "There is only one absolutely successful hedge against inflation: age!"

The Other Side of Disaster

Like Hayek, I seldom add "unless we's." Hayek's vision of the future is too compelling. It is too consistent with the goals of the messianic state. Thus, I save my "unless we's" for the far side of the disaster, whether it is a mass inflation-depression disaster, or a repressed inflation (controls) disaster. The key to the future is not held by autonomous man. The messianic state is self-defeating. It cannot calculate rationally. It is totally parasitic. Without free men acting responsibly in their particular callings, the modern world would grind to a halt. The international and even domestic division of labor cannot survive under full international socialism. In all of history the socialists have only been able to nationalize successfully one item: socialism. The competing waves of tariffs, quotas, exchange controls on money, capital controls, and all the rest of the tools of the modern socialism can lead only to the fragmentation of international trade and productivity. We will be visited by the ghost of the Smoot-Hawley tariff, and the result will be the same: the destruction of wealth. But when the messianic states finally exhaust their resources in an orgy of planning, there will be pockets of resistance. Direct controls—the means of enforcement in a command economy—can be imposed only at the centers of population, and then only imperfectly. The larger the geographical area, and the more dispersed the population, the more costly and inefficient is the control mechanism. It is too easy to buy off the enforcers. Socialist controls do not apply equally well in every region of a large planning region. With the feudalization of the economy, local pockets of free trade can exist.

When the prophet Jeremiah was told that he would have to go into captivity with his people, he was also told to go out and purchase a field (Jer. 32:7-25). It was to serve as a testimony of God's covenant with His people. The destruction of the nation was absolutely inevitable, but so was the ultimate restoration. This is the archetype of every period of trial for God's people. We have a stake in the future. Short-run pessimism is no more to be deplored than short-run optimism. It depends upon the historical setting. Those who are perennial optimists would apparently prefer to expunge the Book of Lamentations from the Bible. They would like to think of Christ's hours in Gesthemene as a chapter 87 of *He Believed in Miracles:* "Jesus Goes on a Picnic." If these people were to produce a movie dealing with the life of Christ, they would probably end it by having a Roman cavalry officer ride up to the cross with a reprieve from Caesar, just before the nails were pounded in.

The only reasonable answer to these people is to tell them to quit dreaming and go to work. And while they're at it, to buy themselves a field, a sword, and a trowel.

CHAPTER FOUR
THE THREAT OF DEPRESSION

When financial writers or newsletter publishers want to catch the eye of the general public, all they have to do is put "depression" in the headline. There is no word in the English language that people respond to faster in the field of economics. Depression is the American's greatest economic bugaboo.

This sensitivity to the word should not be surprising. Every textbook on U. S. history devotes several chapters to the depression of the 1930's. The typical historian is pro-New Deal, a defender of the domestic policies of FDR, and woefully ignorant about economics. This combination makes it difficult for any Liberal to resist the clichés that his equally uninformed senior professor taught him in grad school, not to mention freshman courses in U. S. history back in '58 or '47. The biggest and best cliché of them all was (is) that Roosevelt saved American capitalism from itself. Roosevelt gave capitalism a new lease on life. Roosevelt made capitalism work. There is no dogma in American economic history that is more cherished than this one, for it is this one which supposedly justifies the modern mixed economy. It is the one and only defense of Keynesian interventionism and inflation. It is believed fervently by businessmen, Liberals, civics teachers, government bureaucrats, and financial writers.

The interesting thing is that the textbooks never offer an explanation that shows exactly what it was that caused the great depression—or any depression, for that matter. It was "overproduction" or "underconsumption" that caused it! But why in 1929? Why not in 1928? Why is there any such thing as "overproduction"? Why is production evil? Why does it fail to benefit everyone? Another answer is the great farm crisis. Farmers after 1918, and especially after 1921, never recovered their wartime incomes. All right, they didn't. Why did it take from 1921 to 1929 to produce a depression, especially when a declining proportion of the population remained on the farm? Why should it have been that in an era of reduced importance in the economy of farming that the farmer's income should have been the great determiner of American economic life? Then there was the Smoot-Hawley tariff of 1930. Some writers blame the tariff. This unquestionably made the depression worse, since it reduced the division of labor internationally and domestically. Yet the effect of a tariff is to reduce aggregate production, since it reduces efficiency. But this flies in the face of the "overproduction" explanation of the depression. The depression winds up being caused by overproduction and underproduction. But in any case, Roosevelt cured it. (Or Tojo did, with Hitler's help, since they justified the massive deficits and inflation of the wartime years. Roosevelt's foreign policies may well have helped Tojo and Hitler make their decisions, but this is not what the textbook writers have in mind when they tell us that Roosevelt saved American capitalism from itself.)

There are reasons why Americans fear depression more than inflation, price controls, rationing, and other government-created alternatives to government-created depression. Here is my explanation. **People prefer continuity to sharp discontinuity.** They believe that it is easier to deal with 5% price inflation, or 10% price inflation, than it is to deal with 7% unemployment, if they are part of the 7%. There is a fear of being 100% unemployed. Price inflation does not hit everyone equally hard, but few people are completely wiped out by price inflation in its early stages (single-digit levels). Everyone, or almost everyone, thinks he can beat the inflation next year if he just gets a few breaks. If he can just keep on working, he can get ahead of the averages. However, if he loses his job, he is doubly cursed: his income stops, but prices keep rising. He falls too far behind to catch up. So he will vote for those who promise a remedy for unemployment. The fact that married men seldom are unemployed today, except by choice, doesn't occur to him. What he fears above all is that he will wind up in the ranks of the unemployed. The fear of 100% unemployment for those 7% is what keeps politicians in office. It's an all-or-nothing proposition. Inflation isn't, at least in the early stages. Men can live with a reduction of real income of 6% or 10% or even 20%; what they are unwilling to live with is a reduction of income by 90% through unemployment. The discontinuity is too great. **Massive personal indebtedness** makes it all the greater, and today's American is far deeper in debt than his grandfather was in 1932. **Leverage is a two-way street**, and unemployment puts one on the wrong side of the street very rapidly.

Politically, our willingness to suffer a guaranteed inflation rather than risking long-shot personal unemployment is sufficient to keep the inflationists in the saddle. This is why the **minimum wage laws** are so important to Liberals. These laws keep unemployment high among the "less desirable" members of the labor force, meaning blacks, teenagers, black teenagers, and women. The rise in Social Security taxes will accomplish the same goal, higher unemployment. Then the inflationists will be able to justify even more inflation, in order to lower the real wages of the "less desirable," thereby overcoming the effects of the minimum wage laws. Then the indexation effect takes over, minimum wage levels automatically rise, and the whole process begins again. So what is it that Americans are afraid of?

What are the levels of unemployment that so terrify us that we consent to endless doses of "minimum wage law-counteracting" inflation? Take a look. And bear in mind that black teenage unemployment is in the 40% range, and that married white males—the bulk of the labor force—experience rates under 5%. This means that among those people who actually vote, very few are presently threatened by unemployment, yet they continue to elect inflationists who campaign on a platform of reducing unemployment. The significance of this cannot be overemphasized. It means simply that a **combination of fear and guilt** can keep the interventionists in power, since envy from the unemployed is not politically effective. Too few of them vote. The old line that "some people work for a living and some people vote for a living" is a good one. Unfortunately, it doesn't get at the heart of the problem. **Guilt**, not the votes of the covetous poor, is the real problem. This guilt is manufactured.

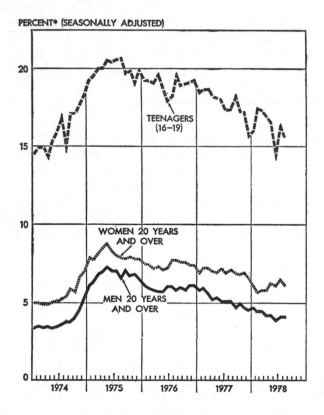

The percentage of unemployed people in the labor force is only part of the story. Consider the far more interesting data concerning the period that people actually remain unemployed. While they are unemployed, of course, most of them are drawing tax-free income from the unemployment offices (which are usually called the Department of Employment). The statistics are most revealing. The politicians whose careers are based on their ability to fan the flames of fear surrounding unemployment never point out how few people remain unemployed for more than five weeks. About 10% of those who are unemployed are out of work for more than half a year, or seven-tenths of one percent of the labor force. One reason why they are counted in the rolls of the labor force is that legislation in 1975 required people on some forms of welfare to state that they are actively looking for work, i.e., that they are still part of the labor force. They have to lie to get their checks. This is one reason why unemployment is not going to drop much below 5-6%, no matter what Washington does. Yet as long as the unemployment statistics report that over 5% of the work force is unemployed, Washington will be unable to balance the Federal budget. Remember, the original version of the Humphrey-Hawkins bill mandated 3% unemployment before the government would get out of the job-creation business. (Fortunately, the bill was passed without this 3% clause.)

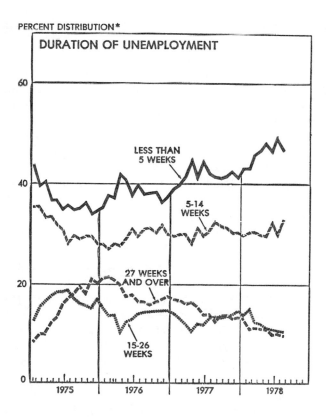

PERCENT DISTRIBUTION*

DURATION OF UNEMPLOYMENT

When Jimmy Carter ran for President, he promised the voters that he would balance the Federal budget before his first term in office was over. He repeated this promise through the early months of 1977, but by the end of the year he had begun to waver. Now the Treasury makes no such claim. Government officials have generally given up the balanced budget idea, assuming that they ever accepted it, a highly unlikely proposition. The pressure from the grass roots to pass an amendment to the U. S. Constitution to mandate a balanced budget is steadily growing, and the economists and bureaucrats in Washington are resisting the move. It is illuminating to realize that even in the projections for an "austere" budget deficit of $30 billion or so, the statisticians have relied on monetary inflation to push people into higher tax brackets, thereby increasing their tax obligations, which is supposed to boost revenues sufficiently to get closer to that elusive balanced Federal budget. Bear in mind also that there are billions and billions of so-called "off-budget" liabilities of Federal agencies, and the Federal government is supposed to be the insurer of these obligations. This statistical cover-up is very popular in Washington, since very few people are aware of Federal agency debt and its ramifications.

The point I am trying to make is this: the voters, meaning middle-class voters who determine who is elected in this nation, have determined for themselves that inflation of 7% to 9% is less foreboding than short-term unemployment rates of under 5%, the rates faced by the average voter. What will he conclude if unemployment rates should increase to 10% or 15%, not to mention 25%, such as we had in 1932? What inflation rate would he tolerate then? What policies wouldn't he accept in the name of reducing unemployment? Charlotte Twight gives an answer in her book, *America's Emerging Fascist Economy* (Arlington House, 1975). It isn't a pretty picture.

The characteristics of the traditional depression include these features: (1) falling prices; (2) reduced output of goods and services; (3) reduction of the money supply, because of (4) runs on banks that topple the fractional reserve pyramid of credit money; (5) unemployed resources, including people; (6) falling investment which results in (7) falling interest rates. **The depression is a massive correction of the free market to prior interventions by the government into the money supply, namely, a prior monetary inflation.** When Professor Ludwig von Mises was once asked by a student what the government should have done about the depression, he replied: "Nothing . . . earlier." If the government intervenes, especially by creating price controls in the form of price and wage **floors**, then the duration of the effects of the depression will be extended, since the response of men to unemployment—the offering of their resources and services at lower prices—is made illegal by the government. Men are then faced with continuing unemployment, or the sale of their below-legal price resources in the black markets. In fact, they have to offer these resources at far lower rates, to compensate the buyers for the risks the latter bear in hiring this below-floor labor or product. This is exactly the position of the illegal Mexican immigrant laborer today.

What I have described is a traditional **deflationary depression**. It is this form of depression that all Keynesian economists think their policies can overcome. It is the depression of falling prices and falling aggregate demand. Their answer: more fiat money to finance purchases by government and those in cahoots with the government. Today we face a new kind of depression, the **inflationary depression**, meaning the kind of depression which results directly from the policies of the Keynesians. The Keynesians are absolutely baffled by this phenomenon. They have no theoretical tools to use on this kind of depression. The features of the modern, Keynesian depression are these: (1) rising prices; (2) slowing and then reduced output of goods and services; (3) increase of the money supply, the result of (4) the creation of fiat money by the Federal Reserve System to finance (5) the increasing Federal budget deficit; (6) unemployed resources, including people; (7) reduced or falling investment which results in (8) falling short-term interest rates, that are followed by (9) rising long-term interest rates that are the result of (10) the increasing inflation premium tacked onto long-term loans by lenders who are trying to evade the effects of a depreciating currency unit. The traditional Keynesian solutions to "depression" only add gasoline to the fire: more government spending, larger Federal deficits, and more fiat money. The intensity of the trade cycle increases. It takes more and more inflation to bring the unemployment rate back down, but only to increasingly high levels. Both unemployment rates and price inflation rates become "ratcheted," never falling back to earlier levels.

The "Crash of '79"

Paul Erdman, Ph.D, the ex-Swiss banker and bail-jumper, has treated us to another book, *The Crash of '79*. It is a fast-moving yarn, filled with lots of pornography, innuendo, character assassination, and realistic assumptions. It has been criticized by Liberal financial writers for its realistic assumptions, which they invariably call "overdrawn." What is overdrawn is the Keynesian intellectual bank account. There has been a run on the Keynesian banks, and there stand Walter Heller, Paul Samuelson, and the *New York Times'* Leonard Silk, telling the fearful depositors not to worry, that there is plenty of capital remaining, only please give them a little more time. "Just one more graph, please," they cry, but the line isn't getting any shorter. It's inside the bank now; if it spills out onto the sidewalk, the Keynesian bankers will be in trouble. Walter Heller, Chief Teller, tells us in the *Wall Street Journal* that the "inflation-adjusted" money supply is shrinking, and that by dividing "the increase in the money supply by the increase in prices, we find the money supply lower today than five years ago." This is the same argument that every German government official and central banker gave the German people in 1922 and 1923. It is the old, pre-Keynesian rhetoric which is supposed to explain the old, pre-Keynesian inflation. It's "the latest stuff" from the boys who do not like to think about the crash of '79.

The key chapter in Erdman's book is chapter 25. Assume the following. Libyan strongman Quaddafi's Marxist-Islamic rhetoric has convinced younger military officers in Saudi Arabia that the present regime has to be scrapped. They find a lower family member who is disgruntled—the typical product of a top-flight American university—and who is willing to allow the military to use him to replace his uncle. The coup is successful. The Saudi government now pulls out all of its deposits from U.S. banks, sells off its investments in the U.S. stock market, and sells off its short-term Treasury bills. It does this deliberately, to "pull the plug" out of Western civilization, which is precisely what Quaddafi's idealogy would accomplish. (I would not be surprised to learn that this was what the 1977 summer battle between Libya and Egypt was really all about, a preemptory strike by Egypt against Libya in response to some sort of Libyan underground infiltration against Egypt, Saudi Arabia, or both. There is no doubt that Quaddafi is the Castro of the Arab world, and it would be naive to imagine that he would not be organizing and training men to infiltrate the military and bureaucratic posts of the richest pro-West Arab nations. I think Erdman's scenario regarding Saudi Arabia is too close for comfort, though I would think that the Saudi Air Force would be the more likely target than the more traditional, feudal army.) Assume also that the public is no longer trustful concerning official statements from anyone in power in this country.

The stock market begins to break. The bond market follows suit. Huge losses are sustained in the portfolios of the New York banks. The Arabs have dumped their money. Now the Europeans begin to follow their lead. Erdman writes:

> Already back in 1976, the two largest New York banks—the First National City and Chase Manhattan—had been declared problem banks by the controller of the currency. Sure, they tried to correct the situation. They were even taken off that list. But in 1978, the folly of lending long and borrowing short, of lending good money after bad to avoid having to write off bad loans, of pouring billions upon billions into the developing world, lending to governments which could not possibly repay in this century, or maybe even the next, of purchasing the notes and bonds of essentially bankrupt municipalities to keep politicians in line—all such practices had left the banks wide open for a run on their deposits.
>
> But runs never occur in the atmosphere of general prosperity and confidence—especially confidence in the institutions of government. For healthy governmental institutions can save anything in the public mind: even the banks. However, by 1979, public faith in public institutions was approaching zero.

The currency of the United States is backed by the "full faith and credit" of the U.S. government. So are government debt certificates. There has been a massive run on the "faith and credit" reserves of the currency and the debt certificates. The "full faith and credit" reserves are in inverse ratio to the dollar-denominated price of gold. This is why the Treasury sold a token quantity of gold when it went above $175/oz in the spring of 1978: to reduce the extent of this inverse ratio. They are vindictive at the Treasury; they want to get even with gold speculators. But if the scenario set forth by Erdman ever takes place, the Treasury won't have sufficient time or gold to keep the price of gold down. In the short run, they can do it, and all gold buyers should be aware of the fact. **Gold might be driven back to the mid-$150's if the Treasury dumps enough of it.** But Erdman's vision will return to haunt the boys at Treasury.

Remember, the justification of Keynesianism is in terms of the New Deal's "victory" over the old version of depression. The Keynesians have waved the "bloody depression" in front of the voters in the same way that Republicans from 1865-85 "waved the bloody shirt" of the Civil War in front of the voters, to keep them out of the clutches of the less interventionistic Democrats. So the people have never forgotten the great depression, the giant gravestone over the Keynesian corpse. If the great bank run begins, those who have heard the stories of failed banks and wiped out savings will line up. The fact that the problem today is the **failure of money**, not the failure of the banks, will make no impression on them. They have learned their history book lesson. The bank run will precipitate the death of the dollar. Writes Erdman:

> [Says the Chairman of the Federal Reserve System:] "If we start buying up Treasury paper [debt], it will simply flood the market with cash."
>
> "Well, for ******* sake, isn't that exactly what we need?" [Says the President of the United States.]
>
> "Do you realize what you are talking about? This is not money that we are getting from taxes or from borrowings. You are talking about us simply printing up billions and billions of new money, and distributing them in the market."
>
> "Exactly."
>
> "Do you realize where that could lead to? Do you remember what happened in the 1920's in Germany, in Austria, when their governments tried that? The inflation that resulted was..."
>
> "Listen," said the President, "I am not interested in hearing any more theories about inflation, or money printing, or any of that stuff. I want action. I will not accept any collapse in the markets for the securities of the government of the United States. Period. And I will not accept one further bank failure in this country. Do you understand?" And his finger jabbed so close to the FED chairman's face that it damn near shoved his pipe down his throat.
>
> "I ... " was the start of the response.
>
> "You," thundered the President, "do exactly what I say. Otherwise

I will have your ****. If you are not lynched first." The President, theoretically, had no power over the FED. But if he went public with his case, and if the situation deteriorated, there was no chance whatsoever that the chairman would survive the mob reaction. It was better that he temporarily meet the demands of these economic illiterates and survive, to restore sanity at a later date.

So they printed up an initial run of $25 billion, and flew the cash to the banks. They knew that this would restore confidence. It didn't work. The debt pyramid was too large.

> What no one had ever really thought about in the United States up until that time was the unbelievably huge volume of liquid assets in circulation that could be traded in for cash. Just the value of those shares traded on the New York Stock Exchange amounted to $850 billion. The amounts of Federal Government securities in the public's hands in 1979 represented another $879 billion. The corporate bonds in circulation yet another $750 billion. Deposits in banks—$1,000 billion. Plus the public's holdings of bankers' acceptances, of commercial paper. Etc. Add it all up, and in 1979 there were perhaps $4 trillion in assets which, theoretically at least, could be converted into cash instantly.
>
> What would happen if even 1 percent—just *one* percent—of these assets were sold, traded in, withdrawn for money—in one day. Well, we found out on March 20, 1979. Chaos. The scenes were frightful on the exchanges in New York, Chicago, San Francisco, and in front of the banks in almost every city and town in the United States. But the system held. Because the central bank had anticipated the run. By the dawn of that day $25 billion in new cash had been distributed around the country to thousands of banks. This, together with the normal cash holdings of America's financial institutions, was sufficient—barely, in some cities, but sufficient to meet every demand of every person who wanted cash.

For one day.

Chapter 26 of the book provides the epilogue. This epilogue is Erdman's answer, descriptively, to the "inflation or deflation" debate.

> It is estimated that on that Thursday the American public converted well over $100 billion in liquid assets to cash. And on Friday another $125 billion. Within a span of just one week, the total money supply of the United States had been artificially increased, by printing of new money in the amount of $250 billion. Thus the money in circulation in America had essentially been doubled—but not one bank failed. And, with the weekend at hand, there was no reason to believe that the tide would not turn. People would realize that the system had held. And on Monday, very sheepishly, they would start putting their money back where it belonged: in banks, not in their pockets.
>
> But that Friday, and that Saturday, and that Sunday, a new phenomenon developed. Cash in vast hoards was now being converted into tangibles—into food, clothing, gasoline, shoes, houses, horses,

furniture. Twice the normal money in circulation was now chasing, in full fury, the same amount of goods which had been there before the madness began. Soon price was no longer an issue. It was a classic case of instant hyperinflation. It was not the banks that were first forced to close. It was the Safeways, the Sears' the Levitzes. They simply ran out of stock. And on Sunday every McDonald's in the land closed. For their proprietors realized what was slowly dawning on everybody else: the dollar had become a worthless commodity. It was insanity to accept any more. It was the same with the yen, the mark, the pound, the lira. The amounts of these currencies in circulation had risen explosively as a result of the flight from the dollar. Then, as the "American madness" spread, governments everywhere had been forced to flood their countries with even more currencies. Now they were also worthless.

The banks did not open on Monday. In fact, the majority never opened again. For they had been broke long before all this had happened. The run merely brought this truth into the open.

Peace was maintained by the national guard. So the story ends, with the narrator returning to his thousands of acres of northern California ranch land.

Where were the Soviets in the collapse? On the sidelines. Would they really remain on the sidelines? Would their economy break down too? Would their internal repression be able to survive, or would it be made easier by beginning a war of international liberation? The book doesn't speculate. All that survives is land and gold coins.

Can we take Erdman seriously? Yes, I think we can. However, the coming of the psychology of inflation might be slower. If people take money out of the bank to hoard it, fearing collapsing prices, prices might well collapse after the initial stages of monetary inflation. If so, then more money would be drawn out of the banks—until that $4 trillion of liquid assets was converted into 4+ trillion of fiat dollars. At some point, the psychology would reverse, but I doubt if it could happen on one weekend.

Erdman's main point is correct: to offset any Arab withdrawals, the FED would unquestionably intervene to shore up the sagging market for government debt. This would inject billions into the economy. If cash was needed, then the FED would provide cash. As long as it's fiat money, the FED can supply it, cash or credit. They may not have much faith, but they can offer full credit.

The talk we hear about the non-green secret currency stored in Federal vaults is probably true. There is no direct evidence of it, but why not believe it? What is inconceivable is that such a currency would be substituted, as Dr. Franz Pick says, at a 10 to one or 20 to one ratio. What government ever revalues its currency by knocking off only one zero? Currency revaluations are last-ditch efforts. Governments knock of two, three, or a dozen zeros. Only when the public cannot be skinned with the familiar currency will governments substitute a new, unfamiliar currency.

Perhaps the new currency will be distributed in response to the imposition of the Emergency Banking Regulation #1 of 1961.* It doesn't matter; the real currency unit will be privately created. The best you can hope for is to **pay off your old debt with the worthless greenbacks** before we get red-backs, or bluebacks, or whatever.

Conclusion

Erdman's scenario could happen. We might get an **initial** deflation. I think that the process will be more gradual. War or revolution could speed up the process, but I think we have to bet on gradualism. The debt pyramid will get larger, and the fiat money necessary to finance it will continue to be spewed out. It is a question of **fiat money chasing fiat debt**. I don't expect deflation in the next 10 years.

I will only say this: there may be a way out. We may be able to avoid a deflationary depression. If we get a **repressed economy**, with price controls, long-term shortages, and rationing, then the economy could be broken. A low division of labor—common to deflationary depressions and repressed inflations—would result. Per capita wealth would continue to collapse. If the destruction of exchange and production is widespread enough, then a currency revaluation and the abolition of controls might not produce a depression. As in Germany in June of 1948, when Ludwig Erhard reduced the money supply, by fiat, by 90%, simultaneously abolishing the price and wage controls, our economy might rebound—if it was completely on its back, with nowhere to go but up. The Keynesians may yet avoid another traditional depression, simply by giving us something far worse and calling it successful.

---

*See Chapter Six.

CHAPTER FIVE
BLUEPRINT FOR TYRANNY

I joined the research staff of Congressman Ron Paul of Houston in June of 1976. Dr. Paul, a physician, had come to Washington in April of 1976, having won a seat in mid-term. His predecessor had resigned to get a new position in the Federal bureaucracy. Dr. Paul lost in November by 268 votes out of 193,000, which has to be one of the tighter races in recent years.

A few days after I went on his staff, President Ford issued Executive Order #11921, one of the all-time catalogues of governmental horrors in American history. Few people read it; few people ever will. It is no longer available from the Government Printing Office or from the White House. It is a blueprint for tyranny, the latest (as far as I know) in a long series of such blueprints that have been drawn up by Federal bureaucrats in preparation for some undefined national emergency in the future. The real emergency will be the imposition of this Executive Order. For those of you who have remained skeptical of what you have read so far in this book, the implications of Executive Order #11921 may remove your skepticism.

The Decline of Congress

To understand the nature of the problem, we have to understand what has taken place to the relationship between Congress and the President. The topic is a vast one, but I think it is significant to make a few comparisons. This term the Congress will introduce about 25,000 pieces of proposed legislation, a figure which includes about 1,500 resolutions. Out of these 25,000, possibly 400 will eventually be enacted into law, or about 1.6% of those introduced. Some of these bills are virtually automatic, such as raising the Federal debt ceiling or the passage of National Whatever Week. In short, with 535 members on both sides of Capitol Hill working full time, less than one bill per congressional office gets signed into law. For this we can be thankful. It might have been two bills per office every two years.

To accomplish this "vast output" of legislation, hundreds of millions of dollars are expended each year. A Congressman receives $240,000 to run a staff. They are limited to 18 people, which is why there is never enough office space for congressional staffs in Washington. Senate staffs cost between $400,000 and $650,000 to operate. Then there are printing costs. A typical issue of the *Congressional Record* runs about 200 pages at an estimated $286 per page. The *Record* is filled with reprints of essays, articles, or in the case of the late Sen. Wayne Morse, 20 pages of fan mail introduced from time to time. What appear to be speeches are frequently merely printed remarks introduced so as to make them look like speeches. Debates are rewritten that afternoon to make the speakers look less like incoherent dolts. And each issue of the *Record* arrives on each Congressman's desk the next morning. There are few typographical errors. This kind of work is expensive.

Then there are the hearings. A few bills on each side of the Hill make it to the hearing stage. Experts are flown in to testify. No one listens. Then they fly home. If they are big-name experts they wait a few weeks until the parallel committee on the other side of the Hill takes up a similar bill. They are asked to testify. Both houses of Congress may print up 10 or more volumes of hearings on the same subject with the same people testifying. But no one reads hearings, and few committee members show up at any given hearing. Sometimes only the chairman of the subcommittee appears, and he may leave for a quorum call, leaving a subcommittee staffer to ask questions. That's when the questions get more intelligent. Then the bill dies. So it gets introduced the next term, and the same process starts over. This can go on for years.

Contrast this process to that of the bureaucracy. Congress slowly passes laws. The bureaucracy implements them. Every day, a book equally as large as the *Congressional Record* arrives at each office, the *Federal Register*. Unlike the *Record*, the *Register* means business. Its fine print is law. Anyone who doubts the scope of the *Register* owes it to himself to order one issue from the Government Printing Office. Or call the special hot line number which provides a 90-second summary of the next day's catalogue of disasters. Here it is: (202) 523-5022. Every day of the work week, 52 weeks a year, the *Register* is published—about 60,000 pages a year. This is the law of the land. Congress may have 30 calendar days to "comment" on a law so promulgated. Hearings might be held if Congress comments. Some laws, however, are immediately applied—no comments, no hearings. Congress seldom reverses one of these laws. No Congressman has time to read either the *Record* or the *Register*, and few staffs even attempt to keep up on both. What's the use? If Congress gets only 1.6% of its own proposed legislation into law, what chance would there be of systematically reversing the promulgations of the bureaucracy that are made under the terms of the legislation passed by Congress? So businessmen have to keep a steady eye on the *Register*. Few can afford the legal talent to do this.

The *Federal Register* also includes Executive Orders. There are almost

12,000 of these laws on the books today. It takes a two-thirds vote of Congress to overturn these orders, so they do not get overturned. The bureaucracy implements these laws, too. What we are witnessing, then, is a massive defection of responsibility on the part of Congress—a defection which is the necessary concomitant to the quest for total legislation. Congress cannot keep up with the 25,000 bits of proposed legislation it creates for itself, let alone keep up with the executive bureaucracy. By attempting to legislate for everything and everybody, Congress has been brought to the brink of paralysis. It cannot lead, it cannot stop the random moves of the bureaucracy, it cannot even grasp the magnitude of the problem. No one can keep up with even the titles of the publications issued daily by the Federal government. We have seen the fruition of the prophecy made by F.A. Hayek in his 1944 book, *The Road to Serfdom*: the triumph of elitist bureaucrats in the name of participatory democracy. Congress cannot plan Congress, let alone the whole economy. Back in 1944, the academic advocates of "democratic" planning answered Hayek with little more than the refrain, "It can't happen here." What they meant was, "It can't happen here fast enough to suit us, the academic elite."

Executive Order 11921

This catalogue of horrors was issued as Part IV of the *Federal Register*, Vol. 41, No. 116 (June 15, 1976). It reinforces previous executive decrees of this kind, but this latest elitist pronouncement goes farther than earlier versions. It deals with "Emergency Preparedness Functions." Its message is clear enough to anyone who reads it: if the President declares an emergency, you had better be prepared.

Executive Orders began with Woodrow Wilson in 1916, the U.S. Shipping Board Act. The 1917 Trading With the Enemy Act is still in force. In fact, it was under the provisions of this wartime act that F.D.R. closed the banks in peacetime in March of 1933—a suggestion which Herbert Hoover had given to him, or so Hoover bragged in his autobiographical memoirs. Congress was then told to validate this action, which it did. That "temporary emergency" was not repealed until President Ford belatedly signed a law cancelling it, on September 14, 1976. This 1976 law also cancelled Truman's 1950 declaration of emergency Korea,   Nixon's declaration of emergency in 1970 (Post Office strike), and the one in 1971 (exchange rates). They have a life of their own even after the conditions producing them are long gone.

When Congress began to look into this problem a few years ago, meaning a few men in Congress, the magnitude of the problem hit with full force. There was no catalogue of the President's emergency powers. None. There were 86 volumes of *Statutes at Large* to go through. Fortunately, one branch of government had the foresight to computerize the entire U.S.

Code. The Justice Department, right? Wrong. The Library of Congress? Hardly; they can barely even shelve their own books. The Air Force. The whole system is in the computers in Colorado. So with the co-operation of the Military Establishment, congressional staffers went to work. They found a staggering 470 special statutes that can be invoked by the President during a time of "declared national emergency." And he alone has authority to define the emergency, at least initially. Sen. Mathias of Maryland was in no sense exaggerating when he testified before a House Judiciary subcommittee in 1975:

> These hundreds of statutes clothe the President with virtually un-limited powers with which he can affect the lives of American citizens in a host of all-encompassing ways. This vast range of powers, taken together, confers enough authority on the President to rule the country without reference to normal constitutional processes.
>
> Under the authority delegated by these statutes, the President may: seize property; organize and control the means of production; seize commodities; assign military forces abroad; institute martial law; seize and control all transportation and communication; regulate the operation of private enterprise; restrict travel; and, in a plethora of particular ways, control the lives of all American citizens.

Efforts by Congress to restrict or reverse the expansion of these powers have been only mildly successful. The morbidly curious can pursue this topic by ordering the following books from the Government Printing Office: *Emergency Powers Statutes*, 93rd Congress, 1st Session (1973), also printed as Senate Report 93-549; *Executive Orders in Times of War and National Emergency*, 93rd Cong., 2nd Sess (1974). I realize that only one or two of you can follow through on this, but it should be done. High school seniors in government could have a crack at this kind of project. (Again, I want to stress the advantages of the intellectual division of labor. We need many eyes to keep up with the growing economic and political disasters. Only with accurate analyses can we hope to solve the problems of political action, personal preparation, and timing. Every local church or study group should have a mimeograph machine, even a used one, plus a good electric typewriter that can produce **clear, readable** copy. The tighter the screws get, the more valuable will be a decentralized network of information producers, especially at the local level. The C.B. car radio and the mimeograph machine—if people have stocked up on paper and ink—are the Achilles heel of any centralized, bureaucratic "emergency" control program, even more than weapons in the hands of citizens. Co-operation requires co-ordination. Guns will be in greater supply in a crisis than mimeograph machines, and the group that can print and distribute information has a real opportunity to influence local events. The Soviet Army's second shock wave always has a man with a typewriter and a mimeograph machine. And if your group could buy a Linotype machine—dirt cheap for the next couple of years due to "cold type" computerized printing—so much the better. The war of words is the crucial one.)

How bad is this latest Executive Order? Very, very bad. Mindbogglingly bad. Anyone who hasn't read anything about these emergency orders has a rude awakening ahead. The day of the Caesar is already on the statute books. It only awaits a set of circumstances, including a risk-oriented President, to inaugurate that day.

To start with, there is total censorship. Not dirty books, you understand. The section on censorship appears under Part 4, the Department of Defense. There is a National Censorship Agreement between the DoD and the Federal Preparedness Agency of the General Services Administration. As far as I am able to determine, the three major control agencies will be Defense, GSA, and Commerce. Section 22 of Part 4 deals with censorship; section 27 with DoD-FCC "plans and programs for the emergency control of all devices capable of emitting electromagnetic radiation." That means your C.B. radio. Conclusion: **let your FCC license for C.B. lapse.** You sold it to someone at a swap meet—the same meet where you traded your .357 magnum. Who needs a license when he no longer owns a C.B. radio? Since 50% of the public will own C.B. units by 1980, or so some people estimate, it will be very hard for FCC people to trace these signals. If you now have a license, use it to find men who are similarly minded. Then all of you should go off the air. No chit-chat unless it's an emergency. The only reason I might hesitate to let a license lapse is that it can be useful to have a C.B. rig for pre-Caesar emergencies. But there is risk involved. The only justification for keeping a license is to organize a true emergency C.B. radio network, quietly, among friends, and then stay off the air. If Executive Order 11921 ever goes into effect, it will involve the confiscation of private radios that can emit a signal. That's why the C.B. craze is so important for the future. C.B.s are the "Saturday night specials" of communications. And now that the new channels have been added, the older units are very cheap in the used markets. That is a good time to pick up a few of them—just in case your main rig gets confiscated. (See also Part 18, section 5.)

The language of the emergency orders has always pointed to nuclear attack. Indeed, the only possible justification of such plans is the destruction of much of the nation over a few days. But the language is misleading—deliberately misleading. The opening words of E.O. 11921 are straightforward: "WHEREAS our national security is dependent upon our ability to assure continuity of government, at every level, in any national emergency type situation that might conceivably confront the nation; and WHEREAS effective national preparedness planning to meet such an emergency, including a massive nuclear attack, is essential to our national survival;..." The phrases, "might conceivably" and "**including** a massive nuclear attack" give the game away. The breadth of this legislation can be seen from the following extract, which I reproduce for your reading horror:

> (b) The departments and agencies of the Federal
> Government are hereby severally charged with the duty of
> assuring the continuity of the Federal Government in any
> national emergency type situation that might confront the
> nation. To this end, each department and agency with
> essential functions, whether expressly identified in this
> order or not, shall develop such plans and take such
> actions, including but not limited to those specified in this
> order, as may be necessary to assure that it will be able to
> perform its essential functions, and continue as a viable
> part of the Federal Government, during any emergency
> that might conceivably occur. These include plans for
> maintaining the continuity of essential functions of the
> department or agency at the seat of government and else-
> where, through programs concerned with: (1) succession to
> office; (2) predelegation of emergency authority; (3) safe-
> keeping of essential records; (4) emergency relocation sites
> supported by communications and required ser-
> vices; (5) emergency action steps; (6) alternate head-
> quarters or command facilities; and (7) protection of
> Government resources, facilities, and personnel. The con-
> tinuity of Government activities undertaken by the depart-
> ments and agencies shall be in accordance with guidance
> provided by, and subject to evaluation by, the Director of
> the Federal Preparedness Agency (GSA).

Part 9, the assignments of the Department of Commerce, indicate just
how complete the period of "emergency" controls could be, assuming that
the Federal government exercises the powers asserted here.

Part 9—Department of Commerce

> Section 901. *Resume of Responsibilities*. The Secretary
> of Commerce shall prepare national emergency plans and
> develop preparedness programs covering:
> (1) The production and distribution of all materials, the
> use of all production facilities (except those owned by,
> controlled by, or under the jurisdiction of the Department
> of Defense or the Atomic Energy Commission), the control
> of all construction materials, and the furnishing of basic
> industrial services except those otherwise assigned, includ-
> ing:
> (a) Production and distribution of and use of facilities
> for petroleum, solid fuels, gas, electric power, and water;
> (b) Production, processing, distribution, and storage of
> food resources and the use of food resource facilities for

such production, processing, distribution, and storage;

(c) Domestic distribution of farm equipment and fertilizer;

(d) Use of communications services and facilities, housing and lodging facilities, and health, education, and welfare facilities;

(e) Production, and related distribution, of minerals as defined in Subsection 702(5), and source materials as defined in the Atomic Energy Act of 1954, as amended; and the construction and use of facilities designated as within the responsibilities of the Secretary of the Interior;

(f) Distribution of items in the supply systems of, or controlled by, the Department of Defense and the Atomic Energy Commission;

(g) Construction, use, and management of civil aviation facilities; and

(h) Construction, use and management of highways, streets, and appurtenant structures; and

(i) Domestic distribution of health resources.

If you can think of anything they've left out, do me a favor: keep your suggestions to yourself. Pay special attention to section (f). Next time you hear someone advocating nuclear power, whether public or private, consider the alternatives. Decentralized power is the conservative's best answer, since it is that much more difficult to control from Washington. Nuclear power is Federal power. Yet most conservatives who go into print call for extended nuclear power. The conservatives in Congress voted overwhelmingly to support a bill to establish Federal loan guarantees for private firms entering the nuclear power field: 8 billion dollars' worth of loans. These loans will shift private capital into a market that would permit the Federal government to take over all power in the country if, in fact, these power plants worked well. Fortunately, they don't. If Karl Marx were writing today, the nationalization of power, meaning nuclear power, would be found in his 10 steps to eradicate capitalism. He would have to add another step. (The vote in the House on this multi-billion dollar boondoggle was 193 to 192; the vote had tied, due to conservative support of the bill, and Speaker Albert broke the tie and voted yes.) Marx could have written:

Part 14

(2) *Regulation.* Continue or resume in an emergency (a) controlling the possession, use, transfer, import, and export of atomic materials and facilities; and (b) ordering the operation or suspension of licensed facilities, and recapturing from licensees, where necessary, special nuclear materials whether related to military support or civilian activities.

What the Commerce Department doesn't get, General Services Administration will:

Part 22

(9) *National industrial reserve and machine tool program.* Develop plans for the custody of the industrial plants and production equipment in the national industrial reserve and assist the Department of Defense, in collaboration with the Department of Commerce, in the development of plans and procedures for the disposition, emergency reactivation, and utilization of the plants and equipment of this reserve in the custody of the Administrator.

(10) *Excess and surplus real and personal property.* Develop plans and emergency operating procedures for the utilization of excess and surplus real and personal property by Federal Government agencies with emergency assignments or by State and local governmental units as directed, including review of the property holdings of Federal agencies which do not possess emergency functions to determine the availability of property for emergency use, and including the disposal of real and personal property and the rehabilitation of personal property.

The phrase, "excess property," is better understood as property owned by hoarders, meaning anyone who has taken action beforehand and who gets caught. Keep your ideals visible and your strategy quiet.

Naturally, price and wage controls are called for. Big deal.

Remember in 1975 when a bunker of Federal Reserve Notes was discovered in a secret vault in the northern Virginia area? If the boys at the FED have their pile of money buried—yes, money that does not draw interest (Milton Friedman's horror of horrors)—why shouldn't you? Why do you need gold and silver coins? Here are a few good reasons:

Part 17—Federal Bank Supervisory Agencies

Section 1701. *Financial Plans and Programs.* The Board of Governors of the Federal Reserve System, the Comptroller of the Currency, the Federal Home Loan Bank Board, the Farm Credit Administration, and the Federal Deposit Insurance Corporation shall participate with the Federal Preparedness Agency (GSA), the Department of the Treasury, and other agencies in the formulation of emergency financial and stabilization policies. The heads of such agencies shall, as appropriate, develop emergency plans, programs, and regulations, in consonance with national emergency financial and stabilization plans and policies, to cope with potential economic effects of mobilization or an attack, including, but not limited to, the following:

(1) *Money and credit.* Provision and regulation of money and credit in accordance with the needs of the economy, including the acquisition, decentralization, and distribution of emergency supplies of currency; the collection of cash items and non-cash items; and the conduct of fiscal agency and foreign operations.

(2) *Financial institutions.* Provision for the continued or resumed operation of banking, savings and loan, and farm credit institutions, including measures for the re-creation of evidence of assets or liabilities destroyed or inaccessible.

(3) *Liquidity.* Provision of liquidity necessary to the continued or resumed operation of banking, savings and loan, credit unions, and farm credit institutions, including those damaged or destroyed by enemy action.

(4) *Cash withdrawals and credit transfers*, Regulation of the withdrawal of currency and the transfer of credits including deposit and share account balances.

(5) *Insurance.* Provision for the assumption and discharge of liability pertaining to insured deposits and insured savings accounts or withdrawable shares in banking and savings and loan institutions destroyed or made insolvent.

Those people who have high hopes for the stock market had better consider the following warning:

Part 25—Securities and Exchange Commission

Section 2501. *Functions.* The Securities and Exchange Commission shall collaborate with the Secretary of the Treasury in the development of emergency financial control plans, programs, procedures, and regulations for:

(1) *Stock trading.* Temporary closure of security exchanges, suspension of redemption rights, and freezing of stock and bond prices, if required in the interest of maintaining economic controls.

(2) *Modified trading.* Development of plans designed to reestablish and maintain a stable and orderly market for securities when the situation permits under emergency conditions.

(3) *Protection of securities.* Provision of a national records system which will make it possible to establish current ownership of securities in the event major trading centers and depositories are destroyed.

(4) *Flow of capital.* The control of the formation and flow of private capital as it relates to new securities offerings or expansion of prior offerings for the purpose of establishing or reestablishing industries in relation to the

Nation's needs in or following a national emergency.

While the E.O. doesn't mention the commodities markets specifically, I think it takes no great leap of faith to imagine what happens when capital, frozen out of the stock market, starts heading for the unregulated commodities markets. Hence, if you have a system for trading commodities, I sincerely recommend that you practice your skills on the London market or some foreign market. Move to the Bahamas while you're at it; no use paying Federal income taxes in the meantime. A person who is smart enough to beat the commodities markets ought to be smart enough to see what's coming. The free mobility of capital implies free men—precisely what this Executive Order is intended to remove.

My belief that the GSA is the primary beneficiary of this law is not an unfounded belief. The *Federal Preparedness Agency*, a GSA subsidiary, bears watching. I intend to do my best to monitor it over the next few years. I suggest that you do the same.

Part 30—General Provisions
Section 3001. *Resource Management*. In consonance with the national preparedness, security, and mobilization readiness plans, programs, and operations of the Federal Preparedness AGency (GSA) under Executive Order No. 11051 of September 27, 1962, and subject to the provisions of the preceding parts, the head of each department and agency shall:

(1) *Priorities and allocations*. Develop systems for the emergency application of priorities and allocations to the production, distribution, and use of resources for which he has been assigned responsibility.

(2) *Requirements*. Assemble, develop as appropriate, and evaluate requirements for assigned resources, taking into account estimated needs for military, atomic energy, civilian, and foreign purposes. Such evaluation shall take into consideration geographical distribution of requirements under emergency conditions.

(3) *Evaluation*. Assess assigned resources in order to estimate availability from all sources under an emergency situation, analyze resource availabilities in relation to estimate requirements and develop appropriate recommendations and programs, including those necessary for the maintenance of an adequate mobilization base. Provide data and assistance before and after attack for national resource analysis purposes of the Federal Preparedness Agency (GSA).

Administrators of private schools can rest assured that help will be on the way. The government plans "to assist civilian educational institutions, both public and private, to adjust to demands laid upon them by a large expansion of government activities during any type of emergency. This includes advice and assistance to schools, colleges, universities, and other educational institutions whose facilities may be temporarily needed for Federal, State, or local government programs in an emergency. . . ." (Part II, Sect. 1106 (2): Health, Education and Welfare). Don't spend all that advice in one place.

Congress reserves the right to reconsider the imposition of a national emergency every six months after a President declared one. However, President Ford directed his Attorney General to look into the constitutionality of this law, and it is questionable in any case if Congress would challenge a President in a declared emergency. (See the *New York Times*, Sept. 15, 1976.)

Conclusion

We must also be willing to face up to the grim fact that nuclear war is not unthinkable to the Soviet military leaders. If the U.S.S.R. were willing to take the risk of launching a first strike against our missile silos and Strategic Air Command bases, they would probably succeed in destroying the bulk of our warheads. Our only option would be retalliation against their cities with our remaining missiles, especially our submarine-based missiles. But the U.S.S.R. would probably have over half their missiles in reserve — missiles that would be aimed at *our* cities. They could announce with near impunity: "If you launch your missiles against our cities, we will immediately launch against yours, and yours are undefended, you have no civil defense program (as we have), and most of your population is in the cities." Would any American President push the button? I doubt it. The Soviet leaders know this. Therefore, the period from 1981 to 1985 will be a time of enormous danger. The Soviets will probably not strike our cities — they want our productivity — nor would they be likely to invade. But an attack on our military installations, especially our missiles, is hardly unthinkable. We *have* to think about it. The Soviets could neutralize us in an hour. Permanently.

Within 24 hours of a successful strike against our missiles, our government will impose the blueprint for tyranny. Socialist America will at last become a political possibility, perhaps even a reality. In all probability they will impose the *Emergency Banking Regulation Number One.* To find out what that means, read the next chapter.

CHAPTER SIX
EMERGENCY BANKING REGULATION NO. 1

The previous chapter should have warned every reader about the possibilities offered to Federal bureaucrats by the national emergency legislation. The executive orders connected with national emergencies transfer almost total power, officially, to the executive branch of the national government. Of course, total power is never given to man or man's political institutions. but such an exercise of power is nevertheless dangerous to our freedoms. That kind of power will make free market transactions far more difficult and far more expensive, not to mention far less efficient.

The previous chapter merely skims the surface of the national emergency laws. There are hundreds of them, some of them buried deep in the Federal bureaucracy, invisible until they are implemented in the name of an emergency. One of the most revealing pieces of evidence in this regard is almost impossible to locate, but I was given a copy in the mid-1960's. It is the transcript of the Economic Stabilization Conference which was held at the Ambassador Hotel in Los Angeles on September 12, 1961, not long after the Berlin crisis of Kennedy's administration began. It was sponsored by several organizations, including the L.A. Office of Civil Defense, the California Savings & Loan League, Teamsters Local 42, the L.A. County Federation of Labor (AFL-CIO), and the L.A. Chamber of Commerce. This was not a minor conference. The real sponsor, however, was the Office of Civil Defense Mobilization (OCDM).

By the time this traveling road show hit Los Angeles, there had already been three other performances in different cities. The civil defense bureaucrats were trying to mobilize local bureaucrats to serve as front men for the Federal government during a time of attack. Regional officers in Federal planning agencies were brought before the audience to announce a vast new scheme of Federal administration. The official excuse for this centralization of power was national defense during a time of attack. Obviously, most people think of nuclear war when they hear the word "attack." Not so in the minds of Federal planners. To limit the word "attack" to a nuclear exchange would be to limit the intrusion of Federal power into local affairs. Attack is deliberately left undefined. This means that the ability of the President to impose the control system is left "flexible," which is another word for "arbitrary." For example, if the Soviet Union tried to block the shipping of Middle East oil to this nation, or to our European allies, would this legally constitute an attack on the United States? It probably would, and if the President were to declare a national emergency on this basis, the whole structure of national emergency regulations could be implemented.

Consider the words of Edward Phelps at the 1961 Los Angeles conference. He was the Deputy Assistant Director for Economic Stabilization of the Office of Civil and Defense Mobilization. His view of the Federal government's role is straightforward. Furthermore, notice the difference between local political power and Federal power in a nuclear attack as compared to a conventional attack. The latter, seemingly less destructive, will pass far greater power to the Federal planners:

> If we are going to keep our economy functioning, solvent, if we are going to stabilize it following an attack, the people of the country who survive are going to have to do the job! Not a big, benevolent, all-seeing, all-powerful Federal Government. On the other hand in a case of limited war, this all-seeing, benevolent, all-powerful Federal Government will do this kind of work, because it is able to do it and is required to do it, . . . and has the capacity to do it! (p. 34)

I have quoted him exactly as his words appear in the transcript, even including the three dots. His view of the ability of the Federal planners to control ("stabilize") the economy is too typical of those who serve in the government.

Robert W. Winsor, another Economic Stabilization Officer with the OCDM, but in this case at a regional office (Santa Rosa, California, Region 7), announced the following plan. For the first five days after an attack on the United States, there will be **no retail sales** of food, petroleum products, or other consumer goods except perishable goods, and then only on a limited basis. Food will be rationed by local governments on a bag by bag, family by family basis (pp. 26-27). The local rationing boards will do their work only until the Federal government can get organized to ration everything nationally. "The last phase of rationing operations would involve the gradual and eventual national consolidation of local-state operations by the federal government. National policy assumes that this would take several months" (p. 27). He was very specific on one crucially important point: **there must be no alternative zones of supply.** "There must be no supply of the rationed item available except through the rationing system" (p. 28). In short, the government, and only the government, should be allowed to keep people alive. People must depend exclusively on government for their survival, first the local government and then the Federal government.

The bureaucrats occasionally let the cat out of the bag. They keep talking about war, or attack, or some military crisis when they seek to justify the creation of a control system. But once in a while the broad nature of their definition of a justifying emergency creeps out. Claude Phillippe, then an Assistant Supervising Examiner of the Federal Deposit Insurance Corporation (bank account insurance), District 12, used the words "or any emergency," in a revealing way:

> First, let me emphasize that regardless of the circumstances which may result from an enemy attack, or any emergency, it is intended for our banking system to continue to function in the post-attack period in accordance with usual procedure, subject, of course, to rules and regulations deemed necessary in the interest of the economy and war effort (p. 58).

Translated from the original Bureaucratese, this means that **nothing** resembling "usual procedure" is likely to survive the attack, or "any emergency," and new "rules and regulations deemed necessary" will confiscate the wealth of Americans on an unheard-of scale.

Am I exaggerating? Listen to Edward Phelps again. He is a classic environmental determinist who wants us to believe that we have no choice in choosing this new system of controls. "The world is changing. I guess we are changing with it, and we haven't any choice but to learn to live in the environment surrounding us." This means that we have to do it the bureaucrats' way. The Cold War will go on, he said. Therefore, again stressing our lack of choice, "we have no national choice but to learn to live in a new kind of world and to prepare ourselves to respond to whatever may happen" (pp. 9-10). But this "new kind of world" is really the ancient system of central political control which has been popular with rulers and bureaucrats since the days of Egypt's pharoahs. Phelps says that we have four, and only four, choices, and we have to choose the fourth. Watch this sleight-of-hand (mouth?) routine. First, we can do nothing, make no national plans, and wait for an attack. Second, we can let people barter after the crisis, meaning we can leave men free to create their own alternative currency system—a terrifying thought. "Whatever it might be, it wouldn't be our system as we know it. It would be a new and substitute one! Well, this has been ruled out and oversimplified, merely because we are so conditioned to our economic way of life. . . ." Third, we can have an authoritarian control system. That is out, of course. Fourth, we can accept this new control system of the "benevolent" Federal government, to use his term. He calls this system a "going concern." He is quite explicit: "It would be a regulated system beyond our past powers to imagine regulation, I suppose" (p. 14). That takes some imagination! But, of course, it would be our system (ours?) and therefore not tyrannical: "But it would be our system and it would be a 'going concern'. . . ." A "going concern" like this used to be called fascism.

This "going concern" will involve a system of comprehensive price controls. The controls are to be imposed by local governments first. Mr. Phelps spelled out the program:

> So, therefore, I will simply say that the basic objective of what we are trying to accomplish in localities and communities is to develop a capability on the part of those communities "to hold the line" with respect to prices and rents for as long as it takes to let the country organize itself and let the federal government organize itself so that it (the federal government) can gradually assume its basic responsibilities and take over or weld together the first temporary interim responses by local and state people!
> Local and state people, you understand, will be impotent unless business, professional and financial people are helping them in undamaged areas. For the latter have the know-how and experience!
> In general, the basic goal of our suggested guidance to local and state authorities is simply that a freeze of prices and rents be imposed, a self-triggering freeze, which will accompany self-triggering action taken in undamaged areas with respect to banks and financial institutions (p. 33).

Banks and financial institutions: here is the key. The authorities must have control of the banking system if they are to control prices, eliminate the black market, and control the population. This control is now waiting to be imposed. It is called the Emergency Banking Regulation No. 1. It was signed by the Secretary of the Treasury on January 10, 1961, and it received virtually no publicity. But speakers at this conference knew all about it and referred to it constantly as a major weapon in the war against "chaos," meaning the free market.

The Story of a Secret Document

Robert B. Anderson, who was President Eisenhower's Secretary of the Treasury, signed the Emergency Banking Regulation No. 1 just before President Kennedy took over. The document, we learn in the conference's proceedings, was sent to "all of the banking offices in the United States as well as to certain other interested parties" (p. 52). But you have never heard of it, right? Neither has your congressman or senator.

When I mentioned the existence of this regulation to a friend of mine who holds a high position in the Washington congressional research structure, he was dumbfounded. He had never heard of it. Yet his specialty is American banking legislation. He immediately contacted the Treasury Department. He was told that such a regulation does not exist. He assigned a Library of Congress researcher to find it, and the man found absolutely nothing.

My friend grew suspicious. The document didn't bear the Treasury Department's official letterhead. It was printed on white paper with

"Department of the Treasury" typed in, not printed. He though it might be a forgery. But when I sent him a copy of the Economic Stabilization Conference and certain other evidence, he concluded that it must be legitimate. But Treasury denied any knowledge of it.

Finally, he was able to get an official answer. The regulation **did** exist, and it was signed, but since the regulation is implemented only when the President declares an attack on the country, there is no law on the books. **There was therefore, no record of it anywhere in the files available to the public, including the U.S. Congress!** If a California lady who supplied me with the documentation hadn't been diligent back in 1963 in collecting this document and the supporting evidence, no one would now know of its presence—no one except those bureaucrats who stand ready to implement it.

The public, the public's representatives, and even the President have only the faintest glimmer of the massive pile of secret legislation ready to be imposed on this nation in the name of national emergency. It is a frightful legacy. This is why I recommend that you read my book very carefully and take steps to protect yourself.

If you want further information on the Emergency Banking Regulation No. 1, the man to contact is Congressman George Hansen of Idaho. Write to him at the House Office Building, Washington, D.C. 20515. He is probably the only congressman today who even knows of this regulation.

How to Protect Yourself

I happen to have dug out this regulation with the help of my California contact. There are undoubtedly thousands of other similar regulations sitting in dusty files, invisible to the public, waiting to be implemented. This is why you have to be prepared for events that most Americans think are impossible.

When you read the full, dull text of the Emergency Banking Regulation No. 1, you had better read **Chapter V** of the regulation very carefully. Then you had better take steps to get a supply of **dehydrated food** for your basement or storage facility. You had better put some cash aside. You had better be sure that all of your easily marketed assets are **not** in your safety deposit box. (Your wife should own the box, and she should pay for it with her own personal, exclusive checking account. This way, the authorities will not seal the box at the time of your death. This one tip could save some readers the price of this book, if they take my advice. Remember, the Internal Revenue Service can legally break into anyone's safety deposit box to search for incriminating evidence, the U.S. Court of Appeals for the Second District—New York City—has determined: *Inflation Survival Letter*, April 20, 1977.)

Never forget: the government reserves the right to ration your own money back to you. You had better own some "alternative money" that the government will have difficulty rationing.

Here, then, is the document which the Treasury at first denied ever existed and the Library of Congress could not locate in an intensive search. I have also reprinted Secretary Anderson's cover letter which summarizes the regulation.

Department of the Treasury

Statement of
The Secretary of the Treasury to accompany
the issuance of the
Emergency Banking Regulation

In keeping with the objectives of The National Plan for Civil Defense and Defense Mobilization, I have issued an Emergency Banking Regulation that would become effective only in the event that there should be an attack upon the United States. Issuance of the Regulation at this time has no particular significance except that, after months of careful study, work on it has now been completed. It is being issued so that banking institutions may develop and complete their emergency preparedness programs as advocated by the National Plan.

Obviously the effective utilization of the financial capacity of the Nation in the conduct of any war that might befall us must be assured. The Regulation provides, insofar as possible, a reasonable degree of flexibility, as proper implementation would depend heavily upon the knowledge, initiative and judgment of the managements of our financial institutions and the understanding and cooperation of depositors and share or savings account owners. Basically the Regulation is for the purpose of assuring the maintenance of operations and functions of all banking institutions, including savings and loan associations and credit unions, and to facilitate restoration of such activities should they become temporarily disrupted because of such an emergency. This Regulation, should it ever become effective, would be subject to such amendment, modification or termination as might be consistent with the existing monetary needs and the developments in the national economy.

The Regulation has been issued pursuant to the authority vested in me as Secretary of the Treasury, including the authority vested in me by Section 5 (b) of the Trading with the Enemy Act of October 6, 1917, as amended (50 U.S.C. App. 5 (b)), and Executive Order No. 9193. Bearing in mind that the Regulation would become effective only in the event of an attack upon the United States, and that the term "banking institutions" includes every commercial bank, trust company, private bank, savings bank, mutual savings bank, savings and loan association, building and loan association, cooperative bank, homestead association, credit union, and United States postal savings depository office authorized under the laws of the

United States or any place subject to its jurisdiction, or any receiver or conservator for any of the foregoing, the Regulation is summarized as follows:

All Federal Reserve Banks, Federal Home Loan Banks, their respective branches, and all banking institutions and their branches would be required to remain open and continue their operations and functions, and permit the transaction of business during their regularly established hours. The only exceptions would be those unable to operate because they may have suffered personnel losses or physical damage, or may be located in areas declared to be unsafe because of defensive or enemy action. Such institutions would also be authorized to act as agent for each other in carrying out their operations and functions. Banking institutions and depositors and the owners of share or savings accounts would be required to observe provisions that would guard against the misuse of the Nation's monetary resources so that they might be preserved primarily for the payment of vital expenses, reconstruction and essential living costs, taxes, or payrolls. Provisions would also guard against the misuse of credit by directing all lending activities toward the above-named essential purposes.

To prevent misuse or hoarding of goods and material and in order to guard against inflation, Government planning also includes a number of other emergency measures. These would provide for the stabilization of rentals, prices, salaries and wages, and rationing. During an emergency of the type toward which our planning is directed, the cash and credit resources of our financial institutions must likewise be utilized to the end that the best interests of the Nation would be served.

Robert B. Anderson
Secretary of the Treasury

Dated: January 10, 1961

Department of the Treasury

Emergency Banking Regulation No. 1

Chapter I

Authority

This Regulation is issued pursuant to the authority vested in me as Secretary of the Treasury, including the authority vested in me by section 5 (b) of the Trading with the Enemy Act of October 6, 1917, as amended (50 U.S.C. App. 5 (b)), and Executive Order No. 9193.

Chapter II

Time of Taking Effect

This Regulation shall be effective immediately after an attack upon the United States.

Chapter III

Definitions

(a) As used in this Regulation, the term "banking institution" shall include the following banking and financial institutions: every commercial bank, trust company, private bank, savings bank, mutual savings bank, savings and loan association, building and loan association, cooperative bank, homestead association, credit union, and United States Postal Savings depository office authorized under the laws of the United States or of any State to transact business in the United States or any place subject to its jurisdiction, or any receiver or conservator for any of the foregoing.

(b) As used in this Regulation, "operations and functions" shall include the paying Chapter, all Federal Reserve Banks, branches of Federal Reserve Banks, Federal Home Loan in any manner or by any device whatsoever; the receipt or paying out of deposits; the receipt of payments into share or savings accounts or the repurchase of or payments on withdrawals from share or savings accounts; the making of loans or discounts; transfers of credit; the performance of fiduciary, custodial or agency functions; the purchase or sale

Section 2. **Temporary Curtailment of Operations and Functions**   Any Federal Reserve Bank, Federal Home Loan Bank, banking institution, or branch may temporarily curtail, place of business separate and apart from the head office of a Federal Reserve Bank, Federal Home Loan Bank, or banking institution in which any of its operations and functions are carried out.

Chapter IV

Continuance of Operations and Functions
Temporary Curtailment of Operations and Functions
Temporary Quarters, and Emergency Loans

Section 1. **Continuance of operations and Functions of Federal Reserve Banks, Federal Home Loan Banks, Banking Institutions, and Branches.** Except as provided in Section 2 of this Chapter, all Federal Reserve Banks, branches of Federal Reserve Banks, Federal Home Loan Banks, branches of Federal Home Loan Banks, and all banking institutions and all branches thereof, without regard to whether or not the head office or any other branch or branches are functioning, shall remain open and continue their operations and functions and permit the transaction of business during their regularly established hours.

Section 2. **Temporary Curtailment of Operations and Functions**. Any Federal Reserve Bank, Federal Home Loan Bank, banking institution, or branch may temporarily curtail, limit, suspend, or delegate any or all operations and functions if located in an area which is unsafe because of enemy or defensive action, or if essential personnel or physical facilities become unavailable. Operations and functions of any Federal Reserve Bank, Federal Home Loan Bank, banking institution, or branch which have been so curtailed or suspended shall, as soon as practicable, be resumed when the cause of such curtailment or suspension has been remedied, removed or dissipated.

Section 3. **Temporary Change of Quarters**. In the event that the main office or any branch of any Federal Reserve Bank, Federal Home Loan Bank, or banking institution becomes wholly or partially unusable, as a result of an attack upon the United States, the Federal Reserve Bank, Federal Home Loan Bank, banking institution, or branch so affected shall, if possible, establish temporarily necessary substitute quarters. The use of such substitute quarters shall be terminated as soon as practicable.

Section 4. **Loans to and Borrowings From Federal Reserve Banks, Federal Home Loan Banks, or Banking Institutions**. In order to provide the necessary liquidity to maintain operations and functions as required by Section 1 of this Chapter, any Federal Reserve Bank, Federal Home Loan Bank, or banking institution, or branch thereof, may make loans, discount assets, or borrow without regard to the restrictions of Federal or State law.

Section 5. **Notification of Supervisory Authorities**. Any banking institution or branch thereof which curtails or suspends its operations and functions or changes the location of its quarters pursuant to Section 2 or 3 of this Chapter, shall as promptly as possible notify all of the authorities responsible for its supervision, State and National, and if the banking institution is insured, such supervisory authorities shall notify the Federal Deposit Insurance Corporation or Federal Savings and Loan Insurance Corporation, as the case may be, of all such actions by banking institutions or branches thereof reported to them.

Section 6. **Acting As Agent**. Any Federal Reserve Bank, Federal Home Loan Bank, banking institution, or branch may be agreement act as agent and perform temporarily any of all operations and functions of any other Federal Reserve Bank, Federal Home Loan Bank, banking institution, or branch.

Chapter V

Restrictions on Cash Withdrawals
and Transfers of Credit

Section 1. Cash Withdrawals. (a) Withdrawals in the form of cash, whether by the cashing of checks or drafts, the making of loans in cash, or any other form of cash disbursement are prohibited except for those purposes, and not in excess of those amounts, for which cash is customarily used.

(b) Banking institutions are further authorized to restrict and ration cash withdrawals to the extent necessary in the event a sufficient amount of cash should not be available.

(c) Banking institutions shall prohibit withdrawals of cash in any case where there is reason to believe that such withdrawal is sought for the purpose of hoarding.

Section 2. Transfers of Credit. (a) No depositor or share or savings account owner may transfer in any manner or by any device whatsoever any balance to his credit on the date on which this Regulation becomes effective, except for the payment of (i) expenses or reconstruction costs vital to the war effort, (ii) essential living costs, (iii) taxes, (iv) payrolls, or (v) obligations incurred before the date on which this Regulation becomes effective, to the end that the best interests of the war effort and the public will be served.

(b) Banking institutions shall prohibit the transfer of credit in any case where there is reason to believe that such transfer is sought for any unauthorized purpose.

(c) After this Regulation becomes effective, banking institutions shall retain until released by Federal authority the original or a photographic copy (face and reverse sides) of each check and other evidence of transfer of credit in the amount of $1,000 or more.

Section 3. Exceptions to Restrictions. (a) Balances in deposit or share or savings accounts may be transferred from one banking institution to a deposit or share or savings account of the same owner in another banking institution.

(b) The restrictions of Section 2 of this Chapter shall not apply to any check or draft negotiated for value prior to the time this Regulation becomes effective.

(c) The limitations and restrictions of this Chapter shall not apply to the United States, any State or any political subdivision thereof, nor to their respective agencies and authorities.

(d) The limitations and restrictions of this Chapter shall not apply to transactions between Federal Reserve Banks, Federal Home Loan Banks, banking institutions, and branches thereof.

(e) The provisions of Section 2 of this Chapter do not alter the right of any banking institution to invoke restrictions on withdrawals of deposits or repurchases of or payments on withdrawals from share or savings accounts provided for under contract or agreement with depositors or share or savings account owners or by reason of law or the provisions of its charter or bylaws.

Chapter VI

Lending and Extending Credit

Section 11. **Making Loans and Extending Credit.** No banking institution may make any loan, extend any credit, or discount or purchase any obligation or evidence of debt, unless it is established and certified in writing by the borrower and a banking institution that the purpose is to pay (i) expenses or reconstruction costs vital to the war effort, (ii) essential living costs, (iii) taxes, or (iv) payrolls, to the end that the best interests of the war effort and the public will be served.

Section 2. **Exceptions to Restrictions.** (a) The restrictions contained in Section 1 of this Chapter do not prohibit the renewal, recasting, or extension of any loan or credit outstanding prior to the effective date of this Regulation, if in the judgment of the management of the banking institution such action is in the best interest of the war effort. The cancelled original evidence of debt shall be attached to the instrument renewing, recasting, or extending such obligations.

(b) Section 1 of this Chapter shall not apply to loans or extensions of credit to the United States, to any State or any political subdivision thereof, nor to their respective agencies and authorities, nor to loans or extensions of credit between banking institutions.

Chapter VII

Savings Provisions

Any action authorized or required to be taken by a Federal Reserve Bank, Federal Home Loan Bank, banking institution, or branch or its management pursuant to this Regulation may, in the absence of persons authorized by delegation or otherwise to take such action, be taken by any director, officer or employee of such Federal Reserve Bank, Federal Home Loan Bank, banking institution, or branch at the time conducting that part of the affairs of the Federal Reserve Bank, Federal Home Loan Bank, banking institution, or branch to which such action relates. Notwithstanding any other provision of law, no Federal Reserve Bank, Federal Home Loan Bank, banking institution, or branch or any director, officer, or employee thereof and no member or employee of any agency of the United States shall be subject to any liability on account of any action taken or omitted to be taken in good faith pursuant to this Regulation, provided that this sentence shall not be deemed to apply to any liability on account of any contractual obligation.

Chapter VIII

Revision or Termination

This Regulation may be revised or terminated when so ordered by the Secretary of the Treasury.

Robert B. Anderson [signed]
Secretary of the Treasury

[I sent a copy of my report on Emergency Banking Regulation Number 1 to one of the most distinguished legal theorists in the United States, a law professor who teaches law professors. He is also one of the most determined anti-bureaucrats in the country. I had not expected any reply, but he sent me the following letter in the summer of 1977. I have edited it to protect the innocent, but otherwise it is unaltered. I would hasten to add that the scholar in question is not a proponent of a conspiracy view of history, which makes his final remarks all that more interesting.]

In 1962 I undertook a large scale project for the [prominent think tank] on "Post Nuclear Attack Economic Planning by the Federal Government." I knew about Emergency Banking Regulation No. 1 and a vast many other pieces of idiocy equalling or even surpassing that one in potential danger or simple wrongheadedness. I concluded at the end of the study that the only thing that could save us from a post attack disaster worse than the effects of the attack was the fact that none of the plans could ever be coordinated or made to work. I confess that I had not noticed that any of these regulations could go into effect without a nuclear attack, and I am not sure of the validity of any of these regulations other than under such emergency war powers.

Well, I did that extensive study with the help of a couple of law students and without seeing any classified materials. However, when the finished study was presented to the Office of Emergency Planning it was immediately stamped "Top Secret," and I haven't seen it since. I know that they threatened to take all contracts away from [the institute's director] unless he revised it, but I don't know what happened thereafter.

A funny thing did happen to me, however, a year or two after that. The University was remodeling our offices, and a four-drawer file cabinet of mine, an entire drawer of which contained notes from the preparedness study, was put into storage. Somehow that file cabinet disappeared. No one at the University could ever figure out what had happened, and they were obviously mystified by the disappearance. But I think I know what happened. Don't you?

CHAPTER SEVEN
A LEGAL FORM OF TAX REBELLION

A Speech Delivered Before
The National Taxpayers Union Conference
Georgetown University—Washington, D.C.
April 17, 1975

Inflation is a tax. This statement has become almost a truism within hard-money circles. Yet it would seem that no matter how many times we repeat this phrase to ourselves, we are unable to face its implications squarely. There is some underlying psychological barrier that persists in spite of rational attempts to overcome it. We continue to view our inflation-hedging activities as just another form of profit-making activity. True enough, there are entrepreneurial profits involved in successful hedging, since the successful hedger (used in the non-technical sense of speculator) has successfully forecasted the future and has taken efficient action to deal with it. But in the final stages of runaway inflation, a fundamental shift in perspective takes place. It involves successive panic movements out of cash or cash-related paper investments. It finally involves total distrust of the monetary unit. To quote the old Marxian formula, a quantitative change produces a qualitative change. At some necessarily undefined point, a majority of participants on the domestic economic markets adopt wholly new patterns of trade. The psychology shifts from making a profit denominated in legal tender currency to making a profit by getting away from legal tender currency.

What do we mean when we say that inflation is a tax? First, and most important, the expansion of the money supply allows those creating money to purchase goods and services at prices that reflect yesterday's supply and demand conditions, including yesterday's money supply. Those who possess the new money are able to buy these goods before others get access to the money. Only as entrepreneurial forecasts by the public begin to take into account the likelihood of new money coming into existence will the price level begin to respond more rapidly to the new monetary conditions, or even **in advance** of the creation of new money. In short, as long as the

80

so-called "money illusion" operates, and men fail to foresee its impact on prices, those with the new money can redistribute productive goods and services into their own hands. When government has the monopoly of money creation, or when it has first access to any new money created by government-licensed central banking procedures, then government reaps the benefits initially. Hence, monetary inflation is a tax.

Only slightly less important is the **invisibility** of this form of taxation. Not one person in a thousand understands how this process works. (Before Harry Browne scored his publishing coup, not one person in ten thousand understood it, which is why Harry deserves a lot of thanks.) It is too easy for the perpetrators of the redistribution—government politicians—to blame someone or something else: labor unions, businessmen, the weather, Arabs, anchovies, etc. This public is unable to respond correctly to the problem because it has not diagnosed it properly. Historically, it has only been the breakdown or near-breakdown of a nation's monetary unit which brings home the truth of the monetary source of the price inflation. A recent *Wall St. Journal* cartoon is all too typical: a housewife is complaining to her husband about the economy. "The real shortage is our shortage of money." That may be the problem for the individual, but on a national basis, the psychology of inflation can be broken only when the mechanism of inflation is broken: fiat money. But the cry for more money is as loud as the cry against those price increases that finally begin proportionately to outstrip the increases in the money supply, as people foresee each wave of new money and frantically enter all markets, thereby bidding up prices in advance. The wealth redistribution effects become too complex to follow; only those on fixed money incomes are sure losers.

What is the **theoretical limit of price inflation?** The point in time at which **no one will voluntarily give up any further scarce economic resources in exchange for government money.** Then private individuals revert to barter or to some unofficial alternative medium of exchange. The government is then compelled either to confiscate goods directly or else reform the currency. The inflation tax has reached its theoretical limit.

Four Stages of Tax Rebellion

Colin Clark, the Australian economist, has studied the history of government taxation very carefully. He found that in all known cases in which the government tax bite took more than 25% of national income, the governments resorted to the inflation of the money supply in order to accomplish their fiscal goals. Clark has been criticized by Keynesian inflationists for not providing a theoretical reason why this should be invariably true. Obviously, no such proof is possible. Academic Keynesians smugly conclude that Clark's 25% figure is therefore meaningless. It is not meaningless; it is a statement of historical fact, not theoretical inevitability. As a product of historical research, it demonstrates that statists have always encountered political resistance at or below the 25% figure, and they have always taken the same route in "solving" their problem. The smug Keynesians—smug before 1967, anyway—are incapable of showing any theoretical reason why the same old panacea will not be tried once again. It is an argument about comparative economic history, not economic theory, and Clark has all the historical evidence on his side.

The four stages of tax rebellion parallel the four stages of any inflation. They are not absolute categories; they are convenient **classification devices** that seem to **fit fairly well** in a number of historical cases, and may very well be found to fit what is coming in this country. Whether the fit is significant is yet to be seen.

Stage One: non-monetary strategies. These involve sophisticated **tax shelter schemes**, some completely legal (Keogh retirement plan, oil exploration, etc.) and others more questionable, i.e. risky (foreign tax havens, complicated corporate ownership, etc.). These latter avenues of escape are open to only a tiny handful of relatively wealthy people, since the information is difficult to obtain, and those who use them must stay very mobile (e.g., Robert Vesco).

There is also **illegal defiance**. Some individuals just fail to declare portions of their income, especially cash income. This is the most widely used form of evasion. Others declare their ideological opposition to taxation, or some aspect of taxation, and refuse to pay. When the authorities think it is worth their time and effort to clobber the ideologues, they move in. The risks are very high, and the non-ideological nature of most people's tax evasion is such that few converts are gained. As long as people think the state is basically an honest institution, or as long as they think they can benefit personally from an obviously crooked state, the tax revolt is of the "let them catch me" variety. It is not that important fiscally. Most people pay most of what they earn, because most of the money is in the hands of middle class people who are only marginally involved in tax evasion. The tax rebellion has to convert too many people who neither understand the arguments for outright rebellion nor agree with most of them when they finally understand them. In any case, they are not going to take the necessary risks. The tax revolt, as a conscious ideological movement, does not stand a chance—in Stage One.

Stage Two: monetary strategies. When the state inflates in order to get beyond that general limit of resistance at 25%, more or less, of national income, then the public changes the rules. Men who are aware of what is happening to the purchasing power of money begin to hedge. They buy hard goods, sign long-term debt contracts, speculate in foreign currencies, and reduce their ownership of mortgages or bonds denominated in fixed monetary returns. These tax resistance groups are not organized. They are seldom even ideologically inclined, although the original source of their strategies may be very ideological (e.g., Harry Browne). They start taking action in their own businesses; they read about others who are attempting similar moves. **These are tax evasion strategies**; men are escaping the invisible tax of monetary inflation. But since the inflation tax is not seen as a tax (precisely the basis of its popularity with governments), men feel far less guilty about their involvement in this form of tax evasion. In fact, they pride themselves on their skills; after all, profit is a sign of one's intelligence and forecasting skills.

This kind of tax evasion is extremely relevant fiscally. As men increase their skills in hedging against inflation, it becomes even more relevant fiscally. The governments are unable to buy so many economic goods as before, since prices rise in anticipation of the increase in taxation, i.e., the increase in the money supply. Even worse, the state is unable to buy so many votes. Projects become insufficiently funded (rising prices) and voters lash out against rising prices, i.e., the inevitable effects of the inflation tax.

The most difficult aspect about this form of tax evasion, from the government's point of view, is that it is **legal**. Furthermore, it does not create sufficient guilt in the minds of the successful evaders, thereby lessening the control that the priests of statist salvation have over the public. This tax rebellion is basically unorganized, non-political, middle class, and self-sustaining: successful strategies of evasion are imitated. The tax men become desperate to close the avenues of evasion.

Stage Three: controls. In response to the cries against rising prices, the government makes rising prices illegal. This creates what Prof. Roepke called "repressed inflation"—the economy of shortages. Economic goods are rationed by non-price means: power, tickets, long lines, sexual favors, barter, etc. Productivity is drastically lowered. But most important, from the point of view of the government, is that government bureaucrats once again gain first access to "money," whether the money is in the form of ration coupons, priority allocation licenses, food stamps, compulsion, or whatever. Inflation tax evasion is once again made illegal and guilt-producing. Hoarding becomes an immoral act against humanity rather than a rational response to the threat of confiscation by the state.

Those who feel guilty or fear the arm of the law refuse to participate on black markets, at least until they feel sufficiently squeezed financially to make profitable a search for illicit goods and the even more important search for moral self-justification for their search for illicit goods. Eventually, everyone who wishes to survive enters the black markets for at least a portion of his economic supplies, but those who were initially patriotic or fearful pay for their personal qualms by having to start from scratch. They have less information, fewer hoarded supplies, and greater hesitancy than their fellow citizens who simply ignored the laws. Initially, there may be few evaders; eventually, the whole society participates. It becomes dangerous to advocate publicly those economic strategies that are economically obvious but officially illegal. Learn while you can. The night cometh.

Some Americans bought gold bullion long before it was legal for them to own gold bullion. They were willing to buy Austrian coronas or South African Krugerrands. Then the government legalized such ownership, making "fools in retrospect" out of many patriotic citizens. They had missed the bonanza. Thus is it always with the law-abiding man who trusts his government. The government misuses his trust. Then he learns. And with that education comes suspicion, hatred, and a hostility to law. The government debases its citizens whenever it debases its currency. (It works both ways, of course: "a little" inflation is popular with many debtors because there is larceny in their hearts.)

The Soviet Union found from the beginning that full socialism, which involves restraints on private production and private profit, creates shortages and crises so horrible that there has to be some sort of backtracking from the official ideology. Hence Lenin's New Economic Policy (NEP) in the early 1920's: small businesses were allowed increased economic freedom. Hence the garden plots in today's USSR. Food is more important than ideology. Hence the laxity in enforcing laws against unofficial barter. Whenever Stalinist ideologues temporarily get tough on black marketeers, the central economic plan smashes up on the rocks of shortages and delays. These political fluctuations between controls and modified economic freedom make true cynics out of the population. Cynicism is perhaps the one item which economic controls can produce in abundance. After painful obedience to irrational rules comes guilty participation in the survival markets. After guilt erodes, only cynicism remains. Cynicism and fear. And a secret lust for vengeance.

Stage Four: feudalization and the destruction of money. Price controls— laws against the most important form of tax evasion—disrupt markets. Unofficial markets replace the hampered official markets. Barter replaces monetary calculation. The division of labor drops as the size of organized markets shrinks. Productivity collapses. As money breaks down as a means of exchange, **non-monetary income becomes all-important.**

This is the remarkable genius of market responses to artifical impediments: men find ways of escape. When the inflation tax is imposed, men flee to hard goods. When it becomes illegal to flee to hard goods on the legal markets, they flee to hard goods on the illegal markets. When money exchanges finally break down, men begin to escape from the money economy, or at least the **official** money economy.

At the end of an inflation, the tax finally fails to do its confiscatory work. All taxes are denominated in money. Money is being destroyed. By delaying payment of taxes, legally or illegally, citizens find it easy to pay their obligations. They sell a hard good or service for paper money and pay their tax—the exchange now drawing twice as much in currency as it would have drawn a quarter or a month or a week earlier. The governments at all levels in Germany were paralyzed by this problem in 1922-23: they could not collect the taxes fast enough, and by the time they spent the money that had been taken in, it had declined again in purchasing power. The government fouls its own nest so efficiently that every time it tries to get out of the nest it slips, falling ever deeper into its own waste. In the long run, **those who are hurt most** by the invisible tax of inflation are those who are **employed by the government** in all but the highest levels of the bureaucracy, those who are **dependent upon the government** for welfare payments, and those who **believe in what government officials tell them**, e.g., that U.S. savings bonds are a fine investment for one's retirement.

Strategy for Survival

Stage One: official compliance. Understand that long-run survival in the coming **inflation tax deluge** requires flexibility. It is nice to have a clean record, governmentally speaking. It is nice not to have government officials with a personal vendetta for you. **Pay up.** Only nomads can escape. The country is not going to be rebuilt by nomads. Yes, the level of taxation is immoral. The means used to enforce the tax laws no doubt involve legalized extortion. The uses to which your tax dollars are put are clearly preposterous. Pay up. Understand that **the worst is yet to come**, and that survival depends largely on a clean record. You are buying invisibility—a very valuable future good.

Stage Two: speculation. When you see the second stage of mass inflation coming (as I think we can), take evasive action. Buy up distressed property. Buy at auctions. Buy future alternative monies: gold coins, silver coins, common caliber ammunition, high quality liquor, etc. If you use debt, make it short-term (there **may** be another credit crunch ahead—we can never be certain). Make sure it is within your power to pay it off by liquidating a present asset. Use **compensated leverage**; do not extend yourselves beyond your means to pay, in case a temporary credit crunch comes before the final inflationary blow-off. **Speculate in goods, not with your survival.** If you have to have something, own it outright. The main thing is to prepare yourself psychologically for the tax system that is the system of the future: mass inflation. If you think you will have qualms about buying and selling on black markets, buy what you think you will need right now, before such purchases are either impossible or illegal.

Stage Three: new life style. Repressed inflation paralyzes the modern money economy. Shortages will be everywhere. You will need a non-urban location, independence from public utilities, new (barterable) skills, and above all, **invisibility**. Keep your principles visible and your profits concealed. Live in that mediocre home with your mediocre clothes and your aging car. Fly coach. Lend a helping hand. If you've got it, don't flaunt it. Cynical citizens who have lost everything to the inflation tax will be seeking vengeance. Stay out of their way. Remember: **most people will not**

escape the coming debacle. The worst tragedy in our nation's history, economically speaking, is fast approaching.

Stage Four: crafts and knowledge. Contribute directly to your community's production. Support your local sheriff. Become your local sheriff. Know who supplies what goods at what non-monetary price. Pay your taxes—denominated in paper money—with all the enthusiasm you can muster; they have dumped the garbage on you, and now you can shovel it back to them with abandon. Get out of any remaining debt. And if anyone asks you how all these things came about, tell him. It all started in 1913: the sixteenth amendment and the Federal Reserve System.

CHAPTER EIGHT
THE FEUDALIZATION OF THE ECONOMY

In 1973, Doubleday published a startling book, *The Coming Dark Age*, by Roberto Vacca, an Italian technologist. Its thesis was simple enough: the modern world has relied on a technological superstructure that is far too complex for men to predict or control. With the overcentralization of planning in every realm of economic life—planning based increasingly on computer models and computerized data—the modern world has opened the possibility of an unpredictable breakdown that would spread like the ripples produced by tossing a stone into a pool.

What kind of disasters does Vacca have in mind? For instance, he argues, consider freeway traffic. Generally, people will drive onto our superhighways so as to minimize their participation in a massive traffic jam. Other things being equal, men prefer to avoid bumper-to-bumper traffic. Voluntarily, men have learned to time their entry onto the highways to avoid jams. But what if there were one day—statistically possible, given enough time—when too many people hit the highways simultaneously? The jam-up seems endless. Finally, people abandon their cars and walk away. Problem: how to unclog it in order to get the trucks in that supply a major urban area? New York City, says Vacca (and others), could last about three days apart from restocking from the outside. What if panic hit, either preceding the jam-up (fear of a bomb or a plague) or after the jam-up?

Then there is the power problem. What if another power failure hits, as it did in New York City and the New England area back in 1965? John Campbell, the late editor of *Analog*, the science fiction magazine, wrote an editorial shortly after this famous power failure, painting a grim picture. Supposedly, there are two basic theoretical formulas that are supposed to show how such a failure could occur, only they do not agree with each other. After showing how the MIT generator was used to start the silent generators of the power companies (with car batteries used to start the MIT generator), Campbell concludes that no one can assure the public, using either of the two formulas, that such an event will not happen again. Vacca has concluded the same thing. The threat of a major power failure is increasing, as more people come under the administration of the power

87

company bureaucracies, and their ability to deal with problems is unable to keep pace with the multiplication of these problems.*

The key problem is **price**. Vacca never mentions this aspect of the disruption of crucial public services. Again and again, the zones of continual catastrophe and crisis are those which are regulated by the municipal, state, or Federal governments, and which have prices dictated to them by politically influenced regulatory agencies. Power, highways, municipal services: all are either monopolies owned by the civil government, licensed by the civil government, or controlled by the civil government. So the problem of centralization cannot be avoided. Decisions are not being made by entrepreneurs who are fully responsible for their activities, and who suffer losses if decisions are not to the liking of the buying public. There is no open entry, with flagging established firms being spurred into action by newer, smaller, more creative firms. Price competition is not the principle behind the allocation of scarce resources. The existence of a free market is retarded, so the ability of managers to calculate costs and benefits by means of profit-and-loss statements is made impossible. Without economic calculation, central planning agencies are unable to evaluate the contributions of the various parts of the total system.

In a free market, entrepreneurs make mistakes. But they do not make simultaneous mistakes. One wins while another may lose. Therefore, there is **continuity** in the supply of needed goods and services. The existence of a freely fluctuating price mechanism informs suppliers of the goods and services in greatest demand; shortages are then filled rapidly. But when men are not permitted to bid up prices, the incentive to shift production from one area to another becomes economically haphazard: who has the most political pull, what are the priorities of the planning agencies, which disaster is getting the most publicity, etc.? Without the price mechanism and profit and loss indicators, no one can have confidence in his safety. Those supplying him become far less efficient in supplying his needs.

Transportation

There is a kind of law of bureaucratic progression in the regulatory process. The first stage involves **subsidies** to a particular established group, usually in exchange for the right of the government to supervise the affairs of the guild. Granting semi-monopolistic economic power to one group, the authorities feel compelled to make sure that such power is "used wisely for the benefit of the public." **Which** public is left undefined.

The next stage is increased **intervention**. Vested interests clash: buyers vs. sellers, excluded sellers vs. established sellers. Everyone wants the favors

---

*The second New York blackout occurred while the first hardback edition of this book was being typeset: July 13, 1977. The result of this blackout was massive looting.

granted by the government. The regulators increase their intervention in order to balance the many demands of the various interest groups. This decreases the profitability of the once-subsidized members of the protected segment of the market. It may produce bankruptcies, especially since managements are now less efficient, being accustomed to continual grants of semi-monopolistic economic power.

The third stage is **outright control** by the Federal government, since bankruptcy threatens the industry. It should be obvious that this outline fits the railroads of the East Coast rather well. Three generations after the original grants of power were made by the Interstate Commerce Commission, the eastern railroads are about to be nationalized. Then we are treated to the spectacle of the businessmen getting on board the nationalized railroads. "Shocking as nationalization may have been a couple of years ago," write the editors of *Business Week* (March 17, 1973), "it now seems to be the only workable solution left. . . . Nationalization—even of decaying facilities owned by bankrupt companies—is never easy for businessmen to accept. But under such circumstances, nationalization of the rails is the only way out." Actually, nationalization of any business used by other businessmen at below-market costs is so readily accepted when nationalized that it boggles the imagination. To hear a businessman complain about nationalization is about as amusing as hearing one of Xaviera Hollander's guild associates insist that she's not that kind of girl. Not at some ridiculously low price, anyway.

There is a way out, contrary to *Business Week*. Deregulate the railroads. Allow any entrepreneur to bid on the value of the existing property. Allow him to run as few and as many trains as he chooses, over whichever tracks produce the greatest return, at any time of day. Then deregulate the control of trucking, in order to give the railroad managers a strong incentive to keep prices down. Then deregulate the airlines and air freight. Do all of this day after tomorrow, and within a year your problem will be pretty-well solved—if it takes a year. In principle, it will have been solved; it may take time to work out the operating solution. Meanwhile, everyone will have to pay the **full costs** of the transportation services received. No one, least of all the businessman, wants to do that.

Transportation is the Achilles' heel of the cities. The miracle described a century ago by Frederic Bastiat—the fact that milk appeared on the Paris doorstep of everyone who ordered it, each and every morning, despite the fact that no planning agency directed such affairs—rests on free entry and free trade. Take away these supporting pillars, and the guaranteed deliveries become erratic. In Paris of 1789, revolutionaries deliberately impeded the delivery of bread to the city; the result was increased panic and rioting, including attacks on bakers who dared to hike prices in response to higher demand. This could happen again. In any case, the imposition of licensing requirements retards entry into the trucking industry, and in a time of price controls, the ability of individual consumers to predict with precision just who will be shipping in goods will be drastically reduced. Bottlenecks of production are bad enough, but bottlenecks of the supply of goods to an urban population could be politically explosive.

Under the controls placed on prices during the French Revolution, farmers refused to bring their goods into the city. A farmer might do it once, but not twice. Then confiscation by the state was necessary. Farmers were forced to give up their goods. Such actions by the state are always seen as necessary, just as nationalization of the rails is seen as necessary. These acts are necessary only in a world where men are not free to pursue their callings as they see fit.

The threat of confiscation only puts a premium on hiding signs of one's production. It pays to lie about what you have produced. This inevitably fouls up the computerized print-outs that are so crucial to macro-economic planning. The data are progressively debased, along with the paper money. It also puts a premium on barter.

Barter and Local Contacts

The medieval economy, like any preponderantly rural economy, was highly personal. Each man knew his supplier. The extent of the market was limited. Personal contacts were of great importance. This is one very important reason why Jews had a competitive advantage in international trade: family and religious contacts within this ostracized segment of the population were elevated in importance. But there really was not much trade, given the high costs of transportation. Bulky goods did not move very far from major waterways. Barter was basic to the economy, and face-to-face contact between producer and consumer was the standard operating procedure of that era.

Today, consumers almost never see the actual producer of any good. Middlemen provide transport services, retailing, and so forth. Money talks. Bookkeeping entries rule. But when price controls disrupt the reliability of supplies, as producers drop those items that no longer produce profits, the state will be tempted to intervene and demand that certain items are produced at a loss. This is no different, in principle, from the requirement by the CAB that certain flight schedules be maintained in spite of the losses they produce, or the ICC rules that certain train schedules be maintained. Then there will be a temptation to dilute product quality as a cost-cutting measure. The productivity of the overall economy will deteriorate. Independent middlemen will be squeezed out of business, as "vertical integration"—ownership from top to bottom by one firm, as a means of avoiding the bottlenecks produced by price controls—replaces multiple ownership. The free flow of goods and services will be impeded, but goods more than services. Goods leave more records. Records invite investigation.

At this stage, black markets will spring up. These will be markets on which money rules only in part. Safety considerations will put a premium on personal contacts—reliability. This, of course, was the basis of the Capone empire and the other gangs of the 1930's. Those who run the black markets are all too often unsavory characters who are willing to take risks and break laws. But public demand will register itself, and suppliers will be found. Local communities will be able to circumvent both government controls and the Mafia only by imitating the black market supply mechanism on a local level. Personal contact will be more important than it is today. On the other hand, the very requirement for personal contact will reduce the extent of the market, simultaneously reducing the division of labor.

There are other factors that tend to increase the reliance of the buying public on barter. One is the fact that goods which are not priced in terms of money, but are traded directly, are much more likely not to be reported on income tax forms, or if they are, at reduced rates. The imputation of monetary value is more difficult. Furthermore, bartered goods do not leave records in a bank account. Finally, bartered goods need not be sold at official **money** prices—controlled prices. This is why price controls increase the likelihood of barter.

It must be understood that barter represents a collapse of productivity and the reduction of everyone's income. It is not an efficient system. But it is more efficient than the repressed economy of price controls. This is why it would pay people to become familiar with swap meets, auctions, local bazaars, "flea markets," and all other similar institutions. There will be a day when knowledge of "junk" may mean survival. The proverbial horse trader may be seen again in some parts of America. It would be wise to start making contacts now if you are already in a rural area.

The Role of the Churches

There is little doubt in my mind that the local churches, with their face-to-face contacts, their family atmosphere, and the strong element of self-help that should be present, will become important centers for establishing lines of supply. They are obviously one institutional means of overcoming the burdens of a declining division of labor. They can be centers of local leadership, too, and where they take on social responsibilities they will simultaneously become centers of power. Power follows responsibility. This certainly has been true in the history of the American Negro. The local church was more than a narrowly defined place of religious worship. Poverty and a lack of community leadership placed great power into the hands of local pastors. Martin Luther King was not a lawyer, after all. Elijah Muhammed had more power than a typical Chicago alderman. The churches are continuing institutions, and this very feature grants to the churches tremendous power in a time of institutional crisis and economic breakdown.

The problem, of course, is that today's churches are seldom fit to exercise leadership. The social gospel denominations have generally forfeited the support of the laity. They have disbursed the capital of generations of giving. They are in deep trouble, both financially and in terms of the confidence of the members. But the conservative churches have been infected with a retreatist pietism for a century. The pastors are not used to the kind of responsibility that serious economic breakdown would place on them. How many deacons have been trained in their jobs? How many understand the biblical responsibilities, let alone the financial responsibilities? But the diaconate will have tremendous pressures placed upon it in a time of economic shortages. We have not raised up a school of the diaconate, any more than we have raised up a school of the prophets. Thus, a basic local institution has not prepared itself for what would seem to be coming. Even more disastrously, few leaders in the churches have sounded the alarm. The last people who seem to know what is happening are the members of the local conservative or fundamentalist denominations. They have a kind of gut-level conservative reaction to the drift of modern society, but they have done nothing, or next to nothing, to begin to work out alternatives for a time of crisis. Pastors who can get seventeen sermons out of Noah and the ark and five years' worth out of the typological meaning of the wilderness of the exodus, seem unable to comprehend the specifics of either. Thank God that He promised not to bring the flood again; if He planned to use it, the modern Christians would be hard-pressed to come up with anything more impressive than a handful of rowboats. (Excepting the Episcopalians, who might have a cabin cruiser or two, and these would be heavily mortgaged.)

Members of the local churches should take it upon themselves to see to it that they know about each other's skills. They should meet in homes, if necessary, to develop the marketing of these skills. Perhaps some men could decide to take a course in a particular craft, with the crafts complementing those skills possessed by other members of the congregation. If these meetings could become community-wide, so much the better. Women could meet together to share ideas on gardening, sewing, and other crafts that would be helpful during a time of reduced productivity. Children should be encouraged to develop skills, especially during summer vacations. A group of adults could locate and hire the services of some retired craftsman and bring him to the church or private school for training purposes. The demise of the apprenticeship system has not yet been seen for the disaster that it has produced. A depression, or mass inflation with controls, followed by a depression, will call the loss to our attention.

The Revival of Craftsmanship

Back in 1970, I wrote an essay, "Inflation and the Return of the Craftsman." I argued that the imposition of price and wage controls would disrupt the normal markets for goods and services and place a premium on the production of relatively simple goods. In other words, the controls invariably reduce the division of labor, and this in turn bankrupts industries that are too specialized, especially industrial firms. Therefore, we should expect to see a revival of interest in goods produced by simpler production processes. Those who have the tools and skills necessary for such production will, obviously, be immediate beneficiaries of the controls.

No conventional magazine would touch the article. I specifically predicted that Nixon would impose price controls, despite his assurances to the contrary. He did, seven months after the article was published. Only the counter-culture magazine, *The Whole Earth Catalog*, would touch it (Jan. 1971). (This article is reprinted in the next chapter.) I have not changed my mind. I would strongly recommend a good apprenticeship program or trade school for those with any inclinations and skills along these lines. The U.S. government operates a National Apprenticeship Program through the Department of Labor, and it would be wise for interested people to order booklets on the program from the Department's Bureau of Apprenticeship and Training of the Manpower Administration, Washington, D.C. 20210.

This may turn out to be one of the major benefits of price controls. Repairs will be the staff of life. If you are unable to buy new manufactured goods at the artificially low prices, then you will have to shell out the money to keep what you have operating. This is where the incentive factor enters the picture. Young men will see the advantages to learning complex skills. They will have to seek out older men to learn some of these skills, since the schools seldom provide craft training, and certainly not in local communities that are too far from a junior college to commute easily (especially under gasoline rationing). The master teachers of the world may find that economic necessity is the mother of harder working apprentices.

When we look at the horrors that Europe has seen twice or more in this century, we Americans are too apt to turn away and tell ourselves that we are completely different. But just because we have not seen this kind of economic disruption, even in the great depression, is no reason to assume that such events are in some way screened out by the ocean. On the other hand, Europe has maintained its artisan tradition longer than we have. If a breakdown should come, then at least we should make the best of it. We should organize ourselves to meet the difficulties creatively. It is unlikely that churches will take these steps in advance, but sooner or later they must face the fact that there are no political and economic vacuums, and that an institution as central as a church cannot evade the responsibilities of leadership forever.

The 8th chapter of Deuteronomy sketches the development of a godly society: covenantal faithfulness produces blessings; the external blessings produce forgetfulness; forgetfulness produces judgment and disaster; and disaster is supposed to call a faithless people to repentance. The destruction of Isaiah 1 is followed by the restoration of Isaiah 2. Hopefully, the disruptions that seem so inescapable today will be of this nature. We will use our economic trials to learn new skills, including the skills of leadership. This has to be done in local churches.

The feudalization of the economy will impel men to exercise their talents to meet local needs. They will be forced to learn who their neighbors are and what they need and can produce. What we lose in efficiency we hopefully will compensate for in increased neighborliness and co-operation in the community. The wealth of urban life brought with it isolation, anonymity and loneliness. Perhaps the loss of wealth will help us to regain what we lost long ago.

In any case, if the churches and local voluntary associations refuse to carry the torch, the Mafia and other less voluntary groups will. It is best to place the leadership, including self-defense, in more reliable hands.

CHAPTER NINE
INFLATION AND THE RETURN OF THE CRAFTSMAN

I could not find a publisher for this in the conservative press, so I sent it to the incredible magazine (now defunct—the only one I ever saw which folded, voluntarily, in the midst of fantastic popularity), **The Whole Earth Catalog** *(Jan., 1971). Amazingly, some of my radical acquaintances on the campus and off found it persuasive. I received a letter from one lady, obviously a hard-working "proletarian" of relatively little formal education, who said her college senior daughter had given it to her and had said, "This is what you've told me for years, but I never believed it before." Unfortunately, truth is not always its own best testimony in our world; where it appears or who says it is what counts. But some of our "hippie" citizens have more economic sense than some of our presidential advisors on the Council for Economic Development. I wrote this in mid 1970. Obviously my timing was off. I had expected the imposition of wage-price controls in 1973 or 1974; Nixon beat me to it. So far, my predictions are accurate: no controls on art objects, collectors' items, used goods, and small businesses. Now, let's see if the rest of my prophecy comes true. I fear that it will.*

Prophets are seldom popular men, even when they predict correctly. In the area of economic forecasting good men are often frighteningly wrong. Thus, the man who claims to know the future is taking a considerable risk: if he is wrong, he will look like a fool; if he is right, everyone will hate him (at least if he has predicted hard times). Nevertheless, every man has to be a bit of a prophet if he is to survive. There is no way of escaping personal responsibility; men must plan, at least to some extent, for their economic futures. If that future brings what I am fully convinced it must bring, a lot of white collar professionals are going to be disappointed, and a lot of hobbyists are going to reap very substantial economic rewards.

America's greatest economic bugaboo is depression. The memory of the 1930's has left an indelible scar on the American mind. It would be politically safe to say that no political party, especially the party incumbent in the White House, will be willing to risk a depression; the results at the polls would be too devastating. In short, if the government should face an either/or situation of inflation or depression, it will choose inflation every time. There is evidence—I believe overwhelming evidence—that indicates that this is precisely the dilemma we face today.

During the final months of President Johnson's administration, the Federal Reserve System (our nation's central bank) stopped the increase of new money coming into the economy. President Nixon continued to support the FED's decision for the first year in office. The results were (or should have been) predictable: increased unemployment, a disastrous fall in the stock market, falling industrial profits, and decreased tax revenues. Ironically, the end of monetary inflation did not bring an end to price inflation; people apparently could not bring themselves to believe that "tight money"—high rates of interest—and zero monetary inflation would persist. They did not believe that President Nixon would pursue indefinitely a policy of balanced budgets, reduced government expenditures, and higher taxes (which is the way you stop prices from rising). So labor and business kept passing on higher and higher prices to the consumer; and the man out of work, the marginal business, and the self-employed laborer found the economic squeeze disastrous. The general public kept bidding for goods.

Since last spring, the Federal Reserve System has reversed itself. New money is now being injected into the economy. The federal government's deficit (the difference between income and expenditures) is climbing again, and this means the central bank now buys government bonds with newly created credit-money—monetary inflation. Given the psychology of Americans in 1970, this will mean price inflation. A "reinflation" of the economy is beginning. What can we reasonably expect? The cost of living index will climb in the 1970's as never before in peacetime America. Price inflation is the symptom of a previous monetary inflation, and we should expect to see prices rise at an increasingly frantic clip. When this happens, there is always great public pressure put on the government to impose price and wage controls. People do not understand that rising prices are a symptom of a deeper cause, namely, the increase of the money supply (fostered primarily, though not exclusively, by federal deficits). They call for a suppression of the outward symptoms. It would not be surprising to see the incoming President in 1973 forced to begin the imposition of price controls sometime during his administration. The Congress has already granted this power to President Nixon, in spite of his protests. Power once granted is generally used sooner or later.*

Many readers will remember the effect of price controls during World War II. There were shortages everywhere, and all of these shortages were not the exclusive responsibility of the war effort. Anyone who has lived in

---

*Controls were imposed on August 15, 1971, seven months after this essay was published.

a foreign nation during a period of price controls knows what can happen, even in peacetime. Anyone trying to rent a decent apartment on Manhattan Island today knows the effect of rent controls: heavy demand and no supply. Lots of money, but very few desirable goods. Since it is more difficult to make a profit in controlled industry, labor, capital, and raw materials tend to go into the uncontrolled industries where greater profits are likely. So the market for industrial goods begins to dry up. You cannot buy a home appliance easily, and new automobiles get scarce, and electrical goods disappear. And the available goods get shoddier as manufacturers are forced to cut costs to make ends meet. We are already seeing this to some extent, as inflation takes its toll; with price controls, these effects on workmanship are amplified.

If I am correct in my analysis of inflation and in my prediction that more inflation is likely, then the reader should begin to see what is coming. The man who plans carefully at this stage stands to survive the price-wage squeeze, the shortages, and the defective workmanship that are on their way. The hobbyist has one item that will rise in value, will be marketable, and will be in heavy demand: **specialized knowledge**. In some cases that knowledge will be so valuable that a hobby may become a new occupation for those men who take advantage of new conditions. For white collar workers, or those associated with heavy industries that will be hit hard by the economic controls, their skills in the home shop may be more profitable than their skills in the factory or office.

Why should this be the case? Because the official lines of supply will be increasingly empty of the desired goods and services. The black market—an inevitable effect of price controls—will begin to absorb the goods most heavily in demand. It always has in the past; there is little reason to expect anything different for the future. Those with power or prestige or other goods to trade will absorb the supplies, leaving the rest of the population to stand in long lines in front of half-empty stores. The difference between the demand (at the official, legal prices) and supply is where the hobbyist enters his glory. One thing which we can expect to see is that new household electrical appliances and similar manufactured goods will become more difficult to obtain. Governments always place price and wage controls over those industries that are large enough and "vital" enough to be worth the effort to control. All industries are not equally subject to controls. Controls are put on such things as mining, steel manufacture, metals of all sorts, electronics, and automobiles. (About the only industry generally left free in the past has been farming: it is a highly competitive market and constitutes a major voting bloc.) Local businesses involved in retailing any of these products are faced with a man-made crisis: shortages of goods and rising wage demands by employees. Capital flows out of these areas of the economy and into the so-called "luxury" trades: antiques, art collecting, coins, stamps, rare books, rare wines and liquors. All of these industries have experienced rapid price increases since 1965, the year inflation began to be felt by the general public. When price controls appear, their expansion will be that much greater, as more and more people pour a depreciating currency into goods that are not under price controls.

If manufactured goods, especially home appliances, get scarce, then the home repair expert experiences a bonanza. People have to make-do with the old washing machine or refrigerator. The day that price controls are declared, the intelligent buyer will go down and buy every $25-$50 used refrigerator he can store. He will buy old broken motors from junk stores. The junk store man, if he is smart, will try to increase his supplies, holding inventories for as long as possible, waiting for the economic boom. It will not be long in coming. When price controls are in effect, a startling effect is produced: the price differential between new and old goods begins to narrow. In some cases the differential may even shift in favor of the used goods: the used good is not under price controls, while the new good is. People can bid up the prices of used goods in a way that they cannot with the new goods. They can buy what they are willing to pay for—but only in the used goods market. If price controls were imposed in 1975, by 1980 a man might be able to triple his original investment. He could do far better if he were a repairman who had bought junk discards to begin with. That is a good return on one's money; the stock market will never match it, for controls invariably spell the death of blue chip capital stocks; it is these industries that are placed under the controls first. Controls, by definition, are intended to reduce profits.

The demand for repairs will skyrocket, but the larger unions—plumbing, plastering, carpentry—are likely to be placed under wage controls. Being more visible, and being orgainized into a guild, these fields will be more easily controlled by government boards of officials. The result will be a fantastic increase in labor's black market, or as it will be called (as it is called today), "moonlighting." A professional will spend as little time as possible on his official job, saving his skills and energy for his "underground" occupation. Even if the unions escape controls, the market for the amateur repairman will expand as people refuse to pay the going unionized wages. We have seen this take place already.

There is another factor to consider. A dollar saved is a lot more than a dollar earned. An earned dollar is subject to taxation; a saved dollar is not. As people begin to understand this basic economic fact, they will make use of their own skills, or their neighbor's skills, to get repairs done cheaply. We can expect to see neighborhood service exchanges set up, and woe unto the man who does not have a skill to exchange.

The demand for repair manuals and how-to-do-it books will increase, and so will prices for such publications. The smart individual will buy his 10-year subscription to a home repair magazine the day following the announcement of price controls. Editors of many popular magazines will begin to face basic changes in their economic parameters. Paper costs will either soar or else paper will become very scarce (due to controls); advertisers will not be willing to pay high prices for advertising, since all the goods they have to sell will be bought anyway. Men will advertise in order to obtain supplies; thus, the money will be made in classified advertising. The repair journals and the collectors' journals will reap the harvest of these subscriptions, for it will be through information in these hobby publications that men will find answers to critical problems. The man with specialized knowledge of these markets and these skills will be in the driver's seat.

Hobbyists will notice another phenomenon. There will be a vast new audience for the hobby industries. Being essentially "luxuries," they will be the industries free from controls. (The controls are at first reserved for "vital" industries.) With money to spend and few products to buy, people will begin to increase their expenditures on luxuries: travel, camping, entertainment, and all forms of do-it-yourself tools and materials. The amateur hobbyist who has amassed considerable knowledge over the last few years may find himself a professional, for knowledge is not a free economic good. It takes time, discipline, and usually money to obtain it. I would therefore expect to see amateur hobbyists establishing local informal schools (or perhaps even franchised schools) that would impart skilled knowledge at a price. Neighborhood evening schools will become common. Some men may have specialized libraries that can be made into reference libraries at a profit. Where there is heavy demand, some men will find a means of converting such demand into personal benefit. Knowledge does not come easily; it will not be sold cheaply.

This has led me to an odd conclusion (for a college instructor). The young man who has skills mechanically would be wise to stay out of college. He would be far wiser to get into a trade school, especially if he should have a skill that would not require highly specialized machinery. With some 8,000,000* young men and women on the college campuses today, there will be a glut of people holding college degrees. In fact, the glut is already quite visible. The automatic job for the man with the bachelor's degree is not automatic any longer, at least not at the older higher wage. The skilled craftsman is about to have his day. The man who can produce a thing of beauty or of use through his own genius, with simple tools and common materials, should find the coming decade exceptionally profitable. If he must sacrifice the false prestige of a college diploma in order to get such skills, the sacrifice ought to pay off in the future—perhaps the very near future.

The 1970's and the 1980's may well destroy the whole economic structure that is based on the "organization man"—the drone who substitutes activity for production, a glib tongue for knowledge. The days of the

*Up to 11,000,000 in 1976.

instant success through college are numbered; there are simply too many people in college for any monopolistic reward to be maintained by holders of the college degree. Men with skills and knowledge will continue to be paid well, but the skills and knowledge required for economic survival may not be those imparted by formal college instruction. Prestige will come once more to the man who can build with his own hands, the creative person, the man who possesses operational knowledge of how simple things work. For that kind of man, the bonanza is about to begin.

CHAPTER TEN
EMPLOYEE RELATIONS UNDER PRICE CONTROLS

We live in an economy which is a truly **political** economy. It is government which controls the money supply's basic aggregates, although citizens can influence monetary results to the extent that they cash in savings accounts (or create them), or cash in checking accounts in order to hold currency. That, in fact, is the original meaning of "cash-in." If the currency is not redeposited by some recipient of the cash, then the overall money supply is reduced, since the banks cannot multiply cash held outside the banking system. Cash is not fractionally reserved, in other words. But on the whole, government controls the money supply, since the Federal Reserve System will capitulate to the government if the President and Congress are agreed on a particular monetary policy.

This means that the fiat-money-induced boom-bust cycle is the product of misguided or malevolent government policy. The politics of inflation and the politics of envy combine to create the universally inflationary economies of Western Europe (yes, including Switzerland), Asia, Latin America, Australia, and Africa. The only continent which is not presently experiencing inflation is Antarctica. This means that professionals, employers, and corporate managers must find ways to keep their businesses operating after price and wage controls —especially wage controls—bottle up the productivity of the free market. Controls may seem far away today, but inflation is certainly with us, the boom-bust economic cycle is still with us, and it is not too difficult to predict the advent of that old political program of last resort, controls. He who ignores them will find his business disrupted, sooner or later. Probably sooner.

The Pressures on Professionals

Men who do their work well, meaning better than their competitors, are subject to considerable psychological stress, and sometimes even killing stress. The stress can become physiological. Men feel driven to stay ahead and improve their businesses. They want recognition of their performance. They tend to be perfectionists—a dangerous goal in an imperfect and decreasingly efficient economy. Very often, they drink too much, work too hard, and die too young. The slogan of Alcoholics Anonymous, "easy does it," is literally a life-saver for some of its members. These are men, in many cases, who almost destroyed themselves by ignoring the limits on their own human capacities. Their labor was intensive, but they could not keep up the pace they had set for themselves.

There is a loss to society when this happens. We may enjoy the services of the self-driven producer, but then we lose when he can no longer produce. In certain key fields where the progress of the profession is cumulative and very rapid—the sciences, law, medicine—the loss can be even greater. It takes so long to gain the professional skills, gain the necessary experience, build up self-confidence, build up confidence among one's potential customers, increase output, and stay on top of the field, that an early death or crippling sickness is a mini-disaster to the profession and those served by it. One of the chief goals of this brief book is to help men to increase their income, but never forget that this means that each man must increase his output over the long haul. The pressures placed on conscientious managers by price controls are horrendous, and they grow worse over time. The more of a perfectionist you are, the more you should concentrate on relieving expected future pressures while you still can. Controls-induced shortages create problems that cannot be solved by the managerial equivalent of a Chinese fire drill.

The Division of Labor

Without the existence of a market system, and primarily a money economy, the division of labor collapses. This is the chief economic (as distinguished from moral) threat offered by full-scale price and wage controls. Men cannot rely on the performance of contracts by others. This makes the delegation of responsbility that much more difficult. Yet the delegation of responsibility is vital if the effects of the perfectionist's mania are to be overcome. "Please, mother, I'd rather do it myself," is a sure-fire formula for disaster when markets get creaky as a result of the distortion of prices.

The key question ought to be the **total** output of **everyone** working on a project or in an office. No doubt there are some managers who can perform the major tasks better than anyone else in the organization, but the central issue is total output. A century and a half ago, David Ricardo defended the free market system of free trade by pointing out that if there are two nations, and one can produce both apples and oranges more efficiently than the other, it should nevertheless concentrate on what it produces most efficiently, leaving the production of the other product to the second nation. Total output goes up. A good manager is one who can get the division of labor working for his organization.

The high-technology, high-education, high-profit tasks should be performed by those few individuals who can handle them best. Find the job which only one or two men can handle and fill it with the best man, even if he can also do the best job on half a dozen less specialized tasks that others can perform, albeit less efficiently. Those highly specialized producers owe it to themselves, their business or organization, and especially to the consumer, to force themselves to concentrate on the tasks that they, and they alone, can perform.

All this may sound trite. But in a time of controls-induced rigidities, it is absolutely imperative that managers and owners discipline themselves to deal with the reality of the division of labor. No one in a professional position denies the fact that some tasks—answering the telephones, filing forms, finding forms, going for coffee—should not be a part of his normal schedule. A professional in a large company should not serve as a part-time clerk. Yet how much attention do professionals give to the problems concerning clerical help? How many seek out opportunities for transferring responsibility downward? Not enough.

Costs of Replacement

Say that by some miracle, you have located a competent secretary. Someone who shows up 15 minutes early, remembers all of your appointments, can make sense of your billing methods, keeps your customers happy, and brews a good cup of coffee. What is she worth? To estimate her value, try to estimate what it would cost you—really cost you—if she were to quit. First, there would be the applications and the screening of a replacement. Think of interviewing dimwitted teeny-boppers (of whatever age) who are the flower of our government-financed educational system. Think about the confusion in your office during the screening process. Think of the possibility that you, out of desperation, might hire one of these dunderheads. Think of the disruption and problems that will accumulate until you fire her and start the search all over again.

If you think this is a joke, start looking into the future three to five years. When wages are frozen by law, and prices are also frozen, your office or company will start getting hectic—more confusion in billing (you run out of forms, and your supplier is out of stock), long delays in getting paid (the "it's in the mail" syndrome), endless government forms to fill out—the only forms, I hope, which will run out of stock permanently. Meanwhile, you are not permitted to raise the salaries of your clerical help. Clerical jobs are now unpleasant, but you are forbidden by law to match the increase in frustration with an increase in salary. That nice, sensitive, competent assistant or typist or clerk finally breaks out in tears. "I quit!" she announces, and promptly walks out. It really is not worth her trouble any more. She can stay home, do some typing on the side (at black market prices), pocket the cash, fail to report the income, and do quite well, thank you. She can go on welfare for less trouble. The sensitive ones will quit first.

What are you able to do about it? The market for competent secretarial help is already a seller's market today; what about in 1984? When wages are frozen, the employer is prohibited from entering the labor markets and competing **by means of wage increases** with his competition. The competition is not simply other harried corporate executives; the competition includes leisure, black market opportunities, government hand-outs, self-employment. How will you convince some competent replacement to come in and straighten out the mess, or at least try to straighten it out? This is no laughing matter. A man's professional career may hinge on his being able to answer this question.

Non-Price Incentives

As always, the entrepreneur who will prosper under controls will be the man who can seek out legal alternatives to the money-denominated price system. It is not a good use of his time in comparison with what he might accomplish under free pricing, but it is necessary for survival. In the case of secretarial and clerical help, studies have indicated that women respond better to improved working conditions than they do to a comparable amount of money spent directly on salaries, compared to the way men respond. This is economically rational, whatever psychological reasons may be involved. First, women are not usually the primary family breadwinners. (Those who are will really suffer under wage controls.) Second, a money raise puts the family into a higher tax bracket, so that non-monetary incentives, which are consumed directly and are not taxable, can be effective even under free pricing. A professional who yells at his secretary when he is under pressure had better find a way to keep from getting under pressure. Or he had better start disciplining himself to control his temper now, before controls are imposed. A man whose office is continual bedlam is asking for trouble. He will be at a competitive disadvantage under controls. It might even pay him to have a management consultant come in and rearrange his office's organization. By reducing office tensions, these well-paid consultants can improve efficiency now, and insure economic survival later. (A wise consultant would today be thinking through the implications of non-price competition; he will need that knowledge soon.)

Another effective means of non-wage competition is the judicious use of a promotion. A truly competent secretary should be made an executive secretary, preferably before controls are imposed, certainly immediately after they are imposed, and absolutely once labor shortages appear. People are status seekers as well as income seekers. They want others to understand their value to a firm, and a title is one means of insuring such recognition. With a promotion in title, the promoted worker should have more responsibility—true responsibility. If possible, the promoted secretary-clerk should have a full-time or part-time assistant. Again, the principle of the division of labor must be recognized and honored in the price control breach. It is absolutely imperative that people be paid in direct proportion to their economic contribution to production. Price controls make this wage-production relationship very difficult to ascertain with accuracy, but managers must try to discover it. **Every** worker must be paid in terms of the **cost of replacing** him or her. The more successful a man is in determining this cost, the more likely he is to survive economically.

Prior to the imposition of controls, businessmen would be wise to use some form of the **bonus** system of compensation. I think that bonuses are superior to simple salary increases. They stimulate people to greater output. Bonuses, not being "owed" directly and regularly, are not mentally classified in the category of "minimum expected payment," which then serves as a launching pad for even more wage demands, whether actual or mental (i.e., resentment against management for not offering a raise). When raises are given, household budgets are expanded and even over-extended (thereby requiring another wage increase). Bonuses, on the other hand, are seen as special rewards for special efficiencies. Furthermore, a tradition of bonuses established prior to controls might give a manager some leverage in the future. Obviously, price and wage regulators will regard bonuses as disguised raises. The firm that has a long tradition of bonuses may escape the controllers for a time. (Frankly, I doubt it. No one pays bureaucrats to compromise, except directly, and that is called bribery, and people go to jail for it. But a tradition of bonuses might help, and it pays off now anyway.)

An extremely effective means of non-wage competition is to drop a thousand dollars in a secretary's lap and tell her to go out and spend it on the office. Tell her she can do anything she wants with it: new furniture, tape recorded music, new filing cabinets, a new IBM self-erase typewriter, or whatever. Make it clear that it is for her benefit. What will make the office more pleasant for her? Your competitor who may want her services has not designed an office around her needs.

An intelligent manager will discuss the state of the office with his best clerical and secretarial help. Long-term employees may know where a crisis is brewing, since they spend time unraveling them on a day-to-day basis. Tell your best secretary to cure it. Delegate responsibility. Get the problem out of your hair and hers.

The Family

No matter how liberated women may become, the influence of their families will be felt. Women may choose to remain employed in spite of protests from their husbands, and a manager's cost calculation must include a compensating remuneration. Under price and wage controls, there will be a tendency for women to return to direct family service. There are several good reasons for this. First, child-care services will begin to dry up—or at least those that are not black market, cash-in-hand services. But the employer is not allowed to increase secretarial or clerical salaries. Thus, some women will have to drop out of the labor force. Second, the wage may not seem so important to the family, since shortages in the supermarkets will reduce the efficiency of money wages. Shortages actually place a premium on other assets, most notably **time**. Standing in line is one important asset. Getting to half-empty shops before the line gets too long is another. Searching the classified ads, going to garage sales, attending auctions—where prices for used goods are uncontrolled—are all time-consuming alternatives to employment in the labor force. Shortages therefore subsidize those with access to time. This is another reason why baby sitting jobs will look less attractive. Thus, a woman will have an incentive to enter the time markets and leave the money markets. Managers must take action to prevent this.

The pressures from her husband to quit her job will be intensified if she comes home tired and irritable. (Who wants to be married to someone who continually acts like the people in the "before" segment of a "Vallium" commercial?) If her job upsets her too much, she may begin to take it out of his hide. One way to prevent this is to insist that she get out of the office at closing time. She must be informed of her importance continually. A successful manager must let his secretaries know that their families should come first, not the office. Men may be married to the job, but lower-echelon women are married to men. Sooner or later, the manager who cannot admit this risks disaster: her home really **will** come first. She quits.

It would be wise to find out the likes and dislikes of the husbands of key secretaries. It would be wise even to court them. Tickets to sports events are very useful in this regard. Have "all-husband outings" at the firm's expense. Tickets can also be given directly to the wife to take home to her husband (and sons). Such a donation should be made in terms of the argument that "I just had these lying around, but I can't use them." Husbands will believe that executives probably do have access to tickets that they really are unable to use. This is the best kind of gift for someone who is not a friend: something useful to the recipient which does not appear to be a loss to the giver. Envy does not breed in such circumstances. This is not seen as a bribe or something demeaning. If anything, it reminds the husband that the executive remembered that he (the husband) likes this sport or could use the tickets to take his sons. The tickets need not be the best; if anything they ought to be cheaper seats. No use reminding the husband that he could never afford to buy such expensive seats. Envy is a killer.

Anything that an executive can do for an employee's children is doubly or quadrupally rewarded in good will. Help in school, tutoring, scholarship recommendations, or anything else an employer can do to create excellent labor relations, but more important, such assistance is an excellent form of non-monetary, non-taxable income. Furthermore, most of us will accept gifts from non-family members to our children, even if we would be suspicious of gifts to ourselves. This is especially true of immigrants with "Old Country" backgrounds. The family is primary.

Loyalty

Western laborers, time and time again, have demonstrated their preference for the "cash nexus" system of capitalism, despite the cries of horror from traditionalists, rural elites, and Marxists. If you want to summarize the dialectic of economic history, you can come close in two words: money talks. But when money is debased, and the bureaucrats will not allow more than a whisper, then the older means of binding men's labor services comes into the foreground: loyalty. It is a feudal virtue, and in "Western" nations, i.e., industrial societies, only Japan seems to operate in terms of it. Even in Japan, the old system is slowly slipping. Therefore, since price controls will eventually produce what I call the feudalization of the economy, it is best to have a corporate tradition of company loyalty instilled in the employees.

Obviously, loyalty is not created overnight as a mangerial response to controls. This is why this should be a year of crucial importance to managers. Small firms have an advantage over large ones in periods of controls, simply because it is easier for personal bonds to develop inside small production units. An esprit d'corps is not some nice extra that a company may wish to cultivate; it is an economic imperative given the likelihood of price and wage controls.

The economy of feudalism would substitute personalism and localism for impersonalism and internationalism in the realm of economic exchange. Personal relationships and contacts are all-important in a collapsing market economy. Who you know becomes more important than money exchange. There is a kind of loyalty account book in a feudal economy; he who does not have one is in bad shape. A man can buy loyalty but the currency will not be exclusively paper. It will be a tradition of concern for the total welfare of the employees, including their families. The corporate executive who recognizes this early enough will have a competitive advantage.

All of this advice may sound trite—textbook knowledge, Dale Carnegie stuff. That it is. The problem with most of us is that we never apply all those trite, elementary sayings that we all acknowledge. Just because something is trite does not mean that it is not difficult. The Golden Rule has become trite through pseudo-familiarity; nevertheless, it is still valid in principle and practice. So it is with good management-labor relations. But in a shortage economy, that which today appears trite will become essential for survival. We must learn to think in non-monetary terms.

CHAPTER ELEVEN
EVADING THE EFFECTS OF PRICE CONTROLS:
CASE STUDIES

The experience of Germany [1933-48] demands that we consider a little more closely this peculiar policy of repressed inflation. As we have seen, it consists, fundamentally, in the fact that a government first promotes inflation but then seeks to interdict its influence on prices and rates of exchange by imposing the now familiar wartime devices of rationing and fixed prices, together with the requisite enforcement measures. As inflationary pressures force up prices, costs, and exchange rates, the ever more comprehensive and elaborate apparatus of the command economy seeks to repress this upward movement with the countermeasures of the police state. . . . The prolongation of a policy of repressed inflation means that all economic values become increasingly fictitious, and this in a twofold sense: (1) stated values correspond less and less to actual scarcity relationships and (2) fewer and fewer transactions are completed on the basis of such values. The distortion of all value relationships which accompany the division of the economy into "official" and "black" markets, and the struggle between the directives of the market and those of the administrative authorities finally lead to chaos, to a situation in which any kind of order, whether of the collectivist or the market economy type, is lacking.

Wilhelm Roepke
Economics of the Free Society
(Regnery, 1963), p. 104.

It was not only Germany which experienced the effects of price and wage controls coupled with monetary expansion—repressed inflation—but the entire Western world. Germany, however, was the first European state to adopt the policies of repressed inflation as a peacetime measure of the 1930's. And the Allies virtually sanctioned Germany's domestic economic policies by imposing "victors' justice" on the defeated German nation:

maintaining the price control policies imposed by Hitler's Nazi government. All that can be said in favor of the Allies' program is that it gave Ludwig Erhard, Roepke's former student, the opportunity to throw off this "foreign" system in June of 1948. It was a strong political argument among Germans at the time, and without the decontrol of the German economy in 1948, there would have been no "German miracle."

Who Wins? Who Loses?

Roepke's point is well taken: the official prices are fictitious. Fewer transactions, proportionate to total transactions, take place at the official prices. Prices are not controlled by the authorities, for that is not possible; only **visible monetary prices** are controlled. Even more accurately, those **people** who are forced to sell at official monetary prices and those who would be willing to buy at higher prices, but who cannot locate legal sellers, are controlled.

Price controls therefore involve a **redistribution of wealth. First,** some people are compelled to sell at prices lower than they would otherwise have preferred to receive and would have been able to receive. The beneficiaries are, of course, the buyers. The intended beneficiary is the "little guy." The actual beneficiaries—**legal** beneficiaries—are the Federal government, the higher officials in various governments, and those people who are willing and able to stand in long lines for many hours (and whose alternative uses of their time are, in their own estimation, less valuable than the goods they receive). **Second,** wealth is transferred to those who produce goods and services favored by the government, or those who produce goods produced in the uncontrolled segments of the economy ("luxuries"), assuming that these producers would not have prospered so well under conditions of open competition and free pricing. The losers are, of course, producers who would have profited under the free market and those consumers who would have bought from them. **Third,** wealth is transferred to those who have fewer moral qualms or fears about participating on the illegal markets, since available goods and services tend to flow in the direction of these markets. The larger the discrepancy between the legal monetary price of a good and the monetary inflation-induced illegal market price, the more goods are transferred to the alternative markets. The losers are the morally inhibited, or fear-inhibited, or information-lacking, or barterable resource-lacking citizens. Above all, the losers are the propaganda-manipulated patriotic citizens. Under all price control schemes, this law rules: **cynics win, patriots lose.** That is the curse of the government-controlled prices. **Fourth,** repairmen win. **Fifth,** those who own goods win, since used goods are not controlled. **In short,** those who possess the **real** money or monies win: good looks, power, goods, inside information, barterable skills, cynicism, and so forth.

Economically speaking, price controls serve as a subsidy to the cynics.

They subsidize those who would not have fared so well under the free market. They are anti-market devices, and they favor anti-market groups and those who do not prosper under conditions of peaceful competition. Those who do not wish to subsidize the anti-market elements of the population should not call for price controls unless they believe that the benefits of a controls-induced redistribution of wealth somehow outweigh the costs. (The theoretical problem here, however, is that there is no way of measuring costs and benefits outside of a free market, or at least no strictly economic way of making such an evaluation.)

Results of the Readers' Survey

After two mailings of my "Price Controls History Sheet," I received back about a 1.4% response. I wish there had been more, but some of those that came back are quite informative. There are theoretical reasons for concluding that similar policies will produce similar results, so our questions must center on the specifics of the legislation. For example, the experience of controls in the Nixon years may have led government officials to conclude that next time the controllers must set limits on the prices of raw agricultural and mineral products. This, in turn, will necessitate prohibitions on the export of raw materials that are under the controls. For example, writes John O'Donnell, in reference to June and July of 1973: "Nixon froze silver prices at $2.35/oz. in the U.S. This was to create a black market in all gold and silver coins plus bullion scrap, i.e., scrap X-ray film and photographic sludge. U.S. refiners would not increase buying prices at spot [cash] markets, while futures [contracts to buy or sell products in the future] prices increased to $2.85/oz. We shipped our bullion and scrap into Canada (Toronto) to receive full value at $2.85 per troy ounce. Most major U.S. refiners have offices in Toronto. The net effect is a silver shortage... ..When price controls were lifted, silver prices stabilized at fair market value closer to $2.56/oz." A similar crisis was created in soybean production. Farmers have always exported soybeans to Japan—the major buyer of soybeans, including U.S. soybeans, world-wide. So the government banned the export of soybeans in 1973. Why? To lower the price of soybeans domestically. And who consumes most of our soybeans in this country? Dogs. (Yes, sad to relate, even those that eat Alpo, which now contains soybeans. Is nothing sacred?) So we wound up selling wheat to the U.S.S.R. at low 1972 prices, thereby fulfilling our contracts—contracts hammered out primarily by U.S. government officials, not U.S. farmers—and embargoing soybeans, a major export to a major ally. So much for the policies of Henry Kissinger, Earl Butz, and John Dunlop.

The shortage problems people faced in World War II were varied, predictably, depending upon the geographical location involved. Frederic Andre reports: "Price controls did not have as large a dislocative impact on our rural life as it may have had on urban-dwellers. Most everything that was in short supply became a 'rationed' item. Our economy was as much favor-regulated as it was price-regulated. Consequently, scarce (rationed) items such as meat, sugar, coffee, gasoline, tires, and batteries were items for swapping among acquaintances. From time to time we would hear of black markets selling sugar and meat at prices 2 or 3 times the grocery store price. Perhaps the item whose shortage most curtailed our normal living was the gasoline shortage. To cope with this, Dad secured both the regular 'A' category of gas rationing coupons and also the 'C' category (perhaps because he was entitled to it as a minister). Anyway, when gasoline ran low, Dad would somehow persuade a friendly farmer to direct the hose of his 200 gallon farm vehicle tank into our car gas tank and into miscellaneous gas cans in the truck." (This "farmer-supplied fuel" scheme is operating today in the case of diesel fuel, since "farm only" diesel fuel is tax-free.) Even more devious, however, was the scheme related by S.E. Barber: "In the area of gasoline rationing I can't remember all the details, but the various categories for civilian use were 'A,B,C' (stamps worth 3-5 gallons each) for autos, 'K' stamps for trucks, 'J' for utility, etc. The dodge lay in (1) plant a 'victory garden' (officially sanctioned by Fed. Gov.); (2) buy some form of power equipment (rototiller, small tractor, etc.)—even if it doesn't run, you've still got a model number and serial number—and apply at local ration board for gas stamps to run the thing. Garden by hand and use the 'J' stamp gas in your car." (On the next page, a reproduction appears of several of Mr. Barber's mother's ration stamp books. Younger readers should not feel sad that they never owned such wonderful items. Have patience. They're coming.)

Another way used to beat any price control scheme is to reduce product quality. For example, oil companies reduced octane in their gasoline during the 1974 OPEC embargo-price control period. This was made illegal when the government found out, but these discoveries take time. Meanwhile ... One anonymous expert in the field of hides (of animals, but also voters) reports: "During WWII to Korea, leather gradings (normally 1,2,or 3; or A, B, C) all became #1 or A. Also, lower grade leather was put into high category lines and price categories. Also hides did not yield the same—higher moisture, salt, manure content. Again, the #3's became #1's." Bill Bowers reports that municipal services in his small Kansas town declined steadily during the war. This is a common feature of both wartime and peacetime price control periods; current operations are financed out of captial expenditures, and total per capita investment declines. This eventually leads to reduced output and reduced wealth.

Building materials are always a problem under controls. Marshall Tilden's comments are especially revealing; where there is a will, you may get away: "As a general contractor primarily building custom homes, I experienced serious difficulties in obtaining metal building products at any price.

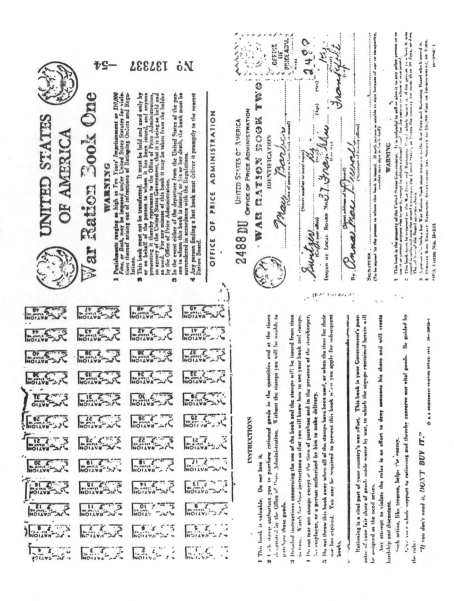

Several contractors got together at a luncheon and decided to have a bi-monthly meeting for the purpose of exchanging ideas to circumvent price controls and keep in business. One of the methods was to bid government jobs in order to obtain priorities for materials. We usually were able to buy under priority more material than was actually required for each priority job. Each of us stockpiled all critical material we were able to purchase through any source and then we used these stockpiles for exchange. I had a salesman travel through the Midwest states buying stucco netting from material suppliers a roll at a time. These rolls were accumulated and then shipped to me. The same way with nails. These materials were used for trading purposes and kept me in business. In some cases we paid double the control price. The fact that I was buying one or more projects under priority made this possible." In short, **priority slips served as the real money supply in the construction industry**.

As soon as the war began, **automobile construction** was brought to a screeching halt. Anyone who had real foresight and a bit of cash on Dec. 8, 1941, would have been wise to go down and order a new car, or late-model used car, plus several sets of tires, spark plugs, points, condensers, oil, and so forth. Even if he had been forced to mortgage his home to get down-payment money, it would have been a smart move. But for sheer entre-preneurship, nothing beats this anonymous reply: "Anticipating difficulty in obtaining a new automobile after the end of active hostilities, I made an interest-free cash deposit with a local dealer permitting him to use my funds in return for priority delivery of a car. This agreement was honored with complete satisfaction after about two years with no further inducement on my part." He was less successful in this same arrangement with another car dealer who later refused to place him high on the priority list. He thinks in retrospect that a lawyer should have been brought in to set up the original agreement. "In the end, the reliability of the dealer was more important than the money or the car." He refers to his second agreement, in which he had traded in his 1942 Plymouth as an initial deposit. This, it seems to me, was a less than thoughtful move in the first place. First, 1942 cars were bound to become collector's items. Second, giving up a new scarce resource for a hoped-for future scarce resource is extremely risky, especially during wartime, when the duration of the war is in question. He con-cludes: "I believe this system will work with any major appliance or equip-ment, but one should take care to contract only with financially sound and established firms who may be expected to continue in business and value their reputations for fair dealing in the community." This sounds good, but firms that take paper money when price controls are on, are not being managed by very rational people, unless the dealer himself is presently very active on the black markets and the money still functions on those markets to some degree. Under today's conditions of massive deficits, price-inflation expectations, monetary expansion, and a high division of labor (meaning extreme personal vulnerability to shortages), the man who accepts paper money for hard goods is likely to go bankrupt before he can deliver, or else he may be dishonest. Winning the Second World War was one thing; winning the war against envy-produced socialism should take a lot longer.

People living on a **national border** may have a distinct advantage, assuming price controls are not already in effect across the border (e.g., Canada in 1976) and assuming that currency controls are only loosely or ineffectively enforced. Writes Mrs. A.C. Reed: "Nothing was a hardship for us, primarily due to our access to Mexico. Nothing was rationed there, so the residents of south Texas towns went across the border for gas, sugar, meat, shoes—anything we needed. As a matter of fact, sugar is still 6 cents to 12 cents per pound there, while ours is about 4-5 times that amount." The reason for the modern sugar price discrepancy is that the U.S. has rigid sugar import quotas to protect domestic sugar manufacturers and also to produce incomparable bribe opportunities for those who are connected with the establishment of the annual import quota formulas. ("Latin American sugar exporters are to U.S. officials as Lockheed expediters were to . . . ." Fill in the blank and send your answer to Prince Bernhard, Bilderbergers Co., Netherlands.)

Rev. R.J. Rushdoony, then a missionary to the Western Shoshone Indians in the Elko, Nevada area, offers this assessment: "During the war years, I found that I was able to get everything I wanted, without any resort to the black market, when I wanted. Only once was I delayed about a month in securing a new tire. I drove to and from California and Nevada for church meetings, and never had trouble securing extra gas coupons legally, or tires. My principle was a simple and Biblical one: do unto others as you would have them do unto you. On the whole, it paid off handsomely. I traded with people, irrespective of price, if I felt they were good and trustworthy businessmen. My shipping or buying was exclusive. As a result of my loyalty, I received loyalty. People went to bat for me to enable me to get what I wanted when I needed it . . . My loyalty to various retailers was religiously, not pragmatically, principled, and it was appreciated. In brief, what I am saying is that economics is more than economics: it involves people, friendships, loyalties, and a variety of non-economic considerations. It is the economic fallacy to view anything, such as economics, in purely economic terms. Life is unity. Because I was not thinking of tires or gas first, or my slight economic advantage with another merchant, but had a unified motivation which made economics subordinate to a unified principle of life, I came out far ahead. This principle works in both war and peace, in time of rationing, and in times of plenty."

Conclusions

Applied economics has got to be more than applied econometrics, applied indifference curves, or applied utility theory. Bringing down rarified academic models or "ideal types" into the real world necessarily immerses the graphs, charts, and abstract chains of reasoning in a universe in which other things never remain equal. Those "other things"—loyalty, principled action, commitment to goals that are higher than profit and loss in a double-entry record book-can be the difference between hardship or leisure, alms-taking or alms-giving.

Yet at the same time, ethics—applied moral principle—cannot ignore the realm of economic theory if it is to stay practical. An impractical ethics is as impotent as an immoral economics. Thus, those who intend to achieve certain ethical goals need resources in a world of scarcity. And the world of price controls is a world of government-induced scarcities on a massive scale. Men need information, as well as accurate economic theory to evaluate the information. The fusion between a reliable ethical position and reliable economic analysis is what Christian economics is all about. If we are going to lead, we need economic resources. If we want economic resources, we need to understand the effects of price controls and the best ways around them. Some people win and most people lose under a system of controls. We should be the ones to win, not for the sake of oppression, but for the sake of reconstruction.

CHAPTER TWELVE
THE INEVITABLE BREAKDOWN OF THE CONTROLS

> There are reports of widespread disregard and violation of the price-control law. Experience shows that this leads to a tendency to disregard the sanctity of other laws of our country. I need not point out the danger of such a public attitude.
>
> Pres. Harry S. Truman
> speech announcing the
> termination of price
> controls (Oct. 14, 1946)

Thus ended another social and economic experiment inflicted on the American public by the great experimenter himself, F. D. Roosevelt. Naturally, it ended in failure. Five and a half years before, on April 11, 1941, Roosevelt had created, by executive order, the Office of Price Administration and Civilian Supply (OPACS), the forerunner to the Office of Price Administration (OPA), which Roosevelt set up by executive order on August 28, 1941. Pearl Harbor, you may recall, was not hit by the Japanese until Dec. 7, 1941. Roosevelt hit the country with wartime price controls before the Japanese dropped their bombs. The controls were to stay on the books until 14 months after we dropped the two atomic bombs on Japan.

Truman gave his stirring speech in favor of decontrol in direct response to an overwhelmingly successful strike on the part of cattlemen who refused to send their beef to the offical markets. They forced Truman's hand. He was quite willing to slap on price controls during the Korean War, indicating that he didn't believe his own rhetoric. Richard Nixon repeated this performance when he slapped on price controls by executive order on August 15, 1971, despite his earlier assurances that controls are bad, controls don't work, etc. He knew from experience, he said; he had begun his career as an obscure official in the OPA.

The lessons of the price controls of the Second World War are still useful, for the effects of price controls are everywhere quite similar.

Truman was correct; the widespread violations of the controls did lead (and will always lead) to skepticism about the validity of the law. Milton Friedman commented on the phenomenon of public trust and law enforcement in a brilliant and completely neglected essay that appeared in the Summer, 1962 issue of the now-defunct *New Individualist Review*. Governments always rely on the willingness of individual citizens to employ self-restraint; no law enforcement system can employ sufficient resources to enforce the law on a recalcitrant population. Self-restraint, local sanctions like ostracism and censure, and private institutions like churches and schools must co-operate with public law agencies. Without such co-operation, there is no respect for the law, and society disintegrates. But legislators and bureaucrats tend to misuse this store of public trust. They pass law after law, thereby disrupting the daily lives of all citizens. The public begins to lose confidence in their public leaders. They begin to resist the laws by evasion. The legal capital available to politicians and bureaucrats—voluntary self-restraint on the part of citizens—begins to run out. The politicians refuse to use self-restraint in their legislative activities, and the loss of restraint escalates. The law enforcement agencies cannot hope to compete with a growing army of citizens who refuse to co-operate. Either politicians turn back and rid the society of their own legal baggage (for example, England in the 1840's), or else the whole jerry-built structure of laws collapses. Only outright tyranny—a tyranny that acknowledges the necessity of at least some lawbreakers who supply the needed goods and services through their illegal activities—can hope to subdue the voluntary actions of men, once those men have lost confidence in the legitimacy of public law.

This is precisely what has happened throughout history when politicians have attempted to impose price and wage controls. They cannot last. In the meantime, however, they can literally destroy those who attempt to abide by them. They can create a sense of guilt among those who try to abide by these insane laws and then give up and violate the statutes. They are bad laws, and they lead to bad results. **The first step in learning how to cope with price controls is to realize that they are immoral, unworkable, and ultimately doomed.** They do not deserve respect. They will not long maintain respect, at least not as far as compliance among the broad population is concerned, no matter what citizens tell public opinion pollsters.

World War II Controls: The United States

Controls are based on economic **ignorance** and **envy**. I am not sure which factor is more important, but both operate in the minds of controllers and the controlled. **Ignorance** leads men to believe that an official price ceiling that is lower than the market price of a good will not reduce the supply of that good, while simultaneously increasing demand for it at the artificially low price. In short, shortages are the inevitable effect of controls—a shortage of goods in comparison with demand. This demand can be registered in numerous ways, such as a willingness to pay illegally high prices or a willingness to stand in long lines, but the artificially low legal price will draw people to the shops and shelves where they think the goods will be available. Seldom will the disgruntled buyers, or potential buyers at the low price, grasp the fact that the artificially low prices set by bureaucrats have led them to make errors in estimating available supplies. Instead, they call for more controls, more enforcement procedures, so long as it is the **other guy** who is controlled. This brings us to **envy**: the desire to bring down the other guy. If someone is profiting from the war, he should be stopped. After all, aren't our boys dying overseas? Yes they are; and if controls are enforced, and profit ceilings are imposed, producers who could produce better weapons, cheaper weapons, and more weapons will have far less incentive to produce them, thereby keeping the death figures higher for our side. But this sequence of events is not understood, which gets us back to the ignorance component of the support for price controls. So support grows for controls, even as individuals do their best to evade them.

Controls are most enforceable during wars. Self-restraint is greater, men are willing to eat up their capital in order to keep the war machine going, more citizens are willing to serve as unpaid informers (500,000 "volunteers" during WWII, though only 275,000 at one time, the peak period), and more price controllers are employed. Yet the war years demonstrated how very willing Americans were to violate controls that involved hardships. When the pinch was on, they evaded the controls.

Gasoline rationing was the biggest bureaucratic problem for the OPA. There were too many cheaters. Everyone knew there were ample supplies of gasoline (the controls had been imposed to reduce the consumption of rubber by tire users), and Americans, then as now, wanted to use their cars. The OPA bureaucrats tried to give some groups special treatment because of their special needs (ministers and physicians), but everyone wanted preferential treatment some of the time. So the evaders went to work. First, there were millions and millions of **counterfeits**. The ration coupons were really money, so they were treated as such by private printers. The "money" was less familiar to gas station attendants, so they could be passed fairly easy. But the gas station owners became buyers of counterfeits. They would sell gasoline to buyers who didn't have ration coupons; then the station owners would turn in the counterfeits that they had bought. If they were caught (which was seldom until after the war), they could always plead ignorance. "Some shady gasoline buyers just fooled me, your honor." Chester Bowles testified before Congress that the profits were a billion dollars a month in 1944 (I think Chet's days as a big-time advertising man may have gotten the better of him). Profits were there, certainly, and the risks really were minimal. While surveys of stations by OPA enforcers indicated that 60% of them were participating to some extent in illegal sales, only 15,094 sanctions were imposed throughout the war. Yet there had been 250,000 stations in 1941. Only 3,500 of these were actually brought to court under criminal sanctions. In 1944, there were 124,000 cases revealing violations; sanctions were imposed in 8,700 cases. Risk? Not much. And everyone knew it.

There were other forms of gasoline evasion, however. Counterfeit coupons were only part of the story. Station owners mixed regular gas with premium. (Reduced quality is a traditional means of evasion for most goods and services.) Buyers were asked to buy repairs or products that were more easily available or even unrationed. There was almost no way to police these violations. The same techniques were used during the 1974 gasoline shortage. In fact, this is always the case: you can buy something you don't need to get what you do need. **Get all your gas and auto repairs down at your friendly local station; midnight gasoline may be available after the place is officially closed.** A Christmas bonus is also called for. Your car may run on alcohol after all—Jack Daniels, to be specific.

Investigations conducted by OPA in 1944 of America's large manufacturing and wholesale firms revealed that about 70% of them were in violation of OPA rules. In that same year, 57% of all businesses investigated were in violation. These were not random samples, although part of the totals were sampled randomly, but the very high percentages at the very height of war (and appeals to patriotism) indicate that the control program was a massive failure. Bowles, who headed the agency in 1945, admitted in an OPA memorandum that a major weakness with OPA's public relations efforts was the fact "that so many violations go on unchecked, and that when violations are found the action taken is not strong enough or vigorous enough. I have met this criticism every time I have been away from Washington, regardless of where I have gone. More and more, the public tends to blame OPA for lack of effective enforcement." The public participated in the alternative ("black") markets, yet cried out against lax enforcement by OPA bureaucrats.

Public attitudes regarding controls are always paradoxical. In November, 1941, a Gallup poll revealed that 64% of those surveyed in cities over 100,000 favored price controls. It was 54% in cities under 100,000 and 46% among farm areas. In 1943, National Opinion Research Center found the figure had climbed to 94% nationally. In 1945, it was up to 97%, and 65% of those surveyed wanted an across-the-board freeze. Yet the whole nation was violating the existing laws daily. In January, 1946, 83% still favored continued controls. In April, 1946, NORC found that 85% still favored rent controls, and 52% wanted them for more than a year. And everyone was cheating. There were raids on commercial frozen food lockers, for example. *Business Week* (May 5, 1945) reported that one check of a Chicago meat locker revealed that 87% of the meat in the lockers had been obtained illegally.

Where there are bureaucrats, there will be inefficiency. Local rationing boards were notoriously lax about records, safety, and general procedures. When OPA officials inspected local boards periodically they found some true horror stories—from the OPA's point of view, that is. Frequently, some boards would have 5-10 years' worth of gasoline ration coupons. In some cases, the figure soared to 40, 80, or 90 years' worth. In two cases, inspectors found 137 years' supply of the gasoline coupons. One board had a century's worth stored in an unlocked garage; the wooden cabinet's lock could be picked with a hairpin. At 10 cents per coupon on the black market, the coupons were worth over $950,000—WWII dollars, of course. Thefts were common, and only after the war did the OPA devise fairly successful procedures to deal with gasoline coupon violations of various kinds.

Local boards, understandably, hesitated to impose strong sanctions against local violators of OPA regulations. Decentralization is basic to any bureaucracy that has to police a geographical region as large as the U.S.A., but localism spells favoritism. There were 96 OPA regions, and district directors had remarkable latitude to hire, fire, and enforce selectively the laws that they agreed with. This means that local friendships, local contacts, and local bribes could postpone or even eliminate the day of judgment for violators.

There wasn't much of an investigating staff in the OPA. In 1941 it was 200; 1942: 900; 1943: 1,800; 1944: 2,800; 1945: 3,100; 1946: 3,600. There were never over 800 lawyers to prosecute. Obviously, you can't police a hundred million buyers and sellers with that kind of staff. Even with 500 information officers ("flacks"), the OPA couldn't convince all of these citizens that violators would be inevitably tracked down and prosecuted. Ironically, it was only in late 1945 that a full-scale program of fear was introduced; OPA news releases then concentrated on successful prosecutions. (The Internal Revenue Service uses this same technique.) Furthermore (also like the IRS), the staffers were not the best men in the civil service program. Few applicants for OPA investigating jobs had any kind of experience in the field, since it was a new field. Enforcement attorneys were unfamiliar with this kind of case, and many were hostile to the idea anyway, having been recruited from private industry. The OPA never did overcome this problem, which is one reason why we won the war.

Marshall B. Clinard, who served the OPA faithfully from Dec. 1942 to Sept. 1945 as its Chief, Analysis & Reports Branch, has given us this interesting statistic. The total number of criminal convictions in cases prosecuted by the OPA from 1942 to 1947 was 11,600. This was a 94% "hit ratio" of the 12,415 completed criminal cases. Of these 11,600, only 25%, or 2,970, received prison sentences; 3,318 received suspended sentences or were put on probation . To say that it was safe to violate price controls in the U.S.A. during WWII is not doing the statistics any justice. (Clinard's book, *The Black Market,* provides a good introduction to the whole incredible story of OPA. It was reprinted in 1969 by Patterson Smith Pub., Montclair, New Jersey. It came out first in 1952.)

This does not mean that enforcers will always be equally lax or impotent. But it does mean that bureaucrats are inefficient people who work in inefficient organizations. They cannot hope to police a population that does not believe in what the bureaucrats are trying to accomplish, or what the bureaucrats **do** accomplish (assuming that the public officially professes faith in the general goals). The history of WWII price controls in the U.S.A. is the history of black market activity so widespread that it was more a case of white market activity; the phony markets were the OPA-controlled ones. They cannot enforce the unenforceable. The law is a sham. People who realize this will truck and barter on the illegal, private markets. He who believes that the controlled markets are the real markets will suffer the consequences: **shortages**.

One of the excuses given by Clinard for the failure of OPA is the time factor. The OPA didn't get moving soon enough. It didn't impose strong enough sanctions early enough. If the OPA had been given sufficient staff, sufficient resources, and sufficient funds to employ sufficient numbers of local informers, we are asked to believe, the price controls of WWII would have worked. The control system was "voluntary" until Feb. 11, 1942. On that day, two momentous events took place: Leon Henderson took over the reigns of OPA as our first Price Administrator, and I was born.

The Emergency Price Control Act had been signed into law on January 30, but even before that date, the OPA had begun to ration auto tires. There was a crucial time lag between late December and late January; people still had the ability to go out and buy goods on legal markets. Even after January 30, a few precious days remained for sellers to take legal evasive action and raise prices. But after February 11, prices of key commodities were frozen, and in April all others were frozen. The straight-jacket was in place.

This means that it takes **time** before the controllers can get the enforcement mechanism rolling. It is in the pre-control period that buyers can take advantage of their freedom and buy whatever they can afford. Then come controls. There are always several weeks, at least, to buy goods that are still on the shelves. In fact, for some goods there may be many months, especially in less populated regions where supplies are not being monitored closely and local people do not understand the threat of shortages. Urban dwellers learn far sooner, since they are more closely watched by bureaucrats and, more importantly, they are more completely dependent upon goods that are brought into the city daily and sold for money at money prices. **The controls are felt in the cities first**. Anyone who thinks that controls are likely to be reimposed should remember WWII: there were several weeks when free market prices still were related to existing supplies and existing demand. The wise buyer took advantage of that brief period of rational prices. A man can buy at many stores in order to maintain invisibility. In fact, **buying in a community 50 miles down the road would be wise.** Local people do not know what is in your basement or attic when you have purchased goods out of town. Once controls are announced, it would be wise to take a vacation, or even annual sick leave, to spend time buying hard goods. This might even mean getting a loan at the bank. It might even mean refinancing the house. Debt is unwise, but in emergencies it can be used to provide necessities. Swift action is critical during the **first month** of price controls. I cannot emphasize this strongly enough. Let Jan. 1942 teach us well.

World War II Controls: Germany

Survival-oriented newsletters place a lot of emphasis on the German experience of 1921-23. This was the period of the great German inflation, the worst to hit a modern industrialized nation in this (or any) century. The Hungarian inflation of 1946 was worse, but Hungary was not industrialized and was not so vulnerable to movements of monetary prices. Yet I think this interest in the German inflation of 1921-23 is misplaced. That inflation was not a **repressed** inflation. Prices were free to rise. The money markets were relatively free, and the dollar served as the standard. The Weimar government simply didn't have the political clout to impose full-scale price and wage controls. That's why I am firmly convinced that the crucial period of modern history for us to re-examine is the period 1936-1948 in Germany, for these were the years of full controls imposed by strong central governments: first the Nazis and then the Allies.

The Nazis were essentially Keynesians in their economic policies. Crude Keynesians, no doubt (not that many equations and charts), but Keynesians nonetheless. Keynes himself admitted in the 1936 German edition of his influential *General Theory* that a totalitarian state (total state) like Germany could impose his program far more effectively than a free market society could. (For a complete translation, side by side with a photocopy of the original German, see James Martin's *Revisionist Viewpoints*, published by Ralph Myles Press, Colorado Springs: 1971. I assure you, you won't find it in any issue of *The American Economic Review*.) That's what Hitler thought, too, apparently. Exchange controls on currency transactions went on almost as soon as Hilter came to power. Yet to an extent seldom mentioned in the textbooks, Nazi policy was an extension of Weimar socialism. But the Weimar socialism was democratic, so the textbook writers look the other way. The Nazis simply tightened up the controls. Full-scale price controls went on in 1936.

An incredibly complex system of national economic planning was imposed on the German economy. A summary of its structure—little more than an outline—takes 25 pages of Nicholas Balabkins' book, *Germany Under Direct Controls* (Rutgers University Press, 1964). In 1939, there were

7 national groups, one for each major industry, under the National Economic Chamber. There were 46 economics groups under them. There were 328 trade groups under them. Finally, there were 323 trade subgroups at the bottom. This is central economic planning in a nutshell. It's a pretty huge nutshell. And evaders cracked it constantly.

The Germans really did monitor official prices. If 1913-14 is taken as a base year, the cost of living index in 1936 was 124.5. (Don't pay too much attention to price indexes, except as crude estimating devices for comparison purposes; they can be misleading except as broad outlines.) In 1944, the index stood at 141.4. That's where the **index** stood. By 1944, that's about all of Germany that was still standing. Maybe the Nazi burcaucrats couldn't control Allied bombing, but they sure did control prices, meaning **reported** prices.

Percy Greaves, author of *Understanding the Dollar Crisis*, was a representative of the European division of the Pet Milk Company in 1936. He once described the kind of games that were played by German retailers. They would buy cardboard imitations of cans of Pet evaporated milk and stack them up to make it appear that there was plenty of milk available. Naturally, there was rationing. Prices no longer served as anything but propaganda devices, both domestically and internationally. It was all show.

The standard of living in Germany by 1944 had collapsed. The war had done its work. Yet the illusion of stable purchasing power was preserved by official prices. There had been controls on some prices since the pre-Nazi days; the total freeze came in 1936; the bombs blew away Germany's houses and industry; but the bureaucrats controlling official prices went merrily onward. Sadly, the Allies extended this Nazi nonsense until June of 1948, when Ludwig Erhard unilaterally announced an end to price controls and currency reform. General Lucious Clay backed him up, and the nightmare ended. The German miracle began.

But in 1945 there were no signs of a miracle. There were bombed-out houses. In the English-American zones of occupation, about 25% of prewar housing (urban) had been destroyed. Yet millions of displaced Germans poured into these two zones from the Soviet-occupied eastern zone. The Nazis had rationed housing for years, even going so far as to assign people to private homes. Prof. Hans Sennholz says that he knew one man who would seal off rooms that had been assigned to outsiders; he would knock a doorway if necessary to let them in and out, but they could not enter his home's living quarters. Sennholz also reports that relatives of his in various cities would "assign" him a room, so that if housing authorities came by, they could say that the room belonged to cousin Hans. He said he was very popular—just so long as he never actually showed up to visit.

But after the war, housing was at a fantastic premium. Adults were assigned minimal living space. Officially, this was 4 square meters of floor space (about 36 square feet). Anyone under the age of 14 received half this space. An infant under a year was assigned nothing. Prior to 1947, there had been no central plan, so at least refugees could truck and barter for space more easily. Building was mostly confined to "gray" and black markets. Rents were frozen in 1945, but of course this was a freeze on **money** prices, and money didn't talk in Germany by 1945. Barter did. Rents in 1948, just before the currency reform, were what they had been in 1936. Money, as an allocation device, was dead. It was good for paying off debts, paying taxes, and presenting (along with a ration ticket) to sellers. The sellers seldom had much to sell. In 1947, if you had a roof over your head and some coal, you were thankful.

The Allies set 1,500 calories as a daily ration for Germans, including coal miners. Usually, they received 1,000. Yet it takes over 2,000 to maintain adequate nutrition, and over 3,000 for heavy labor. Food was at a premium. So Germans did what other captured people have done: they bartered with their captors. Americans sold food and cigarettes, and Germans worked as servants or sold family heirlooms. Cigarettes became the coin of the realm. They are fairly divisible, transportable, and they have a high value in relation to supply. They are not very durable, but they are smoked, and this keeps them scarce. Probably the highest paid workers in Germany were those who worked as cigarette producers, since they were paid "in kind," that is, with cigarettes. They could buy food.

This brings us to a curious fact. **People living in abject poverty want to smoke.** There was a market for cigarettes in every POW camp in the war. There was a market in Germany right up to the currency reform of 1948. A person who is thinking about a highly desirable investment for a period of price controls might consider cigarettes. They can be canned, using dry ice to drive out air from the container. But more simply, you can buy canned cigarette tobacco (one brand: B & W Bugler) and cigarette paper. A hundred cans stored in a basement would be a highly marketable good under a control economy. Another good like cigarettes is (and was) **coffee**. It, too, was a premium good. It, too, can be stored inexpensively. Buy it now that coffee prices are down from their 1977 highs. Prices will rise again.

Barter became the means of economic survival. Thus it always is under price controls, for prices are denominated in official money. Balabkins estimates that in 1947 and the first half of 1948, fully 50% of all production went into the black markets or into barter. This meant that **hoarding**—a pejorative term for **saving**—was necessary for family survival. Saving money was insane; money bought nothing. A man had to save hard goods. Balabkins writes for all official currencies under price controls: "The Reichsmark preserved a stable purchasing power for the legal food ration, rent, gas, electricity, taxes, and fares. The Reichsmark remained a unit of account and a medium of exchange, although it bought virtually nothing more than the highly inadequate food ration. But distrust of its future value led, during the last half of the year prior to the currency reform, to flagrant hoarding of goods." Translated from professorial jargon, this means: official prices meant nothing, rationing meant something, and hoarding meant survival. What was flagrant was not the hoarding; what was flagrant was the policy of repressed inflation.

Germans learned that some goods were not under the controls. Immediately and continually, capital (labor, goods, space) began to be devoted to the production of these goods. First, as in the U.S.A. in 1942-46, there were "new" goods. Usually, these were old, familiar goods with new names or slightly modified appearances. The new goods could be set at a much higher price, since there was no existing price guideline. Ash trays, fancy lamps, toys, and other "luxury" goods became staples, for **at some monetary price** or in exchange for some good or service, a man could buy these uncontrolled products. This meant that these items preserved some degree of purchasing power.

What is not discussed very often is that the U.S., meaning New Deal officials, gave the Soviets the plates that were used to print the Allied occupation currency, and in no time at all the Soviets used their new plates to buy up the East German goods at the official prices. Monetary inflation, coupled with price controls, will give you shortages every time. But capital seeks its highest return, and the luxury goods are the ones that are, in effect, subsidized by the policies of repressed inflation.

Balabkins argues that the policies of controlling prices were maintained by the Allies as the basic tool of stripping Germany of its remaining industrial wealth. The Americans and the Soviets wanted to reduce Germany to a third-class agricultural power. The British were skeptical. But the price controls made any British doubts superfluous. Balabkins writes: "In a war the aim of direct controls is to bring about speedy, efficient, and maximum utilization of available resources for the war effort. But in postwar Germany the Allies aimed not at the maximum utilization of industrial capacity but at precisely the opposite. Industrial disarmament of Germany required that only minimum industrial production be permitted. Thus, the reinstated direct controls were considered proper means to attain the envisaged retrogression of the German economic status for security purposes." As a program of industrial paralysis, price controls are uniquely efficient.

Conclusion

If the justifications of controls are wartime stability and social peace, rather than production, then the experience of the U.S.A. indicates that price controls can work, assuming: 1) citizens are ignorant of economics; 2) citizens are envious and will support the war effort only if they can exercise their envy; and 3) the controls are not seriously enforced. The experience of Germany under the Nazis and the Allies indicates that if the controls are enforced, they will destroy output and therefore destroy income. They lead to distortions that are mitigated only by such devices as black marketeering, barter, hoarding, production of luxury (uncontrolled) goods, and rationing.

Controls cannot last. No matter what men tell pollsters, they will not live under price controls forever. Three years, five years, even two decades; but sooner or later men either abandon the controls (Truman, 1946) or they abandon the currency (Germany, 1946). In 1948, Germany threw out controls, reformed (shrank) the currency, and started over. They went back to marks after having used cigarettes.

If controls are reimposed and enforced, we will see the revival of the money of the prisoner of war camps. That's because we will be living under the economy of the camps: controlled, bureaucratized, malevolent, armed, and inhumane.

Plan ahead.

CHAPTER THIRTEEN
THE LOGIC OF BARTER UNDER CONTROLS

During October, 1945, *Newsweek* magazine began an on-the-scene survey of cigarette barter in the principal European cities. Reporting from their assigned bases, the magazine's correspondents recorded that in Vienna one United States cigarette was the standard tip for a waiter and that twelve packages would buy a new Leica camera. Other *Newsweek* correspondents chronicled that in Rome two United States cigarettes constituted a satisfactory tip, ... In shambled Berlin, thousands of "barter boards" had been raised, and on them thousands of Berliners were listing articles they had for barter. Usually the offers were tested in United States cigarettes, coffee, chocolate, or sugar instead of currency. Typical offers were one diesel engine manual for a package of cigarettes. A substantial part of Berlin sidewalk barter was in single cigarettes. ... The single package was an excellent spending unit since it was readily divisible into twenty individual cigarettes. Furthermore, neither ingenious law evaders nor local politicians could duplicate or counterfeit a package of Camels or Luckies. Also, an unbroken package could be held in reserve for many weeks without ruinous loss of value and, even more importantly, a cigarette once smoked is out of circulation for good.

Charles Morrow Wilson
Let's Try Barter (1960)

Wilson's book is subtitled, "The Answer to Inflation (and the Tax Collector)." It is significant that the book, long out of print, has been reprinted in paperback by its original publisher, Devin-Adair (Greenwich, Conn.: $4.95). The editors have sensed the renewed interest in barter that is rapidly growing across the country. They are trying to cash in on barter.

There is a paradox here. Why should anyone want to "cash in" on barter? If barter is the wave of the future, why should people be willing to take paper money in exchange for information on barter? The answer is

127

simple enough: barter is always **supplemental** to paper money transactions, except under conditions of economic collapse. Barter is an alternative to the standard markets. Money still talks on these money markets, but barter certainly whispers. And when people are trying to escape the clutches of the tax collector, a whisper is just about right. Today, the taxes are primarily direct in nature. Once price controls are slapped on, and price inflation becomes repressed inflation, the tax becomes insidiously indirect. The government confiscates people's capital by means of **fiat money** and **priority purchasing slips**—always possessed by high government officials, their beneficiaries, and the people who are willing to take the risks associated with black market activity. If people are entering the barter markets today, it is not because they are concerned about survival. They are looking for something new, something off the beaten path. They are trying to profit from their own sharp trading in markets that are narrow and less determinate, since participants have less knowledge about other bargainers. To have a broad market, you need a money economy. That's the problem with price controls: they drastically narrow the markets, thereby reducing information. Sharp bargainers obviously benefit from this narrowing of the market. Those who have been trading on these narrow markets, sharpening their skills, getting the "feel" of face-to-face bargaining, have an inside track on those who are entering the markets late, possibly out of desperation. Price controls cannot benefit those who have little familiarity with the unconventional alternative ("black") markets. But for the few who are quite familiar with these markets, price controls can be a bonanza. If you think I'm wrong, try buying a new Leica camera today for a dozen packages of cigarettes. (One reason why Leicas were so cheap was that we made it illegal for Germans to own a Camera.)

The Tax Collector

Karl Hess, the ex-liberal, ex-conservative, ex-liberatarian, ex-urban homesteader who once was Barry Goldwater's speech writer, now lives in rural West Virginia. He is absolutely penniless. He gets by nonetheless. The IRS has a lien against his property for nonpayment of income taxes. In response, Hess has earned his living by bartering for a decade. He earns no money by design. He trades his sculptures for whatever he can get. He gets by. The IRS gets nothing.

Admittedly, the IRS has claims on all income, however received. It has a legal right to get its cut from Hess' profits from bartering. But do you know how much it would cost the IRS to collect anything from him? A lot more than it could collect. How can you evaluate the value of the things he buys? How do you collect from him? Take food off of his table? That would force him on welfare. Income derived in cash is more difficult to trace than income from a check. Income from barter is even more difficult to trace. There is little to be gained from following Hess all day long in order to get $5 in taxes out of him. What will the IRS do, go into the hog butchering business? Will it become the marketing agent for Hess' sculpture?

The IRS can afford to ignore a man like Hess. There aren't many of them, and it's the middle-class family that supports the bulk of the government's programs. The middle class is almost completely dependent on checks, bank accounts, salaries that are subject to withholding taxes, and so forth. So long as the middle class doesn't turn to barter—and it couldn't and survive in middle-class comfort—the IRS can afford to ignore tax evasion through barter. Besides, the IRS system rests on voluntary compliance. There is no way that the IRS can collect taxes on transactions that the majority of citizens do not think should be subject to the tax and therefore reported to tax authorities. For example, a middle-class wife may belong to a babysitting co-op: you sit with my kids and I'll sit with yours. Legally, both families must report the total value of the services received on their income tax reports. Do you think they will? Do they know that they should? If they did know, do you think they would comply with the law? Neither does the IRS. So long as only a small fraction of people's transactions are based on barter, there is no reason to worry about them in the offices of the IRS. The problem for the tax collectors comes when the inflation tax avoiders start buying goods, thereby forcing up prices. This produces the government's response, price controls. Price controls lead to the tax-avoiding response of increased barter and black market activity. Then the tax agencies face a crisis. What a shame.

Yet it was not so long ago that millions of dollars a day were being transacted on the barter markets. Specifically, it was in 1973-74. Monetary inflation had led to price inflation. Nixon slapped on controls by pure fiat order on August 15, 1971, and the printing presses kept rolling. Shortages developed in late 1972 and throughout 1973. Then the Arabs put on their oil embargo, and the supply of oil, already in short supply, started to dry up **at the legal prices**. But there were other prices.

In late 1973, the newly created magazine, *Saturday Review/World*, was in a real jam. It couldn't locate paper. There was a major paper shortage during this period, and all magazines were scrambling for supplies. The editor was offered the following deal: locate propane gas (used in the ink-drying process), and a paper company would supply 50% of the needed paper. The editor got the propane, and he got his paper not long thereafter. (He prudently declined to tell the reporter where he had located the propane.) By early 1974, according to a survey of 300 corporations made by the trade publication, *Purchasing World*, almost half of them were conducting part of their business by bartering for needed supplies. R. E. France, purchasing vice president for Sun Chemical Co. of New York, frankly admitted that if it were not for barter, "we wouldn't be surviving." The reliance on barter was especially marked in the field of **petrochemicals**, given its heavy reliance upon oil. Benzene, which had sold for 18 cents a gallon in mid-1972, had skyrocketed to $2.50 a gallon on the world markets by early 1974. Price controls on benzene made it difficult to buy in the legal markets, so firms bartered. *(Wall Street Journal*, Feb. 13, 1974)

In discussing this period with men in the petrochemical industry, I learned what I had already guessed: the primary source of bartered goods was a network of existing personal contacts within the industry. This is not to say that there were no newcomers acting as middlemen. There were, and stories of self-made millionaires who made their money simply by picking up a phone and persistently calling around are stories that are probably based on fact. But the fact remains that an industry will usually generate its own sources internally. Making a bundle of money takes work, foresight, accurate planning, and probably a whole host of intangibles that are simply not available to most people. But the fact that not many can make a fortune does not mean that no one can. In fact, it means just the opposite. There are services to be performed, and if wealthy industries are willing to pay the freight, someone can make a pile of money. And should the day come that money is little more than a hunting license, then he who can supply the service or goods can demand payment in other goods or services.

Strategy for the Big Payoff

Bernard Cornfeld sold a lot of mutual fund shares with his slogan, "Do you Sincerely Want to Be Rich?" I don't want to imitate Mr. Cornfeld, but you have to ask yourself that question. More important, you must ask this one: what am I willing to **give up** in order to gain the outside possibility of making a bundle (money or goods)? The strategy I will lay out is the one that can open the possibilities of wealth, but it takes sacrifice. It does not need to take a lot of money, however.

The age of mass inflation will be the age of the **speculator**. He who forecasts the immediate economic future, acts courageously to meet that future, and then shifts his psychology to pursue another fast-moving market, will be the millionaire of the future. But once controls are reimposed (and I think this will be before truly mass price inflation arrives), the markets will fragment. At that point, the specialist inside the market will have a distinct advantage, since it will not be easy to enter new markets. You won't phone your broker and ask him to buy a thousand of this or a hundred thousand of that. The strategy I recommend is aimed at this secondary period, the period which follows wild speculation on the legal, open markets. The markets I'm talking about may or may not be legal, but they will be crucial for the economy. No matter what the law books say, officials will have to look the other way if they don't want to destroy all production. Legal or not, alternative markets will exist.

There are laws—economic laws—that govern these markets. They must be respected. They are the first step in making large profits in a control economy. I will spell out the most crucial ones again, though I mention them elsewhere.

1. **Face-to-face contacts.** Men operating on black or gray markets bear a heavy risk, namely, the risk of detection by the authorities. One way to lower this risk is to deal with those who are familiar, people who can be trusted to remain silent. This means old cronies, those who want continuing supplies, those who are related to you, those who share some other common bond. In a control economy, it is as much **who** you know as **what** you know. In fact, the **what** that you know may be the **who.** Contrary to popular opinion, in a free market economy, what you know is far more important because **markets to information** are far more open. Competitive bidding— monetary bidding—can offset not having "connections." But a price control economy makes competitive market bidding illegal. This **subsidizes** the **semi-feudal** type of economic system: personal loyalty and personal contacts count for more than bargaining ability on an open, competitive market. If you liked the Middle Ages, you'll love price controls.

2. **Low profit margin goods disappear first.** The secret of success in a controlled market is predicting what goods and services are going to be removed from the legal markets next. These are the ones that should receive your almost full and undivided attention as a **consumer,** and at least considerable attention as a middleman. When controls are imposed, those goods that are mass produced, and therefore price competitive, are the most vulnerable to panic runs and production bottlenecks. The necessities disappear, and the limited production, high profit (per sale) items remain on the legal markets longer. The real luxuries may remain available until the very end. Therefore, your secret of success is **a new way of looking at the economic world**: those items that are **most available** in a free market economy—most familiar, most taken for granted—are the ones that must **never** be taken for granted. It will take months of painful learning on the part of the average American consumer to grasp this fast. The faster you learn this simple, yet inevitably ignored law of price controls, the safer your family will be once controls are imposed.

3. **Closed markets subsidize those who have already entered them.** The genius of the free market is its ability to transfer massive quantities of accurate information to those who need it and are willing to pay for it. But the world of price controls tends to favor monopolists.

Those who learned the ropes beforehand can more easily keep out newcomers. Rationing and even government-assigned labor pools make it more difficult for people to learn the old trade secrets, let alone the new secrets. **Conclusion**: you should take steps immediately to begin to master the supply and demand facts of the present industry you intend to specialize in, but with an eye to the future. You must learn about today's world, but you must assimilate this information in terms of **a vision of the future which few men share**: the end of a world in which money not only talks but shouts. It is far cheaper now to enter a particular knowledge market, for people are not yet suspicious (and that day is coming as surely as controls are coming), the greatest of all barriers to entry (private barriers, anyway) is erected: fear, coupled with jealousy. Today, the information is relatively cheap, monetarily speaking. Within 18 months after price controls, or 24 at the outside, this kind of information will become far more expensive and unobtainable for most people.

Before considering a strategy for successful brokerage operations (middleman), let's consider something more mundane. By looking more carefully at a consumer item that will be in short supply, we can draw more accurate conclusions about the world of manufacturing. Our consumer item: **toilet paper**. In 1973, Japanese housewives became convinced that supplies of this product were about to disappear, and as is so often the case under price inflation, the prophecy became self-fulfilling. They rushed to the supermarkets and bought every roll in sight. This increased the panic. These kinds of panic runs are magnified under price controls, simply because supplies really are limited and prices are not allowed to rise (thereby stimulating producers to even greater output). Here is a **mass produced** product that is highly **price competitive**. It has a **low profit margin per sale**. Off the shelves it goes, and it is not replaced. When it is replaced, it will be rationed. (That, I assure you, will alter a lot of life styles—life styles that people give little thought to.)

What kind of strategy is appropriate? I guarantee you that not one man in a thousand has even thought of the best strategy, and fewer still have acted. Install a bidet. They are seldom advertised in America, but they are well known in Europe. The Kohler Co. sells them, and they are considered to be very exclusive. They are devices that direct a stream of water to the appropriate location, and they are more sanitary than TP. (And they are a lot more comfortable than corn cobs.) I can see a rapidly growing market for these devices within a year after controls are imposed. It will be a good item to begin manufacturing, too, because it is a new product and therefore more easily priced (higher priced). How many Americans would even think of ordering one today? (For those of us who have installed **Frantz Oil**

Filters, that run on TP, the bidet is only a partial solution. The Frantz allows me to reduce drastically my car's motor oil changes, as long as I insert a new roll every 2,000 miles, adding one quart of oil. I change my oil about every 15,000 miles, although I have gone for 45,000 between oil changes in the past, with no ill-effects in my cars. This requires planning: I'll have to buy a case of oil and two dozen rolls for each car. For more information on this ingenious and highly salable product—especially under price controls and oil shortages if you have TP rolls to sell—write: Frantz Oil Filter, P.O. Box 6188, Stockton, CA 95206.) The person who hears that controls have been imposed but who doesn't buy a bidet (beDAY) or literally dozens of rolls of TP, is being foolish. Rolls should be stored in a mouse-proof, dry area, possibly inside those styrofoam or plastic picnic baskets with the lids taped shut.

It is this kind of thinking that should be dominant in the life of the man who intends to make his fortune in a world of controls-induced shortages. Think ahead, preferably along lines unsuspected by your competitors or potential competitors. It is probably wisest to start where you are.

What is your own industry or service? What does it need? What did it need back in 1974? What did it need during the Korean War and World War II? Who can tell you? Search him out and chat. Let him reminisce. Take notes. You already have information at your disposal. If you can start with an existing body of knowledge, you can save time and trouble. But even if your own field is not where you think you can contribute much, there are still great possibilities. Realize beforehand, however, that cracking open a new nut is a lot more difficult than sticking with an already cracked one. In any case, here is a strategy for a beginner.

1. Subscribe to several **trade publications** in the field, especially those aimed at **purchasing agents.** If you don't know which ones these are, ask a purchasing agent. You have selected a particular manufacturing or service industry as your specialty, so you might as well get used to asking questions. Find out which publications are the guide books for the present experts and start learning what they know. Find out who advertises, what products cost, which are produced by several different firms (price competitive). This is a crucial step: know the publications.

2. Find out which items are **absolutely crucial** to the **survival** of the industry. For best results, in terms of your profit, look for durable goods that appear in the used goods markets. It's easier to track down used equipment, if you're a beginner, than it is to track down a hundred thousand barrels of oil or several thousand tons of coal.

3. Start locating suppliers, especially **small, independent suppliers,** of these key goods. These will be the people most likely to deal with a

newcomer once things get tight, if the newcomer is at least a familiar face. Look for those who supply used equipment, or those who might have a used unit in a warehouse, unused. Find out now. Keep a record in a central file of which equipment is available from what small supplier. If these people have their own trade newsletter, subscribe. Some of them have computerized information services. One example is the junk yards that specialize in auto parts. Get very friendly with these guys.

4. You have to create spare time to visit suppliers, purchasing agents, and others who can help you gain information in the field. They can tell you about books that are helpful. **Start collecting a library** of these books. If necessary, read them at the library and then order the ones that seem most useful. Your time must be spent now on gathering information of how things work **now**. Remember, it's your job to figure out how things will work in the future.

5. If you're dealing with equipment, buy the **repair manuals** or get a photocopy. This kind of literature must be in your library in advance. Even if you can't understand them, someone will. But his abilities to repair goods that are crucial to production will be limited if he does not have access to official repair manuals. Those who have them in advance will be able to exploit (that is, use profitably) that inside knowledge when printing becomes difficult and manuals are scarce. A manual for a discontinued product will be extremely useful. Be sure to take care of them. If you know where an item is, and you think it will be needed in the future, try to get the owner to locate the manual for you and Xerox it.

6. Rule: **in a shortage economy, there is no such thing as junk.** There are only unexploited profit opportunities.

7. Once you have devoted enough time to master some of the literature in your selected field, start jotting down questions. If you can locate a library with older issues, check back and see if the 1941-46 issues are still around, as well as the 1950-53 issues. Read about the shortages and how they were solved. Remember: no one else is looking at these magazines. It's all forgotten. It's all history. **Old trade journals** are a gold mine of useful information for the future. Large firms may even have them available. Find out who the librarian is and go have a friendly chat. You appreciate librarians. No one else does. Once you have questions, start going to those who may have answers.

8. Sources of information: **retired old geezers.** These guys are really

ignored data banks, if you find them before the data banks are shortcircuited by time and neglect. There is probably an association of retired men in your selected field. Visit a meeting. Ask about the good old days. Let them spin yarns about beating the bureaucrats in 1943. Assuming you ever get into the middleman business, maybe some of them can get you introductions that you need, or tell you where supplies might be located. If **you're** an old retired geezer, what are you doing sitting around watching daytime T.V. and talking about the good old days with a bunch of old geezers? Go out and make yourself a rich old geezer. Then you won't be an old geezer any more. You will be a distinguished, though eccentric, statesman of the industry. Never forget who it was who fired you when you turned 65. You too may be able to quote Bobby Fisher, who was asked at age 14 what he enjoyed most about chess: "I love to see 'em squirm."

9. **Trade associations** hold annual meetings, and these are important sources of information and contacts. Once you know enough to start asking the right questions, you should attend one of these meetings, even if it's only a regional one. In fact, especially if it's a regional one. Have a card to hand out: "Joe Entrepreneur, Budget Broker." Get the other guy's card. You can always call him, using his name, when you want an introduction to a purchasing agent or other executive. Names are important. They push open closed doors.

10. **Every man likes to talk about his business to somebody.** Be a good listener. Very few people are, and especially newcomers. There will come a time when people may hesitate to tell the truth about how business operates, but now they are eager to share stories. Don't be embarrassed to ask about details, as long as you've gained his trust. If he's a purchasing agent, he ought to be happy to help you get a start in helping him to get supplies. The more suppliers he has competing against each other, the easier his job is.

11. The **local university or trade school** can provide you with gobs of background information. Unemployed students in chemistry—advanced ones especially—can be used to scout around for supplies of materials once controls make their presence felt. Professors may have suggestions and even personal contacts within the industry. They may be able to help. Nobody pays any attention to them, so why not drop one a note if you want information on marketing? If the school isn't in your area, find out which one is the best in the field, and order a catalogue from the school (free of charge). Then look up the name of the man in purchasing, marketing, or whatever, and drop him a letter with your question. Limit your letters, however,

to two or three a year. Don't be a pest or a red-hot. Nobody in academia like pests and red-hots. These people can give you piles of bibliography on your topic. Your taxes support them, so put them to work for you.

12. If you're a **salesman**, get acquainted with purchasing agents in your firm and with the repairmen. The repairmen will make or break the company eventually. Pump them for information. Salesmen are only glorified order-takers under conditions of shortage, and rational firms lower their commissions on each sale. It takes no talent to sell under such conditions. You must develop new talents. If you stick with sales, try to find someone who will pay you and your company off, at least in part, with goods and services, not simply money. This kind of salesman is valuable.

13. Slowly, tentatively, and in great humility, **start trying out your skills**. This may well take a year. So what? We've all got to start somewhere. Once controls go on, time runs out much faster. Then you will have to hustle. But until then, there is time to learn. Offer to search out some missing product at a price that is lower than the purchasing agent thinks he can get. There is always something that someone needs in some department or other. You may have to get chummy with a department foreman. But if you can start making a few sales-purchases, you'll gain confidence in yourself, and you will have done both the buyer and the seller a big favor. Don't expect to get rich on these early sales. You don't need to get rich if you can get experience. What you need is **self-confidence**. This, more than any other factor, is **the key barrier to entry**. Everyone says to himself, "I couldn't do that; I don't know where to begin." Indeed, he doesn't; and now you do.

Getting rich isn't easy. As I said at the beginning, it doesn't take money. It takes will, determination, and a lot of careful, patient labor. It takes a vision of the future that is either frightening enough (if you're a consumer) or beckoning enough (if you're an entrepreneur) to move you into positive action. These problems will be overcome. They always have been; they always will be. The question to ask yourself is this: can I be the one who overcomes these problems? If you are, then profits lie ahead. The key resource, obviously, is **time**. Time, the irreplaceable resource, constrains us all. But if you don't have a lot of money, time is the only resource that can get the job done. Where do you get it? You make it. It doesn't come to you. You must work six days a week, not five. You must give up Saturday T.V. I know of no better way to begin. In fact, I got rid of my T.V. years ago. I couldn't work three jobs, with a fourth and a fifth looming ahead in the near future, if I still were a T.V. addict. There isn't enough time. Either you pull the plug on it, or walk away from it, or else it will eat into your capital like a cancer. If you can't do this, then ration your time in front of it. Take a vow that you'll pay 25 cents an hour, or 50 cents an hour, or whatever it takes to get you to allocate your viewing time more rationally (and, incidentally, get your children to do the same), and then use the money for charity, or for buying subscriptions to trade publications, or going to trade association meetings, or buying stamps. But rethink your free time.

There ain't no such thing as free time. It always costs you. If you do one thing with your time, you can't do another. Ration it wisely. Lost time now could mean the difference between survival in the future or very hard times. It could even mean the difference between a fortune and scrambling. Your competitors and potential future competitors are also hooked on T.V. **Kick the T.V. habit**. You're probably a T.V. junkie. It's taking money out of your pocket. **Pull the plug**.

While you're at it, kick a few other habits. Specifically, reduce your demand for those items that are the big ones under controls: **cigarettes, liquor, sweets, coffee**. If you can reduce your use value of these items to zero, then the exchange value of them can help you to get necessities and luxuries later on. You can use these items to trade your way into a post-controls business. You can use them to buy time, favors, and even survival in a time of real shortages. Better to sweeten up a supplier than sweeten up your coffee (which you just gave up anyway). Buy these goods as a form of capital investment. That's exactly what they are.

CHAPTER FOURTEEN
THE STRATEGY OF EVASION

It is not accurate to apply terms like "gambling" or "betting" to situations either of risk or of uncertainty. These terms have unfavorable emotional implications, and for this reason: they refer to situations where *new* risks or uncertainties are *created* for the enjoyment of the uncertainties themselves. Gambling on the throw of the dice and betting on horse races are examples of the deliberate creation by the bettor or gambler of new uncertainties which otherwise would not have existed. The entrepreneur, on the other hand, is not creating uncertainties for the fun of it. On the contrary, he tries to reduce them as much as possible. The uncertainties he confronts are already inherent in the market situation, indeed in the nature of human action; someone must deal with them, and he is the most skilled and willing candidate.

Dr. Murray Rothbard

The coming era is going to be the era of the speculator. What is a speculator? He is simply a forecaster. He is the entrepreneur who tires to assess future consumer demand. He then goes into the markets to buy up scarce economic resources that are presently underpriced, given the increase of future demand that the entrepreneur expects. Of course, he can be wrong. If so, he will suffer losses. The person who does not serve the buying public better than his competitors will be removed from the economic scene. The consumers, through their purchases of one firm's services or goods, and by their refusal to buy another firm's services or goods, determine who survives. The consumer is sovereign in the free market.

This book is a book about entrepreneurship. It deals with the future. It tries to show you what kind of economy is coming. If you are to evade the devastation that threatens the whole economy, then you must take action today, tomorrow, and next week. Your plans and decisions will be different from those of your unsuspecting friends and associates. You will have a different assessment of the future. We are all speculators, meaning forecasters. Not all of us are gamblers. (I'm not. I have a moral revulsion against gambling. But I am a speculator. I try to forecast the future accurately. So should you.)

W. Allen Wallis was the president of the University of Rochester. He is a long-time defender of the free market. His book, *The Overgoverned Society* (Free Press, 1976), is a grim forecast of what we can expect in the near future: the imposition of price controls. He is even more pessimistic than I am. He thinks that they will not be removed until the end of the century, and they may last longer than that. As he puts it: "The head of a country in which 70 to 80 per cent of the population believes in witchcraft, simply has to practice a little sorcery." We are in for a long ordeal, Wallis says. If he is correct in his forecast concerning the length of the era of controls, then there will be extreme hardships for most citizens, yet incredible opportunities for high-risk profits at the same time, for it will not take more than a year or two before millions of Americans will realize their dependence upon the alternative (black) market. This means that there will be a **growing market for goods and services within the middle class segments of the American population**—the broadest segment of our population.

The strategy I am setting forth can meet the demands of both the short and long runs. But it should be clear that the longer controls are left on, the more difficult it will be for honest, law-abiding (or should I say legislation-abiding) citizens to survive without entering into voluntary exchanges on the alternative markets. For the short run (less than two years), the recommendations I make should carry through those who follow them without excessive legal risk. But if they remain in force for a decade or more, then all anyone can hope to do is to minimize his legal risk. He cannot avoid legal risk altogether.

I want it very clear from the beginning, however, that the strategy I am outlining here is entirely legal for the present. I am rewriting these words in mid-1979. There are no laws on the books that would make any of my suggestions for present action illegal in any way. I am therefore not recommending that anyone break the law. What I am trying to develop is an economic strategy that will permit people to prosper, or at least get by better than their neighbors, without resorting to illegal or questionable activities. But bear in mind that this strategy **will become illegal** once full-scale price and wage controls are imposed by the President and an acquiescent Congress. That is why present action is so imperative.

No one can follow all the suggestions I list. I am setting forth a program that must be adapted and applied to individual circumstances. It will work. It has worked in the past. But it will not do much good if none of the suggestions is taken seriously enough to apply. It is the investment **approach**, the **attitude**, the **way of perceiving economic reality** that will get each family through the storms to come.

Nevertheless, I want to re-emphasize the fact that my strategy is a way to **avoid** participating on illegal markets in the future. Or should I say, my strategy minimizes such participation for those who merely wish to survive **inconspicuously** (a key word). The big profits in a world of price controls are made by those who do participate in the black markets. Those who meet the needs of the buying public can make huge profits, for they fulfil an important social function by bearing risks and delivering the desired services. For those who wish to participate in future black markets in order to supply needed goods and services, I can only say, don't feel guilty. You are providing a very necessary service. But for those who are convinced that they shouldn't participate on black markets (meaning those who are comfortable **today** in a world devoid of controls that absolutely paralyze legal economic production), my strategy provides a legal alternative, **if** they act fast.

If my analysis of controls does make sense, then it is really suicidal, or at the very least foolish, not to begin to follow the strategy I present. Once again, it is not just what you don't know that can wipe you out. It is also what you do know but **refuse to acknowledge in your daily affairs** that can wipe you out just as fast, only you will have your own memory whispering in your ear: "You knew all this, dummy."

No doubt you are familiar with investment books. The chief problem that most people have with these books is not that the reader is unsure of the validity of the advice. If it were simply a question of ignorance, the reader could read more, look into things more deeply, and follow through on the leads provided by the book in question. Ignorance can be dealt with in a rational manner. The real problem is a kind of **psychological paralysis** that hits most of us when we see an opportunity. In fact, it is this paralysis which makes possible far higher profits for those who have the same knowledge about the future but who are not equally inhibited. **The entrepreneur is willing to act**. He does not simply nod "ah, ha!" to himself, turn the pages thoughtfully, and then put the book down, fogotten. The first nine chapters of the Bible's Book of Proverbs instructs us to get wisdom. The rest of the book is devoted to another lesson for us: get moving!

General Strategy

Saving: Discipline yourself to set aside at least 10% of your after-tax income, month by month, for a systematic program of investing in "hard" goods, or in education leading to your ability to repair such goods. Education is very important. It may be that you have little money but more time. Devote yourself to self-education if you have any talent what-soever along these lines. Get into the public library and start taking out books devoted to auto repair, home repair, plumbing, electrical wiring, and so forth. This kind of investment is highly liquid, highly movable, yet (when necessary) relatively inconspicuous. The best kind of capital is **mobile capital**, and education is the most mobile of all.

The habit of regular saving is extremely important, both for the individual and for Western civilization. The foundation of modern mass production is the willingness of large numbers of individuals to forego present consumption, voluntarily, for the sake of a hoped-for future return. Saving is intensely **future oriented**. Furthermore, saving is an **ethical act**. It rests on an assumption, namely, that the future will not take care of itself, that people are personally responsible for their own welfare and the welfare of their families, and that they have a moral obligation to prepare for the future. Finally, saving is an **unnatural act**. You would think that as men grow more wealthy, they would save a greater percentage of their incomes, since each additional dollar would be used to satisfy wants of lower importance. After all, rich people do not starve, go hungry, or suffer cold. But the people of the United States today are saving a diminishing portion of their incomes as times get better economically. They become less responsible. They take the good times for granted. We are the richest nation of the world, yet we save far less, proportionately, than the people of Japan, West Germany, and other less prosperous Western nations. Saving requires discipline. It requires it from an early age. It requires a future-oriented view of the world. It requires a belief in personal responsibility for one's actions. It is hard work, and it is absolutely vital for our survival as a nation.

Yet it is not enough to save money. It is not enough, in the oft-quoted (and miserably inaccurate) words of Eliot Janeway, to have six-months' income in your savings and loan account. Except for emergency money (probably under $2,000), few families that are not close to retirement (another evil) need that kind of money at their disposal. What you must learn today is to **avoid money**. Capital is not money in a world of price and wage controls. Capital is hard goods, useful goods. Capital is experience in repairing hard goods or in providing them in inconspicuous ways. You don't want money; you want the things that money can buy now **and won't buy after price and wage controls are in operation**. This is extremely important in the world of price controls. You must rethink your usual equation of money and wealth. Under full-scale controls, money is less and less the sign or instrument of wealth. Goods are the real wealth. Get away from money. The love of money is the root of all evil; under price controls, it is also the best way to get wiped out. You want goods, not money.

Tithing: I realize that few, if any, books on investing recommend giving away money, goods, or services. This book breaks with tradition. In addition to saving at least 10% of after-tax income, I recommend giving away about 14% of your after-tax income. Those who have read the Book of Malachi in the Bible know why I say this. There is a relationship between the blessings of God and the willingness of men to honor the principle of the tithe. I have tested this principle in my own economic affairs, and I can say that it works. (Even if it didn't, it would still be an ethical obligation.) Our goal should be the reconstruction of Western culture, and this takes money. It takes donated money. It takes schools, hospitals, churches, the arts, and all sorts of charity-supported activities. If our main political and economic problem today is the huge, impersonal, ever-expanding bureaucratic state, then we must be prepared to take over many of the state's activities. Either we pay for these activities and programs with money voluntarily donated to organizations that must give an account of their actions, or else we pay for them with higher taxes, and nobody is willing to take responsibility for anything. The discipline of the tithe is related to the discipline of saving. The sooner we and our children learn such discipline, the sooner we will see our hopes fulfilled. Resolve here and now to honor the principle of the tithe. The buck starts here. Give it away.

Timing: Watch very carefully for any announcement of an act of Congress which grants to the President the authority to impose price controls. This kind of legislation was passed just one year before Richard Nixon imposed the controls of August 15, 1971. It led me to state, in print, that Nixon would use this power. Of course, there need not be any warning at all. Nixon simply closed the gold window on August 15, without any justification legally. He didn't even declare an executive order. He just said that the U.S. would no longer honor its international monetary obligation to redeem dollars for gold. We live in a world of much legislation and little law. Never forget this.

However, when and if you see that Congress has granted the President such power, start to move fast. You will have to devote 20% of your after-tax income to buying hard goods. This is the minimum figure. If absolutely necessary, get a loan and start buying. Take an extra job. Do anything, but start buying. There will not be very much time to spare.

Which goods should you buy? As I never tire of repeating, those goods that are **highly price competitive**, with **narrow profit margins**, and that are **sold in high volume** to the middle classes. Why? Because these will be the first goods to disappear off of the shelves.

I keep thinking of the first presidential debate between President Ford and Jimmy Carter. I keep thinking of that $1.25 electrical part that failed toward the end of the debate. All America was watching, but America wasn't listening any more. For 28 minutes the sound was absolutely dead, even in the studio where they were debating. Finally, the newsmen had to string in new equipment. They never did replace that $1.25 part.

Now, imagine a world in which that $1.25 part really should be getting

$2.50. But the government has outlawed price increases. It has made the production of these parts at $2.50 a criminal act. So what happens to the production and distribution of these "$1.25" parts? They are sold illegally, or else they are not produced at all. Count on it. And if it is your company's $5 million computer that needs that $1.25 part, what happens to your job? Yes, they'll get the part, illegally, but how long will it take, with how many fouled up orders or directives?

Once the "temporary price freeze" is announced, you're on your own. I can only give suggestions. I would go into debt at this point, although I do not normally advise debt. But this is a true emergency. You must step up your buying. Buy as much as you can. This means that your **present** level of indebtedness must be reduced, in order to give you breathing room, or maneuvering room, when the announcement hits. As much as possible, get out of all unproductive debt. Go in debt for a heavy duty washing machine, not a new T.V. Go in debt for tools of your trade, not a vacation. A washing machine, or a vacuum cleaner, or a good wood burning stove are all capital goods. **Avoid debt for purely consumer items,** especially entertainment items. You can be bored with this year's line-up of "great programs" just as easily on a used black & white set as on a new Sony.

When the announcement of controls or guidelines is made, you are literally **racing against time.** The time will have come to start buying and hoarding (saving) in earnest. There will be no more doubts in the minds of those who are familiar with price controls and their effects. They will be buying heavily. They will be getting ready to become suppliers at above-legal prices. There should be no more doubts in your mind then. Speed will be imperative, really imperative.

These percentages are arbitrary. How can I be sure that 10% or 20% will be just right for you? But I do know that 10% is better than 8% or 1%. I do know that the kind of world that is on its way has got to be viewed from a new angle. I do know that most people will not see it from the proper perspective until it is far too late to take advantage of the wide variety of producers' goods that are available on the pre-price control markets. These are **minimum** survival figures. These are what you have to have to get by comfortably for a year or two. The longer controls stay on, the higher the percentage of present saving (hoarding) should be.

I am increasingly convinced that the **controls will be on for a minimum of five years.** I think a decade is not out of the question. I dearly hope that our political system would reverse the effects of the controls after a period of ten years. But I am not really convinced. **We are being engulfed by the ethics of envy.** Controls are ideal devices for bringing out the envious side of mankind. There are great winners, those who are participating successfully on the illegal markets. They become easy scapegoats for the politicians and bureaucrats. They are too easy to blame for the hardships of others, for the shortages, for the economic dislocations. And there will be dislocations. Men who participate on the markets as little people will not shed any tears when their trading partners—the most successful trading partners—are caught and sentenced.

This leads to another rule: if possible, **trade only with those who are in a comparable income bracket.** Of course, you can trade with someone who is richer, if he is so unwise or so trusting of your integrity to trade with you, the little guy. But **don't trade down**, if you can avoid it. Don't let the feelings of envy get aimed at you. If you do trade down, then do so humbly, quietly, and above all, **inconspicuously.** Dress plainly. If you're smart, get rid of the outward signs of wealth the day controls are imposed. Sell that home in the ritzy section of town if you have one. Get a duplex. Get a small farm in the country. But don't be visibly prosperous. Keep your assets out of sight. Do not "buy upward."

I realize that this is strong medicine. A rich man is unlikely to take my advice. But it is good advice for an envy-dominated era. The idea is to preserve and expand your capital during a period in which other men are going bankrupt or are being forced by circumstances to liquidate assets at distressed prices. But when they pass a capital tax, as they have in European socialist country after country, it will be far better to have your assets hidden. These will be sharply graduated taxes, "wealth" taxes, envy-designed taxes. Envy is loose in the land. Maybe you don't have the time or inclination to read Prof. Helmut Schoeck's great book, *Envy* (Harcourt, Brace, 1969), but you can take my word for it: socialism is at root the desire to tear down all the signs of another man's success. It is the great social destroyer. The bigger you are, the more likely you'll fall. Or more accurately, the bigger you appear to be. When they can't get deeply enough into your pocket with income taxes, sales taxes, capital gains taxes, and estate taxes, then they will tax whatever you have left over that is visible.

Barter, Now

Barter is coming back. Several firms have been established in the last few years that supplement the money-denominated markets for goods and services. If you have a business, you should know about these programs. If your area doesn't have one, here would be an excellent business to run on the side. In any case, it will gain valuable experience for you and all who trade through any such organization.

Say, for example, that you have a tire store. You join one of these barter societies. Someone who is already a participating member comes in. He buys your tires at the wholesale price. But instead of paying you money, he pays you in certificates that can be used to buy products at wholesale from another member of the group. The larger the membership, of course, the broader the market. The broader the market, the more specialized and productive the labor is.

Maybe you want a new suit. You go in to the man who sells clothes, give him your certificate (earned from the man who bought the tires from you) and buy the suit at wholesale. This is especially good for a man who (wisely) is reducing his cash flow and laying up inventory. He is getting into hard goods or direct services, yet it isn't eating into his cash. His cash can then be used to invest in even more hard goods for his business or family.

There are even some people who might fail to report the full retail value of such exchanges to the tax authorities. That may shock you. Or it may not.

Don't try to get rich by starting a barter company. And don't try to beat the tax man. Most important, don't invest in a franchise deal that promises to make you rich by avoiding the tax man. There are too many hustlers franchising barter companies these days. Let the investor beware. I can recommend one firm as an example of what can and should be done with a barter company:

> Pentagon Office Park, Suite 100-B
> 4901 West 77th Street
> Minneapolis, MN 55435
> (612) 835-2233

The quicker you and your neighbors get used to the idea of barter, the better off your community will be. In California, the swap meets that are held in drive-in theaters on the weekends have become meccas for sharp traders. There is no reason why a local organization cannot imitate the success of the West Coast swap meets. (Weather is on the side of the Californians, of course.) But these two barter societies have pioneered a broader concept of barter, and their lead should be acknowledged. The one problem with them for the future is the fact that they do leave records. There are charges for each trade, and the tax authorities can compute the value of the exchanges by using the 7% or 8% fee charged by the firms. Still, participation now can introduce you to people in the community who are barter oriented. This information will be very valuable in the future.

The idea is, simply, get started. Get used to the idea of innovation. Get used to the "feel" of face-to-face exchange. Get used to the idea that "money talks." It does, for the present. But someday it will only whisper.

One thing, though. You should have confidence in yourself. You'll make mistakes, but you have knowledge now that most people don't have. That knowledge is your source of future profits. Have confidence, get busy, and help to rebuild this economic mess.

For professional consultation in organizing a barter society, Mr. Jesse Cornish is available on a retainer fee basis. This approach is generally preferable to purchasing a franchise, which several organizations sell. You can contact Mr. Cornish by calling this toll-free number: (800) 328-1860. (He also sells gold and silver coins.)

CHAPTER FIFTEEN
A SECOND JOB AS A SAFETY NET

One of the most difficult tasks of a serious investment writer is to convince his readers that certain steps should be taken in their financial lives in order to protect themselves from a looming disaster, or to take advantage of a new opportunity. I have become convinced that traders' sheets provide information that only a small percentage of the readers ever really act upon. I have concluded this by watching the results of specific recommendations. I remember one popular letter's advice to short the Swiss franc in January, 1973, just before the massive increase in the franc's value when the Swiss floated their currency in order to escape the panic runout of dollars and into francs. Had any trader taken a short position on margin in January, 1973, the one-day leap in the franc would have wiped him out completely. Yet the letter in question still prospers. People take trading sheets for many reasons, but given the volume of the specific recommendations, it is unlikely that any one recommendation will be followed by a majority of the traders who read a particular sheet. In fact, the more recommendations made by a sheet, the less likely that any single subscriber will be wiped out. At the same time, no single trader is likely to profit from those recommendations that do prove accurate. Sooner or later, letter writers who provide many recommendations per week experience a kind of temptation peculiar to the profession: the "filler syndrome." Just say something eye-catching, since so few will act. People seem to want zippy copy more than they want specific recommendations. (I'm speaking here of the more apocalyptic letters, although I suspect that the same problem holds true for the standard market letters.)

With studies like mine that are geared to long-term planning rather than short-term market recommendations, the problem of convincing readers to act is somewhat similar. No single family can afford to take every suggestion, but ideally every suggestion, five or ten years down the line, ought to produce profits (or avoid losses) for those who took action, given the risks of any human action. Each reader should get a few ideas out of this book that warrant its price. Thus, not every recommendation should be acted upon by every reader. This is analogous to the multiple tips in traders' sheets: no one actually follows every recommendation. But there is one crucial difference: the reader may not be sure of the validity of a suggestion for several years. This is why **trust** is so important between writer and reader. This is also why the logic of a major (expensive) recommendation has to be spelled out.

A Family Safety Net

Because of the disruptions that would appear to be inescapable over the next five years, no man can be really certain that his present occupation will insure him against all the potential losses that could come upon him. Civil servants enjoy job security, but not inflation security, and especially not repressed inflation (controls) security. Salaries may come, but purchasing power almost certainly will drop. Credit crunches are produced either by tight money policies or by easy money policies that produce price inflation loan premiums that in turn smash into state usury laws; these crunches can bring a company to a grinding halt. Lay-offs take place in boom times if a particular firm gets trapped. The whip-sawing effects of the boom-bust policies of the last decade are probably going to increase after 1977, and it takes skilled managers to deal with the next crisis rather than the last one. Your manager may goof.

Many families have both husband and wife working. If the family's expenditures are not pushing tightly against income, and if the two are unlikely to be fired simultaneously, then the family has a cushion. But how many families have much lattitude? And the costs of working parents to the family may not be seen for many years, until the children hit their teens. Unless the wife's job keeps her close to home, the costs may prove to be too high in the long run.

This leaves the husband in a dilemma. A second job may drain him physically or financially. It eats up his time. The obvious source of more time—unplugging the television set—is a drastic step for most families. Yet today it is very important for a man to have a second source of income besides his first job. The psychological safety net of a second income is something that few men experience, but in times of disruption it should not be dismissed lightly. We always tend to accept the good times as normal, since our income rises as we mature in our productive economic years. But the normality of good times is under fire all over the world.

What Else Can You Do?

The essence of the disaster we face, economically speaking, is the **overspecialization** of modern life. The moral faith which undergirded this massive expansion of human productivity and specialization is steadily eroding. Envy, the statist abrogation of the right of contract, the inflation of the money supply, the redistribution of wealth, and the inflation-produced boom-bust cycle have now brought us face to face with a horrifying thought: can the extension of the division of labor, and therefore rising real income, be continued? If the monetary unit is destroyed, can it even be maintained? This is the question Prof. Hayek keeps bringing up, much to the disgust of the Keynesians.

Not only can each man do something else for a living, he may very well have to in the next decade. The best thing that a man can do for himself, given this possibility, is to seek out that **alternative employment** which suits his skills, **and which is likely to be in demand in a controls-induced shortage economy**, and to begin to enter that field now, slowly, thereby lowering the costs of transition later on. The wisest employment is that provided by many buyers, so that no single source of revenue can make or break a man's business, should it be turned off. The broader the market, the safer you are. However, it might be wise to develop that broad market within a local geographical area, for reasons which we have gone over in earlier chapters: feudalization of the economy, breakdown of outside supplies, irregular mail service, etc.

Peter Weaver has written a helpful little book, *You, Inc.* (Doubleday Dolphin Book, C546, $2.95). Weaver shows how he broke out of his salaried, safe position by becoming a writer, but many of his reasons for breaking out and his recommended steps for doing so are quite applicable in other professions. There is boredom associated with dead-end middle management (age 40+). There is the risk of putting all your eggs in one corporate basket. There is the psychological problem of overdependence, which in turn can lead to killing stress. There is the stifling atmosphere of any bureaucracy. Your ideas get blocked. "Your soul gets scarred and shrivels a little. Your intellectual growth withers. You can't even make your own mistakes." Finally, there is the overwhelming danger to the middle age man of the **retirement trap**. Inflation eats away his pension, assuming he has been able to collect his pension (and pensions are a major Achilles' heel of the American economy, both public and private ones). The boredom can kill him. The sense of loss can break his spirit. Therefore, Weaver argues, a man should try to break free, if only part-time.

St. Paul, some of you may remember, was a tentmaker (Acts 18:1-3). His independent source of income gave him a measure of independence from the churches which he advised (II Thes. 3:7-9). Not being in the pay of any of them, he did not need to bend his preaching or admonishing to suit the pleasure of his listeners. But he did have to meet the competition in the tent market in order to preserve this ecclesiastical independence, and he also had to labor day and night, as he reminded the church at Thessalonica. He was independent, but not at zero price.

Preliminary Steps

First, discuss the idea of a second occupation with your wife. There are too many risks for you to go out on your own "cold turkey." But if she can see that you and she need the security of a second income, then she will better understand the costs she will have to make. Second, don't expect to be able to make all your decisions immediately. Most new businesses fail within the first five years. They are almost invariably **under-capitalized**. The less capital you have, the more slowly you should embark on a new calling. You cannot afford dangerous mistakes, so reduce the danger by starting slowly.

Psychologically, Weaver says, the best step you can take is to decide on a company title and go down to your local bank and deposit $50 or $100 or whatever in a special bank account for your business. Get that checking account going, and never touch it except for business affairs. If you need a file cabinet (you will), use your business account. Get in the habit of regarding this account as strictly business. Any money coming into this account from sales must also be regarded as untouchable until the business becomes profitable. If you have to take an extra job to finance the new business, there will always be a temptation to spend the money. Parkinson's Law takes over, as expenditures rise so as to absorb all new income. But the key is the first step in establishing a visible symbol of your intentions: a separate business checking account.

Sometimes you may have to sacrifice your present occupation's opportunities in order to gain your freedom. If you want "out, not up," writes Weaver, this may mean turning down a promotion or transfer. You may even have to take a part-time job to finance your new venture, and this could cost you your regular job. But even this seeming disaster might leave you with more time, which is the crucial capital resource in the beginning.

"I'm not saying you should refuse promotions or more money," he writes. "Just remember: Rent them your body for a while but never, ever, sell them your soul. While you are renting your body, keep your mind on extracting portable skills or a profession that you can take with you when you make the break into your own business. While building up these skills, you should keep a little file of ideas for your side venture." **Portable skills** are a form of **portable capital**, and there is no better form of capital. It is untaxable, it cannot be redistributed by governmental edict, and it is invisible.

In some cases, you will probably find that work in your regular job is improved by your new project. I found this to be the case when I began to publish my bi-weekly economic newsletter, *Remnant Review*. I discovered that by having to keep up with the economic news, the relevance of my writing and speaking for the foundation I was working for when I began the newsletter improved considerably. Some employers might not be very enthusiastic about the idea, however. Obviously, a person with outside income developing is going to be more independent in his work at the office, and some firms are so bureaucratic that the managers resent signs of independence. They want safe, docile employees. That's their mistake.

Optimism concerning one's future (if not transferred blindly to the economy in general) is a kind of internal incentive to increase production. But self-confidence comes slowly, or should; careful planning and practice should precede any full-scale operation. Build up your new market slowly, unless you have a product so good that direct advertising is almost certain to create an immediate profit.

Family Business

"He who does not teach his son a trade teaches him to steal," says an old Jewish proverb. Yet in the modern economy, few men can teach their sons their trade. Their trade is too specialized, and it requires professional training, or trade union approval, or some sort of licensing, or a work permit. In short, salaried men do not work with their sons. Moreover, the old Puritan practice of sending sons to an apprentice, and taking in other men's sons as apprentices, has also disappeared, and with the disappearance of apprentices we have also witnessed the disappearance of the old crafts. This has involved a cultural loss to society, but in a time of a shrinking division of labor, it may well involve far more than cultural loss.

The advantage of a family trade of some kind is that a man can pass along his secondary occupation to his sons or daughters. While they may not take up the trade as a full-time occupation, they have been provided with a kind of employment insurance. The habits of discipline, so crucial for successful entry into the marketplace, are established early. A sense of family involvement is also created—not some sort of makeshift togetherness, but community based on shared goals and shared labor. The breakup of the family unit is one of the primary causes of the social crises of our time. The returns to a family business could be far more than monetary.

One of the most disastrous side-effects of minimum wage laws is the denial to ghetto youths of legal access to the low paid jobs that might otherwise have taught them regular work habits. Without these, they are almost as crippled as they would be if they could not read, which many of them can't. But minimum wage laws do not affect pay scales of family members, which is one great advantage the sons of farmers have in this country. They learn how to work. This is no small accomplishment. Businessmen are hard-pressed to find young men who can handle the discipline of labor. This is one reason why the graduates of unaccredited Bob Jones University are sought after by American businesses. Bob Jones students know how to work hard, and that is all the accreditation the school needs.

Children have become an economic burden in our day. It costs anywhere from $18,000 to $30,000 to rear a child today, and this is not counting the economic losses to the mother who stays out of the labor market for two or three decades. As a result, the size of the families has dropped within the middle class and upper class populations. We are literally seeing a kind of self-extinction of the most talented families—a seemingly rational economic response to the costs of specialized education. But socially, this response is more questionable. I keep thinking of Van Den Haag's observation that medieval Roman Catholics took their brightest young men and made celibate priests out of them. Meanwhile, medieval Jews were sacrificing to send their brightest young men to rabbinical schools, and upon graduation they were expected to marry and have a lot of children. Genetically, the latter social policy favored the Jews over the Catholics. What we see today is analogous to what the later Roman Empire in the West experienced: a population boom among those on welfare, and a declining population among urban, tax-paying classes.

A small family business, even if it is initially unprofitable monetarily, can produce long-term family benefits, so long as the budding entrepreneur is careful not to risk too much of his capital in the early stages. Capitalize the business slowly, using "spare" time if there isn't enough money available.

What Kind of Business?

The first and most important requirement is personal. Do you think you would enjoy the work, even if it paid very little for a considerable period of time? Is the joy of doing business worth the sacrifices and risks? This question is ultimately a religious question about your purpose, skills, and attitudes in life. You have to want to do this second business. If you don't, you will give up too easily. Worse, you might even become too successful, and then you will wind up as your own organization man, falling right back into the bureaucratic trap you are trying to escape.

No matter what you get into, there will almost certainly be a trade association around that can help provide you with such benefits as group insurance, trade papers, guidebooks, newsletters, and other important information, including professional education opportunities. There is a book listing these, *National Trade and Professional Associations of the United States*. There are over 4,500 of these associations. If your local library doesn't have it (including the local university's business education library), it can be ordered from Columbia Books, Suite 601, 734-15th St., N.W., Washington, D.C. 20005: $30.

One benefit you should look for, though not make a primary asset, is whether the second business is counter-cyclical to your primary employment. Does it boom when your regular business does, and fall off when your regular business does? If so, be careful; the heaviest demands will be placed on you at the same time, yet the "insurance policy" aspect of the second business may evaporate. If you can find a "sales-repairs" tandem, you have a strong pair. When recession hits, and sales fall off, people will need to repair their existing equipment. A man can cut down on his sales job and concentrate on repairs. Either can be the primary job, but it would seem more likely that those who read a book like this one are more apt to be salesmen than repairmen. An excellent opportunity for a salesman would be to train in minor repairs in his company's service program if he sells durable goods. The firm may even finance some or all of the education costs. This will make him a more desirable salesman—buyers worry about machines that break down, and a salesman who can make minor repairs has a real advantage—and at the same time provide him with a portable skill. But if you do this, be very careful not to take business from the company's service department with your own moonlighting operation. Do not create conflicts of interest with your present employer. This is a fundamental general principle for all moonlighters. Learn what you can from your present employer, but develop your own contacts on the side.

The Harried Professional

The entrepreneur is never able to rest. (A Christian or Jewish businessman takes rest on the sabbath, but it is an act of faith; his time is not wasted, for he is giving God what is due, and God will uphold him.) He always can learn more, plan better, buy cheaper. His business eats up his time. (This is why men pay good money for newsletters. My readers, in effect, are disciplining themselves to read a book each year, but in digestable portions.) He thinks he cannot possibly spend enough time to learn a new trade and still perform well in his business.

This may be true. If so, the businessman absolutely must find other men with skills who need a silent partner. Look for honest, reliable men who are willing to sacrifice for their trade. Then find a counter-cyclical trade to your own business that will be populated with a few such men—the fewer the better—assuming that you can pick out the good ones. I would like to say that a church is a good place to start, but I have seen too many Christian businessmen who have little regard for paying debts on time. But if there is a tradesman in a local church who has started out of debt, but who now needs a lot of money to launch a new part of his business, he might be a good risk. But in any case, a portion of your capital should be put into men rather than pieces of paper. In a time of disrupted capital markets, it is the character of local tradesmen that will count a great deal.

A partnership is difficult to break when it becomes successful. Have a clause written into the original contract allowing one partner to buy the other's share at a price to be offered by the disgruntled partner. The other partner has the option of buying the first one out at that price. This keeps the offer honest. Either can buy the other out, so the man who wants to get the other man out must offer a fair price to avoid a counter-offer to buy **him** out.

The ideal second job for a really busy businessman should have something to do with his hobby. If he has gained knowledge here, and if the time spent on this hobby does not seem to be stolen from his business, then he may be able to transfer his hobby into a second business.

You must know yourself. You must know your strengths and limits. You must know some of the limits of the bureaucrats of the proposed New World Order, which is going to be the familiar Old World Disorder. If you cannot move to a small town, then begin to prepare yourself for productivity on your block in a big city.

If you go ahead on this project, be sure to buy a copy of Don Dible's book, *Up Your Own Organization* (Entrepreneur Press), which is now available in a paperback. It is sold in the B. Dalton bookstores.

The Sure Thing

Is there any occupation today that is virtually guaranteed, given competence and honesty? I have thought it over, and I think there is one. If you have the skills, become a locksmith. Invest in a trade that has subsidies, 24 hours a day. The skills are portable, the demand is growing, and it combines both sales and repairs. There are locks to match every man's skills, and buyers of services at each level. I'd rather have a locksmith for a son than a sociologist. I want to eat in my old age, not read the results of surveys.

Should You Incorporate?

I'm not a big promoter of Subchapter S (small business) incorporating, although there may be some advantages for businesses netting under $50,000. If you do decide to go the corporation route, the cheapest way is to use the services of Ted Nicholas' Corporation Company, a firm that will incorporate you in the state of Delaware for under $100. Your home state may require additional payments, but Delaware corporations are unbelievably loose. You can designate your corporation as a firm engaging in any lawful activity, and you only need one director. For a $25 annual fine, you can even neglect to file an annual report to the state. Nicholas' book provides all the necessary forms: *How to Form Your Own Corporation Without a Lawyer for Under $50* (Enterprise Pub. Co., 1300 Market St., Wilmington, DE 19801; $10.00). I would still recommend a lawyer or CPA to help you set it up. You might also want to read Judith McQuown's book, *Inc. Yourself* (Macmillan, 1977).

A major advantage of a sole proprietorship, as distinguished from a corporation, is that the business can pay salaries to the wife and children (under age 21) without having to pay the Social Security tax.* A disadvantage is that a sole proprietorship cannot pay your family's health

*Internal Revenue Service, Circular E, *Employer's Tax Guide, Publication 15* (Nov. 1976), p. 13.

insurance premiums on a tax-deductible basis. A small corporation can. This can amount to well over $1,000 of tax-free "income" if you buy a comprehensive policy, such as the one sold by Blue Cross-Blue Shield.

CHAPTER SIXTEEN
AUTO MAINTENANCE AND PRICE CONTROLS
by *Edward Powell*

The following important essay was written by Edward Powell, a retired policeman, age 34, who sees the handwriting on the wall. He also is a very good auto mechanic.

There is no doubt in my mind that his predictions concerning the effect of price and wage controls on automobile maintenance are right on target. The man who survived World War II in some degree of style was the man who: a) bought what he needed to keep his car running on December 8, 1941, or b) participated in the black market. The man who pursued the safer first approach had to have knowledge in advance. He had to know what to ask for and in what quantities. Some little malfunction can bring today's $5,000 piece of equipment to a grinding halt. For want of a nail, etc.

For the amateur repairman or totally uninformed driver, the list of things necessary (let alone convenient) is horrendously large. This book's brief introduction should serve as a warning of just how vulnerable we are to shortages. We are completely dependent on our automobiles, yet most of us haven't the foggiest notion of how to keep them going. "Fill 'er up" is about as technical as we ever get. The real experts say, "Check the oil, will you?" Now you know. Start getting help soon. But at least you have some idea of the questions that need to be asked and the costs involved. I know that if I had simply had the brake fluid changed on schedule, I would have saved myself $60. That is the price of a **Remnant Review** *subscription, and taxes being what they are, I had to sell more than one to pay for my negligence. A penny saved is 1.3 cents earned, depending upon your tax bracket.*

Wage and price controls bring with them the disappearance of mass produced, marginal profit, price competitive items. As costs rise, products of limited demand will become unavailable, while those products which will still be manufactured in quantity will be reduced in quality. Herein lies a major problem for the average motorist, for all automotive parts normally used in periodic maintenance are highly competitive. With the imposition of controls, new parts for foreign and older domestic vehicles (pre-1967) will, because of limited profits, stop being manufactured, while quality of auto parts for the later models will deteriorate, possibly to the point of being dangerous.

The proper time to prepare for any event is **before** it happens. Since controls are coming, it is necessary that automotive parts and supplies be purchased and stored ahead of time. But mere storage of these items is a waste of time, energy, and money unless your vehicle is in proper condition. A car properly cared for is the assurance that you will be able to ride out the controls in safety and comfort. Proper maintenance, quality parts, and familiarity with your car are the keys to long life and minimum trouble.

The following information and recommendations are given only as a guide. How long you wish to keep your present car, how many and what kind of miles you drive, etc., are factors that you will have to consider in evaluating the following. This information has been gleaned from practical experience and highly respected automotive publications. Some of these recommendations will be scoffed at, but I have found them useful in preventing trouble and high costs later on.

Maintenance

Careful attention to proper periodic maintenance is the single most important item that will determine the life of an automobile. If you intend to keep your car as long as possible, don't be penny wise and pound foolish. Money spent on proper service pays off in long and reliable mileage.

A periodic maintenance checklist should be developed from owner and workshop manuals. The lists that are generally compiled in these books are **minimum** service requirements. Few garages adhere to the more extensive lists because owners would object to the costs involved. Learn to perform the small necessary items in these lists yourself and leave the major service to your local mechanic.

The following hints are not inclusive but are only intended as a supplement for existing service lists. Remember, it is **preventive** maintenance that is being touted here, not the fixing of some do-dad that has gone ka-put.

The ensuing sections are interrelated, and each section has some repetition from the others. This could not be avoided. Both mileage and time schedules are listed, and the one which comes first should be followed. You should develop your own schedule of service to suit your own individual needs and desires. The suggestions are for obtaining maximum reliable mileage from any vehicle. The average domestic American car is junked at 110,000 miles, but with proper periodic preventive maintenance this figure can be doubled. Tender loving care and full maintenance never hurt an automobile or a marriage.

The following abbreviations are used to save space:
FMR—Follow Manufacturer's Recommendations
CWM—Consult Workshop Manual for your particular car

Lubrication and Periodic Inspection

1. **Engine oil and filter: FMR**, but read the warning. The oil change recommendations are for ideal driving conditions, i.e., dust-free highway miles, not stop-and-go driving. I change my engine oil every 3,000 miles or 3 months unless I do very extensive driving. If you are presently using a single-grade viscosity SE motor oil (e.g., 20wt, 30 wt), better engine wear and reduced carbon build-up in the combustion chamber can be expected by switching to a name-brand premium multi-viscosity SE oil, but I'd stay away from the 10w-30 types. Best bet for the money is 10w-40 or 20w-50. Air-cooled engines and some Chrysler products work best with 20w-50. Consult the latest lube chart and/or book at your local service station.

2. **Suspension: CWM**. On the newer models plugs instead of grease fittings are often used. Have these removed and grease fittings (Zerks) installed. Consult your manual for location of these plugs. Don't forget to look at the upper wishbones, because some cars have plugs here but don't list it in their manuals. Have your suspension lubed when you get your oil changed or every 3,000 miles. Chevies (and some older Chryslers) with manual transmissions should have their clutch cross shaft and linkage lubed **sparingly** every 30,000 miles. **Warning**: New cars use lithium grease with molybdenum disulfide. Don't mix it with others.

3. **Steering**: If you **don't** have power steering, remind the person who greases your car of this fact. Get him to check the oil in the steering housing and refill or add with 90 SAE multi-purpose gear oil (not grease). CWM.

4. **Driveshaft U-joints**: (See parts section, pp. 174-76.) Unfortunately, few cars come with U-joints that can be serviced. They're made as replacement items. Under normal wear they will last 50-70,000 miles. Time and mileage are bad on these units, so have them checked every 6 months or 12,000 miles. If you do have grease fittings on your U-joints, be sure to tell the "grease monkey" who lubes your car; otherwise he might overlook them. NOTE: Some G.M. vehicles (notably Chevies and Olds) have constant velocity universal joints with small flush grease fittings. These are often missed when a vehicle is lubed, so if you have this type of driveshaft on your G.M. product, remind the serviceman of this fact.

5. **Wheel bearings:** Should be **cleaned** and repacked every 10,000-12,000 miles or 2 years. Find someone who is willing and able to clean both bearings and hubs, not merely smear new grease over the old. **Never clean any bearings with solvents. Use Kerosene.** Repack with high-temperature (disc brake) wheel bearing grease containing molybdenum disulfide.

6. **Transmission & differential:** For severe service, such as trailer towing, FMR. Under normal driving conditions, automatic transmission fluid should be changed every 20-25,000 miles or 2 years. If applicable, change filter and/or clean screen and get the transmission bands adjusted at this time. With manual transmissions, I suggest changing the oil every 25,000 miles or 2 years, and the differential oil every 50,000 miles or 4 years. If you have a limited-slip differential **use only factory approved fluid**, which is available from the dealer-distributor. I change the oil in my manual transmission every 12,000 miles and in the rear end every 24,000 miles. **Oil is cheap** and easy to store. Manual transmissions: Check clutch pedal free play every 6,000 miles. This will help to preserve the clutch disc.

7. **Brakes:** Front brakes are automatically checked when you get your wheel bearings repacked. If you don't get your bearings repacked every 12,000 miles, have your brakes checked when you get a tune-up. If your shoes need replacing be sure to have the wheel cylinders rebuilt. If you don't you'll probably end up with leaks. **Important:** The **brake fluid** should be replaced at least every two years. If this isn't done, moisture gathered from the air will settle on the bottom of the cylinders and draw sulphur from the fluid to create sulphuric acid, which will eat pits into the master and wheel cylinders. If you have a hydraulic clutch, don't forget to flush it at the same time. You'll find instructions for bleeding (flushing) the system in your workshop manual. Bleed **all** of the old fluid out of **each** wheel cylinder. Rebuilt kits are cheaper (by approximately 90%) than master and wheel cylinders, and under controls you'll be lucky if you can buy them. **Warning:** Silicone base and glycol base brake fluids should not be mixed. Doing so will lower the boiling point of the fluid and could produce vapor lock and brake failure. When changing fluid, be certain to flush the entire system. Use **only** a top-name brake fluid and read the information on the can before buying. (I use Castrol Girling LMA brake fluid.)

8. **Cooling system:** FMR. Change coolant-anti-freeze solution every two years. Flush your radiator at this time. Also check your hoses. I replace my hoses every two years and keep the old ones for spares. Short trips are murder on a car. If you drive less than 5 miles per trip and can't properly warm your engine by more extensive driving, the ethylene

glycol will settle into the bottom of the tanks and turn into a jelly. In such cases, be sure to take your car for 25 miles on the freeway **each week**. (It helps your battery, too.) If your vehicle does not presently have a **coolant recovery system**, install one. They are inexpensive ($3 to $10) and come with simple do-it-yourself instructions.

9. **Battery**: A good battery will last considerably longer than the guarantee if given proper care (a friend got 9 years service out of his 3-year battery). Check fluid level **every two weeks** and occassionally when taking long trips. Don't let the cells get dry, and refill them **only** with **distilled water**. Keep it clean, make sure that the cables are tight on both ends, and put **grease** (not paint) on the battery post and cable clamps to prevent corrosion. Once or twice a year, pour a mixture of water and baking soda **around the bottom** of the battery, then sprinkle a little soda in the same area. Remember, it takes 20-30 minutes of driving to recharge your battery to its peak capacity after each start.

10. **Tires**: Check the pressure bi-weekly and when tires are cool, i.e., before you go on that trip. FMR for maximum tire pressure, but don't exceed the pressure rating printed on the side of the tire. This will give maximum mileage. Have your tires balanced, either statically or electronic-dynamically (best with a strobe light). If your drums or discs are in balance (and most new cars are already well balanced), then a static balance is just as good as the much touted dynamic method. Dynamic balance costs more and you can't rotate your tires unless you rebalance them which you can do with a static balance. Your car will dictate what you need.

11. **Air & Fuel filters**: FMR but remember that their service intervals are for ideal conditions. I change both these filters twice as often as recommended. **Keeping dirt out of an engine is cheaper than rebuilding one.**

12. **Odd items**: Check all **rubber and neoprene hoses** once a year. Pay particular attention to the hose running from the fuel pump to the carburetor and the one from the gas tank to the fuel line. Also, check the **brake hoses** and the power steering pressure hose from the pump to the steering box. **Change your brand of gas** occassionally for a couple of tank fulls. This will help to reduce carbon in the combustion chamber. Lube your **speedometer cable** every two years and inspect your **V-belts** (fan, etc.) from time to time. Get them replaced if they have cracks. Check your **exhaust system** and tighten all visible nuts once a year. If you have **tubeless tires**, check the valve stems from time to time. Bend the stem to one side and examine the base for cracks. If you have cracks, replace the stems. A good 30% of the air leaks I see in tires are from bad stems.

Tune-ups and repairs

1. **Tune-ups:** CWM-FMR for both major and minor tune-ups, but remember again that their recommendations are for ideal conditions. If the vast majority of your driving is short shopping and/or you live in cold winter country, you should have a tune-up before each fall. Most manuals recommend changing ignition points and condensor at 12,000-mile intervals and sparkplugs between 12 to 30,000 miles. I change my points and condensor every 6,000 miles and plugs every 12,000 miles and save these old parts for spares. Electronic ignition systems should be examined at 10-12,000 mile intervals, not at the 20-25,000 mile recommendations of the manufacturers. (If applicable, have the clearance checked between the "distributor cam" (reluctor ridge) and "points" (Magnet). If this clearance becomes too small the magnet may scar the reluctor ridges.) Question: I wonder how the electronic ignitions will fare under price controls? Will you be able to get spares? Most of them are relatively new, and I wonder if replacements will be available in the automotive junk yards.

2. **Starters:** Normally, a starter will last approximately 80,000 miles before it needs to be repaired or replaced. If you take only very short trips, your starter may need service at 40,000 miles. This usually entails the replacement of the pinion drive gear (clutch assembly) and/or brushes.

3. **Electrical system:** Outside of keeping your electrical system clean, little maintenance is required. I would consult your workshop manual to be sure. Some generators have to be lubed at periodic intervals. Also, generators have to have their brushes replaced at 50,000 miles and above, so it is a good idea to get it examined when you start getting heavy mileage on it.

4. **Shock absorbers:** I know of no domestically made automobile whose original factory equipped shocks will last the normal life of the auto they're on. Their life expectancy seems to vary from 30,000 to 70,000 miles. Outside of a few foreign cars, shocks can't be serviced and are sold as replacement items only. Get them checked when you get a lube job or a tune-up. If you need new ones, get them in pairs and make certain they come with a guarantee for the life of the car. **Buy the best** if you intend to keep your car for any length of time. (A friend has put 150,000 plus miles on his Koni shocks without a trace of problems.)

5. **Water and fuel pumps:** FMR, if they have any, which is doubtful. In days past, schedules were listed for examining, rebuilding, and repairing water and fuel pumps, but that has been abandoned because of costs

and the **new philosophy of replacing the whole car at 50,000 miles.** There's **no way** that you can check a water or fuel pump to determine adequately its life expectancy and condition. Pressure tests on fuel pumps only indicate that something is or might be wrong, but if the test is okay, it does not give any indication of future reliability. Age and miles are bad on both.

Water pumps should be replaced at 50-70,000 mile intervals. If you have to have your radiator removed for any reason and you have 50,000 plus miles on your pump, **get it replaced.** Keep the old one for a spare.

Fuel pumps made today are generally of sealed construction, and parts can't be purchased to rebuild them. Replace your old pump at 50,000 miles and carry it in your trunk as a spare. Exception: some electric pumps can be disassembled (many British cars for example) and new points and diaphragm put in to make them good as new. Don't buy a new pump; just rebuild the old one every 50,000 miles. I wouldn't do this with a mechanical pump unless I also had a spare. Electric pump cores seldom fail, but you can't say this about mechanical pump bodies.

6. **Costs:** Think of **costs per mile**, not lump sums. Replacing parts may seem expensive, but it's cheaper than a new car. **Reliability,** which is what you're buying now for price control days, isn't that expensive **per mile** of operation. Example: cost of replacing my water pump at 50,000 is .04 of a penny per mile. If you add labor, the cost shouldn't go over .1 of a cent per mile.

Additives & Add-Ons

Whenever anyone gets serious about proper preventive maintenance, he is ultimately confronted with the problem of whether he should use additives in his oil, radiator, etc., and the add-ons, the fascinating gizmos that "guarantee" better mileage, or more horsepower, etc. Unless an additive is specifically recommended by an automotive manufacturer as part of the vehicle's regular maintenance schedule, additives will **not** provide **any benefits** that are not provided by the recommended fluids, nor will they extend the life of the vehicle by **any** amount. Add-ons are incapable of providing any material improvement in an automobile's performance. If your car has been properly cared for, the use of additives and add-ons is a waste of money. If your vehicle is showing the symptons of neglect, the use of additives and add-ons for "improving performance" will not provide any lasting benefit. It is better to solve the problem that improper and inadequate care has created, and establish a regular maintenance schedule, than to try to skirt the problem by the use of cheap substitutes.

For example, radiator additives that "inhibit rust and prevent over-heating, and lubricate the water pump" simply provide the same functions as coolant-antifreeze. If you inhibit rust you automatically solve 95% of your overheating problems. Both the coolant and the additive lubricate the water pump. But the coolant-antifreeze and the additive are not the same. The additive is a cheap substitute and does a poor job in comparison with coolant. The latter raises the boiling point of the cooling solution, which prevents the loss of the solution, and lowers it's freezing point to protect the engine in freezing weather.

An example of the add-on is the "gas saver." It lowers the pressure of fuel that is being delivered by the fuel pump to the carburetor. If the pressure is to high, excess fuel can be forced into the carb past the valves in the float bowl. The fuel-air mixture is then too great, and you get excess fuel consumption. By adding the "gas saver" (which is nothing but a pressure valve), you eliminate this problem, and presto, you "save gas." But if you have this problem, isn't it better to get the defective fuel pump replaced rather than spending money on an item that is only temporarily masking the problem?

Stay away from gadgets and the engine oil additive that resemble Karo syrup. Replace parts with factory-approved items and use the money you save from not buying additives for the purchase of the best oil and fluids that you can get. Preventive maintenance is basically common sense and regular, periodic inspection.

[As the author of this book, I would like to offer one possible exception to Ed Powell's critique of additives. You should definitely look into the lubricants produced by D. W. Adams, Inc., 13607 Braemar Dr., Dallas, TX 75234. Adams does not normally sell these products directly to the public. They go to cab fleets, oil drilling rigs, and similar commercial applications, usually in 50 gallon drums. You can buy them in minimum orders of half a dozen one-gallon cans, plus shipping. They are not inexpensive, but for trucks, tractors, commercial vehicles, and heavy duty engines, they are worth the investment. Car owners may also want to consider them. Increased engine life expectancy of 50% is possible, along with fewer engine overhauls. Car owners will want to ask about L.E.C. with "moly"—molybdenum disulfide—the motor oil additive, and also the fuel conditioner, L.E.C. Before overhauling an engine with baked-on sludge, try these two L.E.C. products. A group of buyers might go in together on one shipment, thereby reducing costs.—Gary North.]

Mechanic

The maintenance work and repair work done on your automobile are only as good as the ability and integrity of the individual who performs the work. It is preferable to have an average all-around mechanic whom you know and can trust than a whiz-kid (of whatever age) "automotive genius" who likes to cut corners. This will be especially true under controls. Your future "life style" is going to be more dependent upon the **character** of the people with whom you trade than on any other single trait, and this will demand personal knowledge and contact **before** the effects of controls become disruptive.

There are basically six different types of repair shops, and these fall into two broad categories: dealer-specialty shops and the independents. I'm prejudiced in favor of the independents for the simple reason that I want to know the guy who works on my car and because of my particular view as to what the future holds in store. Naturally your own views will dictate the type of shop you wish to patronize.

Dealer-specialty shops:

1. **Dealer service departments:** Generally speaking, these are the most expensive. They use quality parts, often have the best mechanics, and provide complete automotive service under one roof. Unfortunately, you can't go into the shop area and view the mechanics at work. The workmen are specialists and often lack adequate all-around automotive experience. In some shops the men are transient and this spells unreliability (foreign car dealerships seem to be especially plagued with this problem). The biggest defect is that you can't get to know the character of the people who work on your machine. Do they do the work you requested and use the parts listed? Will they continue to do so when the disruptive effects of controls are being felt and parts are in short supply? Are you going to disassemble your brakes to ascertain whether they used the parts **you** brought them? Present ability and and convenience may prove in the future to be poor substitutes for the personal knowledge of the integrity of the guy who works on your wheels.

2. **Franchisers:** These are the $9.99 special shops run by the Biggies such as Sears, Two Guys, Firestone, etc. What has been said about the dealer service departments goes double with these outfits, with one added attraction: They're big and can't hide from Uncle Sap. They're forced to hire incompetents, and in order to remain competitive they must run the brake-muffler specials. They cut corners, such as not rebuilding the wheel cylinders when they do brake jobs. Remember that **there is no way to cut corners** on proper tune-ups, brake jobs, or brain surgery.

3. **True specialty shops:** These are the shops that have one specialty

such as brakes, tune-ups, transmission repairs, etc. As with anything, quality varies. For specialty work they seem, on the whole,
to know their business, but the service and repairs that they perform can often be done by the local independent. I would patronize one of these shops only if the local mechanic couldn't do
the work requested and then only on his recommendation.

Independent shops:

1. **Independent garages:** These can vary in quality from poor to
   excellent and in size from a couple of men to a dozen. The larger
   independents have the same problems as the dealerships. I would
   also guess that they have a greater transient problem. The **small**
   independent has a bigger service to keep his clientele. A good independent mechanic generally has greater all-around automotive
   experience than a specialist and has a better idea of parts, supplies,
   and manuals that you might want to purchase for your car. He is a
   good source of information on other services offered in the area
   and is much easier to get to know.

   When picking such a shop, go for the small ones which have
   five men or less and where the major mechanics are owner-partners
   who have been in business for awhile. See if they will repair and
   replace **parts** in alternators, generators, and starters rather than
   replace the whole unit, and find out if they provide **warranty
   lubrication service.** Talk shop with them and get an idea of their
   character. Remember the old adage that "the man who cheats on
   his wife will cheat at anything." (When you hire an employee, this
   is an ideal guide for lowering your search costs.)

2. **Filling (service) stations:** To my mind, a station that is owned or
   leased by partners who are trustworthy, conscientious, and reliable,
   where one of them is a mechanic and the other a "grease
   monkey," is the ideal place to take your car for repairs and maintenance. Here you can get just about every service you need for
   preventive maintenance, plus gas and spot checks. Station operators
   love to talk shop and provide friendly service and local news. If
   they are men of character, they are independents because they
   want personal contact with their customers and like having roots in
   their community. Unfortunately, the small station operator is being
   squeezed by both the oil companies and various government
   agencies. Under controls, the "rationing" of automotive parts and
   supplies may force the individual service stations against the wall,
   except in rural areas. He simply does not have the political pull
   that the dealerships and franchisers do. He'll survive in the rural
   areas, but his future looks bleak in the big city.

If you live in a rural area or plan on doing so in the future, this type of shop is the best and it is also the hardest to find with competent help. Consult the local realtors, pastors, small businessmen, etc., in the area. If you plan on storing auto parts, go into your local auto parts dealer when he isn't busy (not a lunch time) and buy a few parts and get friendly. Tell him how much you like the area and the people. Do this several times and then ask about a local service station with a good mechanic. If the area has one, he'll know.

When gasoline is rationed, and the gas station mechanic who knows you, **trusts** you, gets a good chunk of your business, and can help you get some emergency "midnight gasoline," you will be glad you were nice to him and used his services.

3. **Back yard mechanic:** Know someone who likes working on cars? Not a pro by any means, but is conscientious and willing to learn and help others with their automotive problems? Here are the beginnings of a future relationship that may blossom into a part–time business. Most back yard mechanics are total washouts but if this "friend" has a "natural" talent, he may prove to be well worth knowing in the future. He is the perfect guy to barter with in order to obtain maintenance and repairs. If he can do tune-ups and knows something about trouble-shooting and automotive electrical systems, don't forget him at Christmas. If you live in a rural area that has no reasonably adequate garages, you might want to encourage him into the business. Become his good friend, or better yet, his relative. Get your kid sister or sister-in-law to marry him. If you have your own parts, this is one guy you'll want to see more of under controls.

Tools

Individual needs vary so much that it is virtually impossible to recommend tools; if you do your own work, you'll have a good working knowledge of what you need. If not, and you wish to purchase tools in anticipation of a time when you might have to perform your own maintenance and repairs, you'll have to talk to your mechanic and study automotive manuals to get an idea of what is needed. If you have a friend who does his own maintenance, talk to him. This is the ideal source of information, because he too started from scratch. He'll know what you will need and will be able to help you build a kit with minimum expense. Back yard mechanics, if reasonably good, are great fountains of information.

There are two exceptions to the above: 1) every car owner should possess, and carry in his car, a minimum tool kit and, 2) foreign cars made with metric measurements must have a more extensive kit, because many

American garages do not have metric tools on hand. If you get stuck "in the sticks" and have your own tools and a manual, the chances are you'll be able to find someone who can help you fix your car. Not all foreign cars have metric measurements, so check the manual before buying any tools. Notice that the listing for the minimum kit also applies for foreign cars, and that extra or spare parts are also listed. You **must** carry spares with you if you don't want to get stuck waiting for parts. Under controls you'll end up waiting around like Edward K. Smith. (Smith was Captain of the Titanic.)

Minimum Kit

1. Blocks of wood for blocking tires and as a base for the jack stand in soft sand. I use 3-2x4 blocks for this purpose.
2. Bulbs for tail and signal lights. Extra fuses.
3. Distributor cap, points, condenser, rotor, and coil.
4. Electrician's tape, wire, and solderless connectors.
5. Fan belt (optional: power steering belts, etc.)
6. First Aid Kit; hand cleaner and towels if you wish.
7. Flashlight that works; flashing warning light or flares.
8. Fuel pump (see Maintenance Section).
9. Jack and lug wrench (know how to use them properly).
10. Screwdrivers: medium and short lengths, flat heads and Phillips.
11. Sparkplugs and wrench (make certain the wrench fits both car and plug).
12. Tire stem valves (cores) and tool. Carry four.
13. Water, if you're taking a long trip or live in a rural area.
14. Wire, type used to wrap small packages. You can make mini repairs with this until you get to a garage.
15. Wrenches: I prefer combination (open and box) end wrenches ranging in size from 3/8 in. to 1 in. plus several small ignition types. You should also carry 4 in. and .6 in. adjustable (Crescent).

Foreign Car Kit

1. Extra clutch cable, if applicable (VW and Porsche).
2. Radiator hoses and clamps.
3. Workshop Manual.
4. Any special tools that are used for normal repairs and maintenance. Talk to your mechanic.

If your vehicle is metric, add the following:

5. Complete socket set, 9 to 22 mm. I believe the ½ in. drive is the more practical.
6. Complete set of end wrenches, 6 to 19 mm. Also, a couple of

small ignition wrenches if your car uses them.

7. Hex Key (Allen) wrenches. **Be certain they are drop-forged**.
8. Wheel bearings. This is strictly optional Bearings should last the life of the car but seldom do. I repack my own, so I don't worry about them, but if someone else did the job, I'd carry one extra set of inner and outer bearings if I ever used the car out of the Big City. Pack the bearings with grease and wrap in several layers of plastic food wrap, place in a plastic bag, and store in the original container.

One final note on tools: like everything else, you get what you pay for. Cheap tools are cheap. **Buy name-brand** (Craftsman, Snap-on, Proto, etc.), **drop-forged tools**.

Parts

Buying parts for your car can be endless. What you need and will use in the future is dependent upon the present condition of your vehicle and how long you intend to keep it. If you do your own maintenance and repairs, you'll have a good idea of what you'll need. If not, you should consult your mechanic, old repair bills, and owner-workshop manuals. Think in terms of mileage and time left in the old buggy. If you have 200,000 miles on it, you won't have to worry about storing much of anything.

Save all your old parts except items that have come in contact with fluids and cannot be cleaned (oil filters for example), or that are damaged beyond repair, or that will prove hazardous.

Each vehicle has its own bad traits. Ask your mechanic about the effects of high mileage on your particular model and year. Example: some Chevy wagons like to eat up axle shafts, and some Chryslers go through rear transmission seals and bearings. You might want to purchase the items he tells you about.

This section should be used in conjunction with the others and your manuals. It is not complete but is only intended as a guide. This list of spares and supplies is for a vehicle with 50,000 miles or less on it which will need normal and preventive maintenance over the next 100,000 miles. The items marked * should be owned by every car owner unless the vehicle is about ready to expire. If a quantity is listed, this is considered the minimum. Consult your manuals for specifications regarding oils, filters, etc. **Buy name-brand fluids** (Mobil, Castrol, Prestone, etc.) **and spares** (AC-Delco, Champion, Motorcraft, Borg-Warner, etc.).

Fluids

1. Oils: engine (5 qts.), tramsmission (1 qt.), and rear end (1 pt.). One can of high temperature wheel bearing grease with molybdenum disulfide.

2. Ethylene glycol anti-freeze (1 gal.)
3. *Brake fluid: buy only small cans that are **sealed**. Never open more than one can and never leave the lid off it. If you do, **even for a day**, the fluid becomes **contaminated**. (2-3 pints) (See maintenance section).
4. Shock absorber fluid for some foreign cars.

Ignition and Electrical Systems

1. *Distributor cap (1), points (2), condenser (1), rotor (1), and coil (1).
2. *Sparkplugs (1 set).
3. *Extra bulbs, fuses, and signal flasher unit (if desired).
4. High tension spark cable. **Buy only** from the dealer for your car, because there's a lot of junk cable around. Don't bend it. (3 ft.)
5. Small roll of 10 and 16 guage wire, electrical tape, and connectors.

Filters, hoses, and belts

1. Filters: oil (4), fuel (2), and air (2).
2. Drive belts: *fan (1), power steering, smog, etc.
3. Radiator and heater hoses and clamps (1 set).
4. Vacuum, smog, and fuel hoses (2-3 ft.).
5. Power steering high pressure hose (1).

Repair kits and supplies

1. Brakes: master and wheel cylinders (1 kit for each cylinder), clutch master and wheel cylinder, if applicable.
2. Carburetor rebuild kit (1 for each carb.).
3. Fuel pump points and diaphragm, if applicable.
4. Muffler bandage (Duro brand) and cement (manufactured by Yale Engineering).
5. *Tire repair kit (Kex or Camel) and one tire inner tybe (bias ply radial ply tires use different type tubes—get one for your type of tire).
6. Valve stems for tubeless tires (4) and valve stem cores (4). Purchase from your local service station. Get the right size stem for your wheel rim.
7. Generator and starter brushes (1 set each).

Gaskets and Seals

1. Head gasket set (1), valve gasket (1), and thermostat gasket (1).
2. Front-wheel bearing seal (1).
3. Windshield wipers (1 pair).
4. Purchase of one tube of each type of gasket sealer. These

are: 1) Anaerobic (e.g., Permatex Gel Gasket, Loctite Fit-All Gasket, etc.); 2) Silicone (e.g., Permatex Silicone, G-E Silmate, Dow Corning Silicone, etc.), and 3) Solvent Resistant (Permatex No. 2).

Spares

1. Fuel Pump* (1), water pump (1), and thermostat (1).
2. Universal joints. Buy as many as you now have on your drive shaft. If possible, get ones with grease nipples.
3. Wheel bearings. Strictly optional. Talk to your mechanic. If you store any, only get one inner and one outer bearing.
4. Shock absorbers. Use your own judgment. If you intend to keep your car for as long as possible, I would buy a set for the car as soon as controls are imposed. See Maintenance Section. Front-wheel bearing seal (1).

Parts should be of **high quality** and should be purchased from your **distributor-dealer** for your make of car or from a **local reputable parts house. Be sure you get the right parts for the right car. Order parts by model, year, engine and chassis** numbers. Get this info off of your vehicle registration slip. **Don't order by mail** unless you know the firm and have done business with them previously. **Mark** all your parts, particularly the hoses, so you don't get them mixed up. Write **date of purchase** on the hoses and keep the bills. Some parts such as hoses will deteriorate with age, and these bills will help you later in determining the life span of stored parts.

Storage

Gaskets, seals, hoses, belts, and other pliable items should be **stored flat** without any weight put on them. "Hard items" such as fuel and water pumps can be stored anywhere that water or moisture cannot get to them. Small rubber items, such as repair kits, can be stored in bottles, but be sure that there is no moisture in these containers. Fluids should be stored in their own unopened and resealable containers.

I use old army ammo boxes to store my hard items, and small jars (that have been slightly heated in the oven to remove all moisture) to store my small items. Before placing bearings or U-joints in storage, pack them with grease and seal in plastic wrap, then store in sealed containers. Don't mix petroleum and rubber products together. The rubber will rot if you do. If you store **shock absorbers,** follow instructions that come with them. Store **vertically,** and don't dent the bodies.

Those items that will store the longest should be the first acquired. These are the hard items as mentioned. Rubber and neoprene parts should be bought as soon as controls go into effect. This is not a hard and fast rule, but only a guide. Valve stems and cores, anti-freeze, and possibly brake fluid might disappear before controls are slapped on. Those who own foreign cars should experience "hard times" **before** the owners of American cars. Small parts will simply disappear for foreign cars. If you own one, buy small now. (The one exception: the VW beetle. Two decades of junked VW's should provide a large supply of interchangeable **hard** parts.)

Manuals

Every motorist should have a copy of the owner's manual that comes with his car. It lists minimum periodic maintenance and is a helpful guide for the novice in explaining to his mechanic what type of service he wants performed. It should be carried in the vehicle along with a note book that lists date, mileage, purchases, and service performed. This information can be used later for developing a **list of parts** you will wish to store. Purchase can be made from the dealer for your make of auto.

The **workshop manual** is a detailed repair and maintenance book that is geared for the professional and the advanced mechanic. If you own an American car, you need not purchase one so long as you continue to visit a professional garage. If there is the possibility that you may have to work on your own car, this type of book is a requirement. If you intend to move to a rural area, I would also suggest the purchase of one of these manuals. Also, if you own a foreign car, you **must** have a detailed manual with you at all times. Few domestic automotive garages have foreign manuals, and if they don't have the information needed to make repairs, you'll be left high and dry no matter how much someone wants to help you.

The best workshop manuals are put out by the automotive manufacturers themselves. Unfortunately, they have a tendency to get a bit over-detailed in their description of the tools needed to work on their cars. You don't need all the tools they tout. Purchases can be made from the auto dealership where you got your owner's manual, or you can try writing directly to the factory. Be sure you give make, model, year, and serial and engine numbers.

Motor Publications puts out a good variety of foreign and domestic workshop manuals. Unfortunately, they are geared for the pro and just don't have the number of illustrations that they should have to help the amateur. Write to Motor Publications, 250 West 55 St., New York, NY 10019. If you wish you can ask your mechanic to let you take a look at his motor manual, and you'll get a better idea of what they publish than by reading their advertising.

Clymer Publications puts out some excellent manuals for those who have a small working knowledge of automotive mechanics. They also publish manuals for motorcycles. Check with your local parts dealer or you can write to Clymer Publications, 222 N. Virgil Ave., Los Angeles, California 90004.

Chilton Book Co. of Philadelphia, PA puts out some decent books, but they are geared strictly for the pro. It has been some time since I've seen a manual by them. Perhaps they've changed their ways. Check with your local parts dealer.

Popular Mechanics has an excellent automotive section each month. Questions and answers and regular monthly features for the do-it-yourself beginner. Their May, 1975 issue was devoted to "Car Care." Available for 75 cents from *Popular Mechanics*, 224 West 57 St., New York, NY 10019.

For any manual or car book printed, write to Autobooks, 2900 W. Magnolia Blvd., Burbank, CA 91505. They are the world's largest dealer in automotive publications.

VW Beetle owners should pick up John Muir's book, *How to Keep Your Volkswagen Alive: A Manual of Step by Step Procedures for the Complete Idiot* (P.O.Box 613, Santa Fe, NM 87501: $6.50).

Maintenance Check List

The following list is compiled from three different preventive maintenance check sheets of three different automobiles, both foreign and domestic. This list is not applicable to any particular car but is an excellent guide for compiling your own check list. Remember to check your own manuals for your set of wheels. When your vehicle gets to 96,000 miles, start the list over again. If you don't get 200,000 miles out of your machine, you aren't trying.

Warning: high quality neoprene ("rubber") parts are getting very scarce. Cost-cutting has led to thin material. Dealer-supplied parts are probably the most reliable.

Weekly

Check fluid levels: engine oil, radiator, battery, power steering, windshield washer unit, automatic transmission, and air pressure in tires.

3,000 Miles or (those marked*) 3 Months

Carry out weekly service plus: Check: condition of ignition points, timing and dwell, idling speed, level of brake fluid in master cylinders, condition and free play of V-belts, wiring, fuses, lights, *windshield wipers, *possible leaks in oil, water, fuel, and hydraulic systems, adjust valves (air cooled engines), check play in U-joints on drive shaft. *Lube: hood and door hinges, locks, gearshift (Porsche & VW), cables (with powder, not oil), carburetor controls, change engine oil, check fluid level in manual transmission, rear end, and steering box (if unit is without power steering), lube front end and driveshaft.

6,000 Miles or (those marked*) 6 Months

Carry out 3,000 mile service plus: *Get a minor tune-up: check and/or clean spark plugs, ignition points, distributor cap (for cracks), clean battery. *Change engine oil filter. Check: clutch and brake pedal free play, tightness (torque) of valve rocker shaft nuts, and valve clearances.

12,000 Miles or (those marked*) 12 Months

Carry out 6,000 mile service plus: *Major tune-up: change ignition points, spark plugs, PCV valve (smog), air and fuel filters (don't forget air pad for absorption cannister, if applicable). Check: compression, tightness (torque) of cylinder head nuts, smog and water hoses, smog valves and air pump, brake linings, shock absorbers, clean and repack front wheel bearings. *Drain, flush, and refill radiator with 50% solution of water and anti-freeze-coolant.

24,000 Mile or (those marked*) 24 Months

Carry out 12,000 mile service plus: *Drain, and replace brake and hydraulic clutch fluid, oil in manual transmissions, fluid and filter in automatic transmissions (check bands and adjust if necessary). Lube speedometer cable, lifting jack, get front-end aligned, check exhaust system, consider replacing the radiator hoses, tighten all visible nuts to specifications.

48,000 Mile or (those marked*) 48 Months

Carry out 24,000 mile service plus: Clean and tune, or rebuild and tune carburetor(s), consider replacing both water and fuel pumps, inspect starter, generator/alternator brushes and bearings, replace carbon absorption cannister, *drain and refill rear end.

96,000 Mile

Carry out 48,000 mile service plus: Replace the bearings and brushes in the starter and generator/alternator. Get your front end checked by a specialist and go for a quarter million miles.

CHAPTER SEVENTEEN
THE QUESTION OF TIMING

The question of timing is crucial for any entrepreneurial decision. The source of all profit is successful forecasting and efficient planning in terms of an accurate forecast. But there are many different ways to measure profit. In fact, the whole accounting industry is in an uproar because of a continuing debate over the proper way to record profits in corporate reports. In the final analysis, profit must be determined by the acting individual. What does each man think he should do with his assets in order to better his condition? This is what all of us must ask ourselves constantly. We change our minds all the time, sometimes in response to losses, but sometimes in response to what we had thought would be true profits results that we wanted to achieve that turn out to have been unfulfilling. I have to stress this point: the ultimate profit is not necessarily or even usually the positive results on a corporate profit-and-loss statement.

People are willing to spend money in order to make money. They buy information that they believe will help them to make more money in the future. I am all in favor of making money. But we have to bear in mind that in an era of seriously enforced priced controls, "making money" means **avoiding** money. When we say we want to make money, we mean we want to have more goods and services, more power, more of the things we want at the end of a period of time. We equate making money with gaining assets. That is a kind of mental shorthand that is reflected in our language. But in an era of controls, we have to **beware of traditional language** because we have to **rethink our activities** in the market.

The reason why controls are demanded by the public is because people are too dazzled by language and inaccurate perceptions based on a convenient mental shorthand. Prices, denominated in a particular monetary unit, are rising. Instead of questioning the monetary unit, most voters look at prices. The problem is seen as being the problem of decisions made outside the world of money. Someone is greedy, someone is a monopolist, businessmen are crooks, someone is gouging the helpless public. Thus, prices have risen. But the problem is not greed, monopoly (at least business monopoly), crookedness, or gouging. The problem is monetary inflation—an ancient misuse of a government monopoly. But people refuse to see this. So they call for price and wage controls. An error of economic analysis, coupled with rampant political envy, has created a situation that compounds the economic problems. People blame the traditional enemies, such as big business, when the real problem is political.

This is familiar enough to my readers. But we, too, must take care not to become entangled in concepts and language that are no longer accurate in the new world of price controls. We have to time our actions in terms of a new set of external conditions. We will no doubt make a lot of mistakes, but we have to make decisions, and we might as well get our language cleaned up in advance. We may say the old words, for the sake of convenience, but we must know what we really mean.

What I mean is simple: do not expect the ᵲederal government to solve the inflation problem. It is the cause of the problem.

Shortages and Fear

The summer of 1979 brought frightening gasoline shortages to the major cities of America. The gas lines began in California. (In 1974, California was one of the last regions to suffer.) In rural areas, and even in moderately large cities, there were no visible lines. In Los Angeles, San Francicsco, New York City, Washington, D.C., and even in Houston, people spent hours waiting in long lines to buy gasoline. When Americans cannot buy all the gasoline they want at the posted prices, they get angry. They panic. They call for government action.

One fact should be understood from the beginning: **shortages are the results of specific economic and political policies.** Scarcity is a fact of life. Shortages are not. Scarcity means only that **at zero price**, there is a greater demand for most goods than there are supplies to meet that demand. So economic goods command a price. A **shortage** results when prices are closer to zero than the market would otherwise dictate. If you want to clarify the nature of a shortage, so that you will not be misled by experts in rhetorical manipulation, you need a rule. The rule is simple enough. Never, ever think the word "shortage," let alone utter the word, without keeping this qualifying clause in the back of your mind: **"shortage at some price."** There is no such thing as a shortage, as such. There are only shortages of specific goods or services at some **lower-than-market-clearing price.** When there are people willing to buy at a particular price, but not enough supplies to meet their demand, then a higher price is called for in order to clear the market, i.e., equate supply with demand.

Consider the grim reality of modern economic life. The Federal government has a monopoly of dollar creation, at least inside the borders of the United States. It shares this monopoly with the Federal Reserve System and the nation's commercial banks. When the government creates money by selling debt to the central bank, the boom-bust cycle is set into operation. The boom leads to rising prices, as people compete against each other to buy goods and services. They use the newly created fiat money to make their bids. Prices rise.

The government likes the boom but hates rising prices. Rising wages are politically acceptable, and they also lead to higher income tax and Social Security tax revenues. The boom can only be cooled by the stabilization of money, or at least by a failure to increase the rate of money creation. To stifle price rises, the government must follow policies that lead to an economic slowdown or recession.

Bear in mind also that people are short-sighted. They are never quite certain just what it is they want government to do. (My answer, of course, is simple: less.) When prices are rising, they worry about inflation. But when unemployment starts up, in response to inflation-fighting monetary policies, they cry out for government to put an end to unemployment, too. The problem is, basically, that once the fiat money-induced boom has begun, there is no known way to obtain both falling prices and very low rates of unemployment until the market has had time to adjust to the new rates of monetary expansion. This adjustment period is called "recession" or "despression." The public is not sufficiently confident in free market forces to produce economic growth and stable (or even falling) consumer prices. They no longer trust the Federal planners, but they really don't trust the free market. They don't know what to believe, so they do what is familiar. What is familiar is to call on the government to repair the mess created by earlier government decisions.

The boom-bust cycle has been going on for several decades, but the public simply cannot locate the source of the trouble, namely, the monopoly of money creation in the hands of the government. So they demand short-run solutions. What the government is capable of providing is only short-run responses, or multiple responses that in many cases are in conflict with each other.

Eventually, both the voters and the politicians get tired of the never-ending swings between higher prices and unemployment —— swings taking place at ever-higher levels. The troubles just will not go away. People start lashing out at real or imagined enemies: the Arabs, the oil companies, the speculators, the apartment house owners, the supermarket managers, the truckers, and even (miracle of miracle) the trade unions. People decide that the best way to solve the problems of the market, meaning the inflation-buffeted market, is to bang a few heads. Whose head is the preferred one to bang? It isn't easy to predict in advance. It depends on the timing. Who is being singled out by the news media as this month's "public economic enemy number one"? He will be fair game when the axe falls, when the President is forced to Do Something Creative and Forceful.

One of the most fearful aspects of recent years is the willingness of the public to expect forceful actions by the President. The drift of modern political life has created a monster. Men have been led to believe that centralized political and economic power is creative, only to learn that central power means a massive bureaucracy and economic strangulation. They have not learned their lesson. . . yet. President Carter was unmercifully criticized by the American press and by editorial writers for his seeming indecisiveness during the gasoline crisis of July, 1979. His energy policy advisors could not agree on the proper policy, so he cancelled an announced speech on energy. Why not? Why come before the public and say nothing? Of course, it would have been wiser never to have announced the speech. This seeming indecisiveness cost him dearly. The public has been promised miracles by four decades of political scientists, messianic politicians, socialist and Keynesian economists, and most textbooks in the social sciences. That religion, always a false one, is steadily revealing its fraudulent nature. But the public is now savaging those "priests" who are trying to explain away their inability to produce bread out of stones — the trick they had claimed for years to be able to accomplish.

If you are trying to deal with the economic future, be sure of one thing: men do not abandon a political religion easily. In times of peace, they seldom abandon it at all. Only crises can force the hands of the false priesthood. Only economic, military, or social catastrophies are sufficient to get the public to change its collective mind. The trouble is, you and I are trapped inside the arena in which the crises are being turned loose.

What will the government do? Inflate. What will happen to prices? They will keep rising. What will the response of the public be? Outrage. What will the government then do? Lots of things, almost all of them disastrous. You must watch very closely to see the signs of impending doom: the coming of controls.

When you start looking for the "key" sign to watch, you are probably making a mistake. There is no sure-fire, universally valid key economic indicator of the future. If anything, there are too many to watch, and sometimes they seem to be contradictory. There is no known scientific formula for charting the economic future. What is important is that you be aware of several economic factors that seem to be reasonable indicators of a forthcoming political decision. Monitor them carefully. Then guess. An informed guess is the best you can hope for.

The Signs of the Times

Monetary inflation is always a good place to start watching. The problem for most of us is that these statistics are available only intermittently. On the other hand, these figures don't have to be monitored weekly. Serious readers can subscribe, free of charge, to the publications of the St. Louis Federal Reserve Bank. The weekly publication, *U.S. Financial Data*, provides a running commentary on monetary developments. Some people may wish to order its *Monthly Review*, which offers semi-technical articles of importance. (Write: P.O. Box 442, St. Louis, MO) If Money One (meaning checking accounts plus currency in circulation) begins to climb over several months' time at rates approaching the double-digit level, be sure to keep monitoring statistics. It may take six months, or it may take a year, but price increases will follow on the same order of magnitude.

Price Inflation has a psychological impact. The 10% figure is significant politically. The commentators will start writing about price inflation once it goes above 8%, but 10% will be headline news. This will bring out the consumerists and the do-gooders. Something has to be done, they will shout, except they won't be very sure what. So the old political game will begin again. Yes, we partners told those greedy people not to raise prices. No, it didn't do any good. Yes, we have to do something. No, voluntary guidelines didn't work. Yes, price controls have failed in the past. No, it won't do to sit quietly on the sidelines, shouting at the top of our lungs. Yes, controls produced shortages in the past. No, it won't happen this time if we all get together and treat each other in love and think good thoughts and put a few corporation presidents in jail for six months.

Discounts from listed prices will start drying up prior to the imposition of controls. This is a sure sign to anyone who is planning for the future that it is time to start stocking up on raw materials, equipment, and spare parts. It is very important for businessmen to monitor their trade journals carefully. They should check every six weeks or so with suppliers about the availability of discounts. A good working relationship with a supplier is important. Tell him why you keep asking. Let him know that you are interested in how business is going. Don't go out of your way to tell him that as soon as he stops giving discounts, you are going to order like crazy from him. But let him know that you're interested. Any way you can get information on discounting practices in your industry, you should do it. They are a very good "early warning signal" in your field, which is the significant information anyway.

Inventories are important. When the managers start stocking up, the economy will be hailed as ready to take off again. The stock market will probably rise (don't take my word for the stock market, however, since I try to be rational about economics, and the market confuses me), and the newspapers will be filled with glowing tales about how well President Carter's prescription for the economy is working. But in a period of history that is inflation-conscious any strong rise in inventories should be regarded with suspicion. It means that businessmen are trying to hedge against inflation by purchasing goods beforehand.

Interest rates, especially long-term rates, will start climbing again. The short-term rates are more volatile, however. A major move by businesses to increase inventories will drive up short-term rates. But they will try to get long-term loans if they can. They got whipsawed in the last recession. They don't want to get stuck with 90-day notes if the economy should turn downward. But when short-term rates turn upward, be careful. If long-term rates follow, then this is an indication that the professionals think the next boom will be an inflationary one. The long-term rates are the inflation-hedging signal, for long-term debt carries a large price inflation premium (lenders are trying to protect their future assets from the effects of de-preciating money). Thus, when the short-term rates turn upward, watch long-term rates like bonds and mortgages. If they confirm the move of the short-term rates, begin to increase the proportion of your income devoted to the purchase of hard goods. When mortgage rates go above 10%, infla-tion will be on its way, if it hasn't already registered in the consumer price index.

Raw materials shortages are an important sign of imminent controls. Newsprint is an important indicator, and so are the petrochemicals (plastics, etc.). If the firms you buy from start delaying the delivery of their cheaper lines of products, then there is trouble coming. Get into the markets and start buying. Usually, the major shortages will appear after controls are imposed, but some will appear before. Be alert to them.

Strikes. This is simply the method of trade unions to get ahead of the increase of prices. Businesses, I suspect, will capitulate, now that a Democrat is in the White House. But a series of strikes will indicate that businessmen are too scared of price controls to grant the unions their demands. In other words, businessmen will figure out that in this cozy "partnership," they will be the ones first asked not to pass along all in-creases in costs. So they will balk at the demands made by unions. If the threat of strikes is followed by capitulation, then more unions are going to threaten their industries. When the resistance is escalated, and strikes do hit the country, get ready for full-scale controls. The President will want to maintain industrial peace, and controls will be viewed as one way to "put everyone on an even level." And if the strikers are **public** employees, the threat of controls is that much greater.

I have listed these signals in the order that I think is most significant, but there is no way to be certain that events will be so condescending as to follow my outline. But these are the kinds of indicators to watch close-ly. Remember: it is your business, your basket of consumer goods, and your decisions that are most important for you. Don't worry too much about the statistical aggregates; they don't necessarily reflect what is most important in your particular niche in the economy. At the same time, monitor each of these areas carefully. Don't make the mistake of thinking that events in one area (rising money supply, rising prices, strikes) are unrelated. They are related, and it is the coming together of several of these phenomena that should alert us to the possibility of action on the part of "the partners." If shortages hit your industry before the aggregates indicate universal shortages, you will have to take extra risks: to buy or not to buy, that is one of the questions. Is it temporary? But if the aggregates start pointing to a crisis—money is up, prices are up, long-term interest rates are up—then don't sit around calmly, even if your industry is still running smoothly. If one or two of the indicators move upward, take caution; if three or four do, take evasive action.

Timing for Profits

Let us return to the original theme. What are profits? More important, over what period of time? Decisions that produce profits over a year's period of time may not prove to be profitable over a decade's span. This seems elementary, but it has to be repeated. We are living in one world, a world generally free of price controls (energy being the major exception). But we ought to be planning for a very different world. We will have to forfeit short-run profits for the sake of the long haul. **We must expand our time horizons.**

The trouble with this approach, psychologically, is that the short-term events will tend to make us confident. The country has experienced a major recession. Now it has pulled out of this recession. The initial signs of danger—meaning long-term danger from the imposition of price controls—will be interpreted by the press as proof of President Carter's success. Rising inventories, more employment, greater output, and similar signs of boom conditions will be interpreted as **normal**. The other signs, such as rising interest rates, rising prices, bottlenecks in production, and strikes, will be interpreted as unfortunate and even unrelated to the President's program. At the very least, they will be explained as side effects—**side effects that can be overcome by decisive action**. And the results of the recommended decisive action, namely controls-produced shortages, will be explained as being the product of evil, greedy men rather than the product of the controls.

I think it may prove to be important that Carter is a Southern Baptist. I am very fearful that his religious background will combine with his technical and pragmatic background to produce a very dangerous outlook. His pragmatic tinkering with the economy will produce side effects, meaning **unwanted** direct effects, but the innate pragmatism of the man, like the innate pragmatism of the voters who elected him and Nixon and Johnson and Kennedy—pragmatists all—will result in something like the following. **First**, he will like some of the effects. He will like the somewhat reduced unemployment figures, the greater output of goods, the signs of business confidence. (Rising inventories have historically been signs of confidence, but in an economy threatened by controls, rising inventories will progressively be a sign of falling confidence in the future.) Carter and his fellow tinkerers will hail the wanted effects as the products of the Keynesian policies of Federal spending, tax cuts, and monetary inflation. **Second**, the President will not like the other effects of his policies: rising prices, shortages, bottlenecks, etc. He will have a strong tendency to blame evil hearts for these results—a lack of commitment, greed, a failure to appreciate the needs of a decent society, and so forth. **Third**, he and his advisors will design a program to punish evil men. If evil men can be punished, and other evil men see that this punishment is painful, then they will be restrained. If they are restrained, then the successful Keynesian policies will be able to operate properly. **Fourth**, they will see price controls as a way to restrain "a minority of greedy businessmen and militant labor unions" and allow the majority of good men to enjoy the warm glow of Keynesian economics. **Price controls will be imposed to control the greedy minority**. Price controls will be seen as a perfectly rational response to the evil actions of a minority.

For the first time in recent memory, Federal officials will call upon liberal think tanks like the Brookings Institution (assuming that Carter hasn't hired them all to serve in the White House), and the experts will recommend policies of law and order. Or more precisely, **laws and orders**. All of a sudden, punishment will get a good press. Crime doesn't pay, we will be told, under price controls. No more guidelines. No more voluntarism. No more Mr. Nice Guy. Get tough on evil. This will be the New Prohibition. Billy Sunday fought booze. Jimmy Carter will fight price gougers. He and his partners. Justice on a white horse will be promised to all. Pragmatism will chase the evil-doers out of the land.

What I am saying, then, is that a combination of pragmatic tinkering, Keynesian economics, and ersatz religion is a dangerous combination. If you think Carter's theology is shaky, as demonstrated in the *Playboy* interview, wait until you see his applied theology in action in the realm of economics. (I hope I am wrong about his future actions, but Carter's version of Southern Baptist marital ethics did not impress me with its theological rigor.)

CHAPTER EIGHTEEN
A SHOPPING GUIDE FOR SURVIVAL

By now you have at least the general idea of what this country is facing and what a survival-oriented family will have to do to keep its capital intact. If you agree with my general analysis (nobody has to agree with each and every point to make me happy), then you will want to start taking action.

Where should a person begin? There are so many possibilities, so many different families, so many different needs that no single plan will satisfy everyone. But I want to offer an acceptable outline. At least you will have some idea of where to begin.

If you earn in the range of $10,000 a year, it will be very difficult for you to do very much on your present income. You are already hard-pressed financially. If you have **children who can work**, then I would suggest that you let them get jobs, contributing a portion of their earnings to a special family projects fund for long-term survival. Let them know what the money is for and how important it is that the fund be established. I would also recommend that you try to **get a second part-time job**. If you are short of time, give up television, or drastically reduce the time you spend watching it. If necessary, skip a vacation. Go to the library and start reading books that will help you develop a skill or trade. Go to night school, if necessary. But start using the one resource you may have, even if you don't have much money. That resource is **time**.

If you earn around $15,000 a year, you have some breathing room. Not much, but some. If you can do any of the suggestions suitable for the $10,000 family, do them. But you should be willing to set aside some money each month to make investments. One place to start is with the suggestions in John Kamin's *How to Make Money Fast Speculating in Distressed Property*. If you can find a copy of the $1.25 Pyramid Books edition, fine. If not, order it for $12 directly from Kamin. (I list the book in the bibliography section.) If you have a skill, especially related to making repairs of machinery, develop that skill.

If you make over $20,000 a year, you should put at least 10% of your after-tax income into such investments as American silver coins, gold coins, handguns, rifles, tools of your profession, and a library. If necessary, take your kids out of college, or reduce the payments to them. (I never recommend taking them out of a Christian day school, however.) Let them earn more of their way. Time is getting scarce. This is an emergency.

Anyone who makes over $30,000 a year has the ability to hedge against the controls and even make the big money. It may necessitate moving into a less expensive home and using the after-tax profits for long-term hedging. It may require other stringent controls on the family budget. But there is no reason not to take the necessary steps. There is a lot of slack in the budget. If you must, **sell off some status.** Your investment in status may be too high anyway.

Survival-Hoarding-Saving

The steps you must begin to take should have the primary goal of long-run survival for your family. Let the dreams of big profits wait until these steps are begun. There is still time to begin, but once controls go on, there will be far less time. **Your plans should be formulated now.** What do you intend to do? How soon do you expect to reach your goal? How much do you estimate that it will cost to meet your goals, stage by stage? What are the resources available to you right now. Start taking inventory **today.** Count the costs. Estimate the benefits. This is the necessary preliminary step. If you don't start here, you really don't mean business.

Every family should try to make the following purchases (starting at top):

$500 face value worth of silver U.S. dimes
A six month's supply of dehydrated food
A home water filtration unit
At least one .38 caliber handgun
A 30.06 or .308 rifle with at least a 4X scope
Reloading equipment for both weapons
50 pounds of one-pound cans of coffee (barter)
50 pounds of 7-ounce tins of cigarette tobacco (barter)
   six cigarette rolling machines
   100 packs of cigarette paper (100 to a pack, gummed)
20 pounds of inexpensive pipe tobacco (barter)
An inexpensive spring-loaded air rifle (ElGamo 300)
One case of expensive whiskey (barter)
10 one-ounce gold coins (Austrian 100 corona, Krugerrand)
20 quarter-ounce coins (Austrian 20 corona)
30 Mexican 2-peso gold coins
10 U.S. $20 gold pieces (St. Gaudens)

Whenever possible, make all purchases in cash. This leaves fewer records. It is a good rule of thumb that the fewer records you leave of items to be stored for future use, the safer you are.

There is no doubt that few families in this country have anything like the recommended list of goods before a panic hits. Go at your own pace, but do start setting aside money for these purchases. You can buy the silver coins in bags of $100 face value. You can buy the cigarette tobacco, the liquor, and the gold coins in small parcels.

What should I buy first? That question must not be used to justify buying nothing. The answer depends on where you live, what your income level is, what savings you have, how old you are, and how much you believe in this book. The silver coins are "survival money." They can be easily sold at a local coin store, or sold back to the firm that sold them to you, or bartered, should a total panic hit the economy. They are very important. Food is important, too, but only with this proviso: you really do intend to locate a safer place to live than a city of 100,000 or more people. It does no good to store food unless you store water, and it does less good to store food for the expected looters. If you say to yourself, "What good is my food when I live here?" you have just provided yourself with a first-rate reason for moving. Don't blame the vulnerability of the food; blame your geography. If you live in an area where the food is too risky to store, then you absolutely have to move. Not maybe; absolutely. Soon.

Where can you buy silver and gold coins? At a coin store, for cash. Through the mail. At some banks (not many). Buying and selling coins is easy, for the present. And if you say to yourself "Some day it may be difficult to sell my coins," you have just given yourself the best reason to buy them now. The only thing that would make it difficult to sell coins is the imposition of full-scale price controls and even tyranny. That's precisely the time when you have to have the coins, for barter purposes. I have listed several honest, reliable firms in the appendix on "Services and Products." If you refuse to buy any coins, then you haven't understood (or believed) this book.

It is true that coins "earn no interest or dividends." It is also true that the value of silver American coins increased 700% from 1971 to 1979. Gold coins did as well or better in this same period. Rare coins did far better. The chatter about "no interest" is not that impressive when you consider the capital gains involved. And never forget: capital gains profits are taxed at a lower rate than interest or dividend income.

Another very interesting proposition is the availability of loans for coins offered by Deak National Bank. The bank will offer up to 50% of the market value of the coins (for example, $2,000 on a $4,000 market value bag of $1,000 face value). This means that you can invest $1,500 and get the right to take delivery of a full bag of coins. You get the interest deduction on the loan, which helps lower your taxes. There really is a bag, stored by the bank or in a warehouse (the bank makes the loan on the basis of a warehouse receipt). Most bankers refuse to make such loans. For full information, contact R. Hyler at

Deak National Bank
Main Street
Fleischmanns, New York 12430
(914) 254-5252

For a higher-risk proposition, but one which would seem to be legitimate, given the inflationary nature of the crisis which is facing us, the man with $15,000 to invest in a home, whether his actual residence or an income-producing unit, might want to buy 5 bags of coins using $7,500 of his money and a $7,500 loan. He could then take the other $7,500 and put the down payment into the house. He would wait for the appreciation of the coins, selling off the coins in two or three years, or even longer, paying off the loan against the coins and the loan (or a big chunk of it) outstanding on the house. This is a rational use of debt, since the likelihood of the coins or the house falling in dollar-denominated value is rather low. The government subsidizes this transaction by offering the interest rate deduction on the annual income tax report. You use an appreciating asset to gain access to depreciating paper money; the money is then used to pay off a loan. Or, if the dollar **really** collapses, the man can pay off both loans, take delivery of the coins and possession of the house. Dollars would not buy much under such a scenario, but they are useful for paying off dollar-denominated debt. I call this approach **compensated leverage**. The debt is backed up by appreciating "hard" assets.

The **water purifier** is not very expensive. A good one is the Water Washer unit, which sells for $21.45. It can be ordered with Master Charge or Visa from

Reliance Products
P.O. Box 2000
Alamo, CA 94507
(800) 227-1590

As for **air rifles** and **air pistols**, I cannot recommend them highly enough. Here is the way to learn to shoot safely, inexpensively, and accurately. When I say air rifle, I don't mean a Daisy BB gun. I mean a precision sporting weapon. Two companies offer catalogues, and you would be wise to order both.

Beeman's
47 Paul Drive , 25-B
San Rafael, CA 94906
$1.00

Air Rifle Headquarters
P.O. Box 327
Grantsville, WV 26147
Free

I recommend the purchase of the ElGamo 300. It will get you started, then hooked. The ammunition is incredibly cheap, and the weapon is very accurate up to 25 feet. It is remarkably accurate up to 30 yards if you pay to have it accurized (about $20 extra). The weapon sells from $85 to $95, depending on which company sells it. Beeman's is less expensive initially, but ARH has a large parts department and does fine repairs. The finer weapons go up to $600. These weapons do not have to be registered . . . yet. The Feinwerkbau 124S, coupled with a good Beeman 3-7X scope ($50 from Beeman's), is a terrific weapon. The deluxe model costs $210 from Beeman's, more from ARH. But these are superb weapons, not toys. They are excellent for competition, but also for hunting small game. They are very quiet and very accurate. As for air pistols, the Webley Tempest at $70 (Beeman's) is a good one. You can pay up to $300 for the better pistols, but these are sporting items, not survival guns.

A good **rifle** for the money is the Browning semiautomatic in a 308. You need a **shotgun**. Recommended: Remington 870, 3" magnum. Get the shortest barrel legal, 20 inches. It is a real crowd subduer. As for **handguns** I think the Colt or Smith & Wessen .357 magnum is the best bet, since it will shoot the .38 caliber standard amunition and the high-powered .357 shell. Some people say only the .45 caliber Colt army pistol will stop the bad guy, but a .357 magnum still seems good enough to me. (A word of warning: keep your **reloading equipment** out of sight. The presence of such equipment alerts neighbors and local authorities that, in all likelihood, more than one weapon is owned by the sportsman. Some people buy cheap weapons and plan to turn them in, if forced to, while keeping the good ones hidden. If that's your plan, keep the reloading equipment equally hidden.)

An unconstitutional law prohibiting the ownership of such equipment will raise the value of existing units.

The **barter** items are the traditionally high-demand products, vices for the most part, but widely indulged in. Tobacco, good liquor (which can't be brewed up on a local still overnight), coffee: people will trade to get these items. They make very good presents for people like local sheriffs, especially good whiskey like Jack Daniels black label or Wild Turkey. You will need the co-operation of men like the local police chief. Make Christmas nice for them. Or their birthdays. Or Groundhog Day.

Personal Items

Such things as toilet paper, toothbrushes, tooth flossers, hair brushes, sanitary napkins, aspirin, bandages, antiseptics, and similar items should be stored up regularly. Watch for sales in the supermarkets and buy in bulk. Or join a co-op. The problems of deterioration (aspirin) can in part be overcome by freezing; box them up and stick them in the rear (or bottom) of a freezer. Photographic film can be frozen, too (allow 24 hours for it to defrost before using). I strongly recommend the purchase of a 35 millimeter camera ($100-$200 range) and bulk film (black and white), plus developing chemicals (dry packed), paper, and an enlarger. **Memories** are going to be very precious in a time of real trouble.

The problems of storage space are not easily overcome. How do you stock up on enough toilet paper for a family of five for a period of six years, ten years, or more? It is a troubling thought. The use of styrofoam containers, tightly sealed with wrapping tape, is one way to keep out mice and rats, at least for a while. The picnic box kind of containers are ideal, the kind you keep the beer on ice in when you go to the Big Game. For paper products, the attic is a better place to store them than the basement, since moisture is a real problem. For food or other perishables, the basement is better because of the cooler temperatures. People who live in apartments in a city shouldn't. Nevertheless, if they have to stay where they are, it might be wise to rent some square feet in one of these mini-warehouses that are springing up around the cities. (They are a good place to go to **auctions**, too, so don't forget to meet your payment schedule. They will sell your stuff.)

The food storage program wouldn't do much good if riots, fires, or war were to break out. The food on hand would be stolen, or if not stolen, would be useless if the city's water or power were cut off. Food storage in a city is recommended only because people can pick up and leave a city, if necessary (maybe), and they can eat stored food if food supplies get tight for a couple of weeks. They add more protein to a diet. There will eventually be food rationing inside the major cities. It pays to have some food on reserve. Also, in the country, a drought or fire or flood could hit the crops. A reserve is wise. I hate to say it, but **peanut butter** really is an ideal food as far as storage, protein, cost, and acceptability with children are concerned. Large cans of it can be ordered, but if you can get the non-hydrogenated (oil at the top) variety, pay double. It is far better for you. I fear that Jimmy Carter's economic policies will place a real premium on large cans of peanut butter. Cans of **honey** can serve as the family's main sweetener. Buy a small can, and if you like it, order it in 5-pound or even larger cans.

Light Bulbs: Convert incandescent bulbs (which burn out continually, run expensively, and are likely to get scarce) to flourescent lighting. Look into the KillerWatt conversion units that are sold by Montgomery Ward and Penneys. These are very fine long-term investments. They can be attached to existing lamps and to ceiling lights.

Salt: You have to have it. Buy it in inexpensive boxes, and buy lots of it. Buy 30 or 40 boxes. Keep them sealed, thereby reducing the threat of moisture. If you're in the country, I'd buy a barrel of it from the local grocer. He can special order it. If there is trouble with refrigeration salt will be a crucial preservative.

Sugar: An excellent barter item. Give it up yourself, and buy a barrel of it. Keep it in the attic, away from moisture. It's a preservative, too.

Nails: Buy a barrel of them.

Tools: Any time Sears has one of its special sales on its Craftsman tools, buy all you can. Even if you can't hammer a nail straight, you can always swap the use of your tools (in your shop or garage only, of course) for services from a skilled, but tool-less, worker. Tools are a great investment. The prices only go up.

Dehydrated food: Taste various brands in advance. Some companies sell inexpensive sample packs. Simpler Life Foods are the Arrowhead Mills brand. Most health food stores carry Arrowhead Mills foods (not dehydrated, however).

Now is the time to get started. It takes determination. It takes money. It takes planning. It takes the courage to examine what the future seems to have in store for us, and then the courage to start dealing with that future. But the family that follows these suggestions will be far less troubled when the trouble hits.

I have made special arrangements with one firm to supply sample food packs to readers of this book on a special basis. For $25 (as of late 1977), they will supply the sample, and this $25 is applicable to the purchase of one-year's supply of food for one person, or two six-month units. The program was designed by Howard J. Ruff, a nutritional authority. Ask for the Ruff recommended reserve. When you write, please mention that you are taking advantage of the special offer. Contact

Martins Distributing Company
P.O. Box 5969
Tahoe City, CA 95730
(800) 824-7861 (toll-free, USA)
(916) 583-1511 (collect, Calif.)

I recommend Ruff's book, *Famine and Survival in America* ($4.95). Order from Target Publishers, Box 172, Alamo, CA 94507.

Capital Gains

I distinguish survival investing from conventional investing for the purpose of making increases in one's risk-oriented capital. Of course, all investing must bear risk, but some investments are riskier than others. They should offer higher rates of return as a result. I offer the following suggestions to those with extra capital. This means those who have taken the steps listed under "survival-hoarding-saving." Since it would cost several thousand dollars to complete the earlier program, many of you will not have the resources left to pursue these strategies. However, if you have taken the recommended steps, you are far more protected than most urban-dwelling Americans. The "personal items" alone will set you apart.

Real estate: The most useful approach for the person with time, but not as much money, is to go with the Lowry-Nickerson approach (see Bibliography). This involves locating run-down or "problem" properties, buying them with little or no money down, correcting the problem, and **trading** (not selling) the now repaired property for more or larger run-down properties. By trading, you defer capital gains taxes. This makes it possible to build up your resources far more rapidly. You use debt in this system, and unfortunately the proponents of this approach never warn you against the possibility of collapse. They also do not mention the threat of national rent controls. Therefore, you have to go very carefully. But the technique is sound: locate a poor property in a decent neighborhood, correct the problem, and move on. It is the best way to build assets rapidly. It takes a lot of work and courage. I would recommend only small-town investing in single family dwellings, duplexes, triplexes, and quads. No apartment houses, please; the threat of rent controls is too great. If you must invest in a city, make sure there is public transportation nearby: gasoline rationing threatens suburban investments in some cities (such as Los Angeles).

Precious gems: This is already a big field. A one-carat diamond is a very safe, very profitable investment. Reliance Products sells them in the wholesale range. Call them at their toll-free number, (800) 227-1590. The best way to buy diamonds is at a pawn shop. If you can get the owner to sign a 48-hour right of return, you can buy the stone or ring, take it to an appraiser, pay $5 for an appraisal, and keep the stone if he says that it's worth more than you paid for it. The closer you are to a military base, the better the selection. Too many men receive "Dear John" letters. Used engagement rings are a glut on the market, and few men are willing to keep them for their investment value. They think that lost sentiment somehow destroys their world market value. So many of them think this way that the market for used engagement rings really is depressed close to military bases. Be an entrepreneur. Buy the other guy's mistake and hold for long-term appreciation.

The problem with diamonds is simple: you are at the mercy of the appraiser, unless you have the time (and stomach) to bargain. There are other investments, most notably rare coin investments, that provide comparable appreciation but greater liquidity. But for hiding huge amounts of capital in easily hidden, easily transported, always valuable forms, nothing beats a high quality, investment grade diamond (one carat or larger). As a "buy and forget" type of investment, diamonds are excellent. Again, you must have a reliable dealer, and you must allow up to two months waiting time for your dealer to get the best price, at least in some instances. Never sell under pressure, unless it's really life and death.

The stones are very good investments for putting into a Keogh or IRA retirement account. They do well in inflationary times, and they do reasonably well in deflationary times. They are relatively liquid, unlike real estate, and they are durable, transportable, and scarce. They have most of the elements of money. They can be hidden. They can be moved quietly. It is difficult for tax collectors to tax them (again, unlike real estate). Once you have 20% of your liquid assets in "survival" gold and silver coins, meaning the so-called bullion coins, you can consider gems. The aquamarines and topazes are "poor men's diamonds," and the percentage increase of their price over the 1970's has been as spectacular as the rise in diamonds.

Rare coins: For liquidity, safety, and capital appreciation, nothing beats rare coins. They are not as subject to fluctuations in the gold and silver bullion markets, unlike the bullion gold coins and "junk" silver coins (pre-1965 U.S. coins). They rise far more rapidly in inflationary times, at least until the final weeks of panic collapse, when the bullion coins may perform better, and food probably does best of all. The trouble with rare coins is simple: it is very difficult to get good advice about when to buy and sell. There is one answer to this problem: **Numisco**. The Numisco Company of Chicago is a brokerage house that also publishes a fine newsletter for $48 per year. If you are after long-term capital gains, there is no newsletter available that is more likely to give you the advice necessary to get you those returns. I would advise starting with type sets of U.S. gold coins and British gold coins. These are collections of each of the gold coins in a series, such as the various denominations of U.S. gold coins, or the monarchs' faces on the British gold sovereigns. You can contact Numisco by writing or calling

> Numisco
> 175 W. Jackson Blvd.
> Chicago, IL 60604
> (800) 621-5272 (toll-free)

I think that at least 15% of a person's liquid assets (not counting his home) should be in rare coins. I think that 25% would be preferable. For any portfolio above $100,000, at least 30% should be in rare coins, with 25% in precious gems, 20% in bullion gold and silver coins, with the rest in mining shares, income-producing real estate, and/or three-month Treasury bills. This kind of portfolio will withstand everything except outright confiscation and dictatorship, and the coins and gems will even help to mitigate the effects of tyranny, since they are easily concealed forms of wealth (not to mention the bribery potential). Before starting in rare coins, you might want to read the following book: *High Profits in Rare Coin Investments*, by Q. David Bowers. It can be ordered from Bowers' company; price: $7.

> Bowers & Ruddy Gallery
> 6922 Hollywood Blvd.
> Los Angeles, CA 90028

"Penny" gold mining shares: If we ever see gold going above $300 per ounce, we will be viewing true "gold fever." When this strikes the investing public, there will be a rush to buy gold mining shares. The South African shares have a bad press. The familiar North American shares are few and far between. They will be overpriced. That leaves only the exploratory, high-risk, low-production "penny" shares, which sell from a few cents per share to several dollars. If gold fever hits, these could pay off at 10 to one or 50 to one. They are a good crap-shoot for about $2,000 or up to 5% of your portfolio. Warning: this is very speculative, or can be. But the goal is to buy thousands of shares and hold them until gold panic hits. Then sell them at high prices to the lemmings coming in who want to gamble, really gamble.

There are many risks. The big ones are these. First, gold prices get controlled by the government. Miners cannot sell the gold legally at a true market price. Second, gold mining equipment gets scarce because of price controls on industry in general. Third, a major World War breaks out, and conventional investments are frozen. Fourth, your broker is a crook and loads you up with shares in a lot of "goat pasture." The goal is to buy several mines, hope for the best, and unload them in the midst of "gold fever." Then use the paper money to pay off all your debts, especially real estate debt. Maybe "penny" gold shares will get you off the debt pyramid.

One broker who specializes in the exploratory mining shares of North America, both silver and gold, is

Sam Parks
Sam Parks Co.
2601 Elliott Ave.
Seattle, WA 98121
(800) 426-0598 (toll-free)

I would advise getting in slowly. Set aside $500 or $1,000 and nave Sam put you into half a dozen or more companies, $100 to $200 per company. Set the shares aside. Then when you have another $500 or so, call him up and order more. There is no need to rush in all at once. There will probably be several "gold dumps" by the U.S. Treasury before true gold panic hits. **Never buy in a panic market**, if the market is skyrocketing upward. That's the time to be steadily, quietly, and profitably **selling**. That's the time when the brokers will be calling you in an attempt to locate shares to sell to the late-comers who have just read about penny shares in the *Wall Street Journal*. They won't publish anything favorable in the *Journal* until it's time to start unloading. When the "unconventional gamble" starts looking somewhat conventional and "a reasonable high-risk investment" in the bulletins of the large brokerage houses, it's time to start unloading. Don't call them; let them call you.

The thing I like about these shares is that the upside potential in a panic gold market is 5 to one, 10 to one, or more, yet there is no downside risk apart from the money you put into the original purchase. Unlike the highly leveraged commodities markets, if gold falls, they can't come and confiscate all you own. You get maximum leverage and minimum downside risk.

Life insurance: I do not recommend anything but **annual renewable term**, with guaranteed renewals to age 70. These should be **nonparticipating** policies, since all the "participating" policy allows you to do is to participate with other uninformed buyers in paying higher annual premiums. This allows the company to use your funds through the year. If you have cash-value life insurance, you should get yourself a term policy. Then cancel the cash-value policy, or borrow against it, and buy some coins, gems, or income-producing real estate. Never, ever become a long-term creditor in a time of price inflation or price controls. If you have a cash-value life insurance policy (whole life, ordinary life, straight life, etc.), you must take immediate steps to get rid of it. Furthermore, your wife (or the stated beneficiaries) should be the sole and exclusive owner of any life insurance policy, paying the premiums with her own, exclusive checking account (not the joint account). This insures that the insurance pay-off will not become part of the husband's estate for estate tax purposes. If your insurance salesman didn't tell you this, you need a new insurance salesman. Also, never tell you present insurance salesman what you intend to do. ("Never ask the barber if you need a haircut.") Find an independent agent, buy your term policy, and then tell your present agent that you are going to let your present cash-value policy lapse, or that you intend to borrow the cash values.

How much insurance should you buy? At least three years of the bread-winner's income. This means you probably need at least $50,000, unless you have a lot of equity in your other property, that is, a net worth of well over $30,000. You can use $100,000. The place I recommend to get up-to-date information on the least expensive policies available (these will change from year to year) is

The Life Insurance Truth Society
P. O. Box 117
Cross Plains, TX 76443
(817) 725-6635

Ask to speak with David Holmes. A $5 or $10 donation is appropriate, since the information will save you hundreds or even thousands of dollars.

At present (mid-1979), the best easily available $100,000 term policy seems to be the one offered by **United Investors Life Insurance**, located in Kansas City, Missouri. Your independent insurance agent should be able to get the policy for you. If not, call the company and ask which broker sells it locally. Telephone number: (816) 283-4242. This policy allows you to decrease your coverage as you grow older, a very important feature. The rates are cheap. A 35-year-old man (or more properly, the wife of a 35-year-old man) will pay a premium of about $230 for one year of coverage. That's not much money for $100,000 of protection. If you can't afford this much, then try a $25,000 policy from **Old Line Life Insurance** of Milwaukee. In any case, never, ever convert a term policy to a so-called "permanent" life insurance policy, meaning a cash-value policy. Your term policy is 100% permanent to age 65 or 70 or 90, depending on the contract. What isn't permanent is the purchasing power of the dollar. **Avoid**

all cash-value life insurance policies. If you are too old to own term insurance, you are too old to own **any** insurance. Cash it in and buy some gold coins. But if you are converting to term, be absolutely certain that the new policy is in force **before** you cancel the old one.

I realize that most of my readers will not have taken this advice in the past. About 85% of all policies in force are cash-value policies. The commission structures discourage any life insurance salesman from selling annual renewable term policies. Remember, it is not your personal responsibility to offer employment to life insurance salesmen. It is your responsibility to see to it that your family is protected. An agent gets a first-year commission of over a thousand dollars, plus renewal commissions, for the sale of a $100,000 cash-value policy to a man aged 35. A term policy earns him about $100 the first year, and practically nothing thereafter. Which will he try to sell you? For more information, read Norman F. Dacey's book, *What's Wrong With Your Life Insurance* (Collier, $3.00).

"Pure Equity" Trust: Some people are being approached by salesmen who are not lawyers who peddle an incredibly overpriced gimmick called a "pure equity" trust or "family equity" trust, also called "Constitutional" trust. It involves giving your assets to the trust, and you and a second party, normally your wife, become trustees of the trust. Then you contract with the trust to provide your services to it as an independent contractor. The salesmen tell you that you can "split the income" by filtering it through the trust. The beneficiaries of the trust (wife, children) get their share of the income, and of course most of them are in lower tax brackets. Salesmen fail to mention one slight complication: the courts have denied the legality of income splitting through a trust (in 1978), and the Supreme Court refused to reverse the decision. Thus, those who set up these trusts are in store for some very unpleasant audits and back tax assessments, plus interest.

Now salesmen are peddling an "off shore" (foreign-based) trust package very similar to the now-defunct "pure equity" trust. It is easy to predict what the results will be. Before you set up one of these off-shore trusts, write for the printed opinion ($10) of a specialist in trust law, B. Ray Anderson, located at

Anderson, Nearon & Falco
1924 Tice Valley Blvd.
Walnut Creek, CA 94595
(415) 933-6760

These trusts are not the same as the simple inter-vivos trusts like those found in Norman F. Dacey's book, *How to Avoid Probate* (New York: Crown Publishers). For people with estates under $100,000, the Dacey book is probably very useful, despite the opposition of legal profession. A good trust lawyer is expensive. Better to rely on Dacey's book than not to do anything about your estate before your death. Dacey is better than nothing, and nothing is what most American men do about their estates prior to death. (Nothing is what all of them do after their deaths.) However, if you need some advice on trusts, and you can pay a per-hour fee that is reasonable compared to the costs of unraveling a legal mess after you have acted by yourself, I can recommend these names (in addition to B. Ray Anderson):

Michael Ushijima	Peter Lind
6300 River Rd., No. 100	P.O. Box 3426
Rosemont, IL 60018	Bellevue, WA 98004
(312) 696-3466	(206) 455-4240

For those who need expensive advice concerning the possibility of establishing a foreign trust or other off-shore entity — a form of business operations that has, as a possible secondary benefit, some important tax consequences — I recommend Quentin Breen. He can be contacted at 728 Montgomery St., Suite 36, San Francisco, CA 94111. Telephone: (415) 421-5670.

Survival home: Probably the most important decision you can make concerning the possible crises that are coming is to move to a safer geographical location. A rural or semi-rural area is ideal. You may choose to live in a small town (under 25,000) and garden in your back yard. You may live a few miles outside of town. But by far the best thing you can do before making your decision about where you need to locate on a permanent basis is to buy and read Joel Skousen's critically important book, *Survival Home Manual* ($25). It is not available in book stores. Skousen tells you the safest regions of the country, what their climates are like, what sites to look for, and what kind of a home to build. No serious survivalist can afford not to read this book. It can be ordered from the book distribution division of the American Bureau of Economic Research. Send a check for $25 to

Survival Book
American Bureau of Economic Research
3536 N. Wellington Ave.
Indianapolis, IN 46226

Conclusions

I realize that this chapter could cost an investor thousands of dollars in order to implement its recommendations. I realize that many of my readers just don't have this kind of money. Still, as I have said repeatedly, it is far better to start some kind of long-term capital preservation program than none. It is better to take a few of the proper steps than to stand pat with conventional investments and savings programs. You can do **something** about your future, even though you can't do everything. You should not be paralyzed into inaction just because you think you can't accomplish every-thing in this book. Unless I sell a lot of these books, I can't afford to take all the steps myself. What I am trying to do is to take those steps that fit my circumstances best. I offer many avenues of investing and buying because I have to cover a lot of different circumstances that my readers may be in.

I want you to get out of conventional investments. I want you to be able to look back at your decisions over the next few years and say to yourself, "It's a good thing I took that book's advice, or I would be in poor shape today." If you can do that, we will both be better off. The only ones who will be worse off are employees of the government and government dependents who believed political rhetoric. For them we need shed no tears. If it weren't for the present governmental policies of theft, forced redistribution, and the subsidizing of the indolent all over the world—necessary if a government is to replace the family and local voluntary agencies in the government's quest for total power—we would not have to take such drastic investment and survival measures. Let us never forget that the Federal, state, and local governments got us into this mess. It is up to us, as individuals, to take action to get ourselves out of the government-created mess, and then put government on a crash diet. If we are going to build a better world after the coming collapse, we had better have some resources left in our possession. We will not be able to rebuild if we perish in the meantime. Start taking evasive action.

CHAPTER NINETEEN
LOOPHOLES IN THE CHAOS

Price controls work. Let no one tell you differently. They accomplish their statist goals, though not their stated goals.

Why do governments impose price controls? The main reason, of course, is to stay in power. That's why governments do everything they do. More specifically, legislators impose controls to satisfy the demands of the public to "do something" about rising prices. If legislators take what appears to be positive action, then any negative results can be blamed on those people in the community who are not law abiding.

The purpose of price controls, politically, is **to provide nongovernmental scapegoats** for the failure of government policy, and to provide self-serving explanations for any part of the program that the public favors. Every failure is explained in terms of the failure of private citizens to abide by the rules set forth by the government. Every success—meaning either unde- tected failure or aspects of the economy untouched by the controls—be- comes a Brownie point for the regulators and the statist philosophy of messianic salvation.

People inevitably fall into the intellectual trap which some economists have called "the fallacy of the thing unseen." The public looks at the "positive" government program. The program is launched in terms of uni- versally agreed-upon **general** goals. The program is staffed by "experts." It is comprehensive. It offers the public hope. When it fails, the program cannot be scrapped. Too many special-interest groups have grown accustomed to the benefits of the program—benefits that come from the pockets of the majority. The potential opponents, meaning those who pay for the benefits of the minority, either do not recognize the nature of the wealth redistri- bution scheme, or else they find it too expensive to organize all the potential opponents of the program. The beneficiaries are a concentrated pressure group with a direct interest in the continuation of the program. So the failure is blamed on someone else. The public sees the program, listens to the rhetoric, and hopes. The failures are blamed on others. The bureau- crats get lodged in their Civil Service-protected positions, and the program becomes permanent. The costs of the program cannot be estimated easily, and the government and its beneficiaries have no incentive to get those costs estimated. They advertise the benefits and suppress knowledge of all costs. The things unseen—all those projects that might have been begun had men been allowed freedom—go unseen for generations. They are forgotten. The government advertises the successes, suppresses the failures, blames others for whatever failures become apparent, and the public pays the freight.

Don't people learn from history? How many times have I heard that phrase? The phrase is ridiculous. The next time you start to use it, bite your tongue. The very fact that critics of contemporary insanity, which is in fact the ancient insanity of messianic statism, keep repeating the phrase indicates that the critics don't learn from history. What history teaches clearly is that people don't learn from history.

History teaches nothing to those who hold a philosophy contrary to the truth. All historical facts are reinterpreted by the statists to conform to their philosophy of statism. Does Galbraith learn from history? Did Hubert Humphrey? History is not some systematic collection of indisputable facts; it is an excerise in faith. It is factual, but different men interpret the facts differently. You have to start with first principles of interpretation to learn anything from history, and history does not advertise these first principles, or at least not loudly enough to catch the attention of the utopians.

Price controls lead to shortages, production bottlenecks, crises, family disruptions, and a long list of demonstrable disasters. But the demonstration can be made successfully only by someone who believes and understands economics, as well as the proper use of historical documents, and the demonstration can be convincing only to someone who at least has some grasp of economic theory, or at least the principles of liberty. There are very few teachers today, and the listeners who can make use of what the teachers have to say are also few in number.

The results of price controls are abhorrent to most people who are the victims. But the victims almost never understand that the results are actually the product of the price control system. Herein lies the awful truth. Price controls produce bad economic results, but the public universally misunderstands cause and effect in economics. They call for even greater enforcement of the controls in order to alleviate the results which are perceived to be burdensome. They do not learn from history because they do not understand the blessings of liberty or the logic of economics.

The Chaos of Regulations

How, then, can we escape the seemingly inevitable drift into price controls? For the individual, there are ways to mitigate the effects of controls, temporarily, in some cases, for some families, so long as the controls don't last too long and are not rigorously enforced everywhere.

What we need to survive are loopholes. Fortunately, every system of law ever devised has loopholes, and every enforcement mechanism provides even more way to escape. The mills of justice grind slowly, but they grind exceedingly lumpy.

First, and foremost, the regulators want to achieve contradictory goals, and they have competing programs to achieve them. The bureaucrats are not able to devise a truly comprehensive and complete system of controls. (In fact, we are told by mathematician-philosopher Kurt Goedel that the human mind is theoretically incapable of devising any system that is both comprehensive and complete, meaning completely in agreement with original premises.) So there will be loopholes in the original legislation. The idea is to slide through the contradictory and incomplete regulations for as long as possible. There are holes in the government's many dikes. Never forget, **the government doesn't know what it wants to accomplish,** other than tenure.

Edward Knight, an economist in the industrial organization section of the Library of Congress, has produced several studies of price controls in recent U.S. history. His study of Nixon's early controls, "The New Economic Policy," was published by the Library of Congress' Congressional Research Service on August 30, 1971 (71-202 E). His comment on the 1942 price freeze is revealing:

> However, from the very outset it was realized that the administration and the enforcement of the regulation would be complicated by a number of unresolved issues namely: What products and producers, if any, should be exempted from price control? What standards should govern exemption? What factors were to determine the setting of maximum prices? Where should ceilings be set to be generally fair and equitable to both consumers and producers? If profits are a measure of fairness to producers, how were they to be measured? Should profitability be applied to each of an industry's products or to all of its operations? Should profits be computed as a return on investment or as a return on sales? Should a single ceiling be established for all sellers in a trade or should different maxima be established for different classes or sellers or for individual firms? What allowances should be made for decreases in costs and increases in profits? Should maximum prices be established through base-date freezes, through formulas, or set forth in dollars and cents? (pp. 6-7)

This is one of the finest statements of the problems that I have ever seen. Back in 1920, Ludwig von Mises gave us the answer: the government cannot possibly find the answers. There is no other answer. Without a free market, it is not possible for the government to assess true costs. Only acting participants can make such estimations, and the continually shifting results of their continual evaluations and re-evaluations are prices. Yet it is the price system which all socialist governments are trying to abolish or at least control. Thus, the bureaucrats cannot answer even one of Knight's questions, let alone all of them, and not by any stretch of the imagination (or computer print-out) could they answer all of them so as to produce an integrated, effective, cost-efficient economic plan.

Does this impress the controllers? Not a bit. Did they find answers to these problems? Not a one. They didn't have to find answers. This is the very heart of the price control system. The government does not have to find answers because the goal of the control system is **to create a scapegoat mechanism which is a political substitute for answers**. That's it. If you try to seek out the inner truth of controls, you will search in vain. The truth of price controls is best seen in a cartoon of a ring of men, each pointing to the person on his left. Better yet, a massive crowd of bureaucrats pointing to another crowd of productive citizens who are trying their best to satisfy consumer demand with a diminishing quantity of resources.

The second fact of price controls is that there are not enough regulators to enforce the controls. There is too much paperwork, too much confusion. They can harrass an individual proprietor, whether or not he has done something wrong, but they cannot enforce their regulations on more than a handful. The whole system rests on **voluntary compliance**, and the more people comply with irrational pricing directives, the more crises hit the economy. This eventually leads men to try to evade the regulations that they say they believe in. What producers want is simple: "Let the government enforce controls on my **suppliers**; let me alone to sell at a free market price (unless the state grants me a monopoly and the right to charge a monopoly price)."

There are not enough resources available to controllers to confiscate all resources. They will try, of course, but they cannot succeed. Their success creates built-in resistance. The public starts to hide resources. Men cheat. They evade. Only a few can be caught. They vote for the controls, but they do not act as though they believe in them. They are schizophrenic, and their confusion allows clear-thinking men to survive.

Fast Action

The secret of profit is knowledge. Your competitors are ignorant. They are also inveterate optimists. When Nixon imposed price controls on August 15, 1971, He promised: "Our best days lie ahead." In the midst of a massive, thoughtless destruction of American liberties, Nixon announced to the American electorate:

> As we move into a generation of peace, as we blaze the trail toward the new prosperity, I say to every American: Let us raise our spirits. Let all of us contribute all we can to this great and good country that has contributed so much to the progress of mankind.
> Let us invest in our Nation's future; and let us revitalize that faith in ourselves that built a great nation in the past and that will shape the world of the future.
> Thank you, and good evening.

About all that you can say about that speech is that he obviously wrote it himself, and it is covered by Ford's pardon.

But Americans cheered. The polls showed that over 75% of the voters favored the move, and the majority of businessmen did, too. He offered them hope—hope in the results of government coercion. That hope dominates our age.

While there is hope, there is time to act. While the lemmings who believe in the theology of statism glow in the sunlight of the latest cure-all out of Washington, the intelligent strategist can act. *The Wall Street Journal* for August 26, 1971, reported: "Progress Report: After 10 Days, Firms Say Equipment Orders Aren't Pouring In Yet." There was no rush to buy capital goods.

That meant that rational executives had ten days to begin to prepare for the shortages that the 90-day price freeze guaranteed. It also meant that there are few rational executives nationally. There will be more next time, but not many. Optimism and ignorance—a potent drug combination—work on the side of the man who takes fast action. Your competitors have faith; this gives you time.

Another fact: your actions will not be observed in the early stages of a price freeze. Your order for capital goods or consumer items will not be part of a wave of orders. It will not be large enough for anyone to worry about. If you spread your purchases among several suppliers, you will leave no traces worth mentioning. People simply do not act in time. They seldom know what to do, and even when they do, they do not take those steps. In the early stages of a price freeze, there will be time.

Stages of Controls

First comes the freeze. This is what the public wants to hear. The government has at last taken action. It has answers. It has shown its mettle. People are reassured. There must be answers, and the government will provide them soon. The "cooling off period" will help give the economy a breather.

Nixon declared a universal freeze. Only raw agricultural products, interest rates, stocks and bonds, exports, and (for one week) school tuitions were left free. Oh, yes; taxes were also left free to rise. The consumer price index had been rising at about a 4% clip then dropped to about 2%. But the 2% rise came in the middle of a universal price freeze. Conclusion: freezes are more like melts. Freedom dribbles back into the economy.

The pressures continue to build. A universal freeze is not politically possible. The government has to backtrack. The normal response is to freeze prices and wages of the largest, most visible, most central businesses, especially manufacturing. This has been true since the price control edict of the emperor Diocletian back in 301 A.D. About 800 different goods were covered. Violations were capital crimes. Thirteen years later, the system was scrapped. The empire was falling apart at the seams. This, of course, didn't prevent the pagan emperor Julian from trying the same thing 60 years later.

There is a kind of escalation of controls, with each series far easier to impose on the public. **First**, monetary inflation creates price inflation. The statistics begin to worry the planners who are running the budget deficits that are being funded by the monetary inflation. So they call for restraint on the part of the public. This makes about as much sense as calling for restraint in the middle of an auction—an auction being innundated by new bidders holding fresh, crisp dollars, hot off the presses so to speak. "Quit bidding so high," says the President. Meanwhile, the Treasury is borrowing a few billion from the Federal Reserve System, which in turn creates more money to fan the passions of the auction. And this auction can be paid for with credit, unlike conventional auctions. No wonder the bidders lose control of their emotions.

Second, when the bidders keep bidding up the price of the goods, the government imposes guidelines. These are usually voluntary at first. They may or may not have any effect. This was what happened during the first year of price guidelines of Roosevelt's war years, from February of 1941 until March of 1942. The guidelines had no teeth. Sooner or later, the Congress or the President will buy the bureaucrats a set of dentures.

Third comes the freeze. This is the freeze that doesn't. The best strategy is to begin to make purchases of long-term durable goods. Prices really are not frozen, especially prices of **services**. It is very interesting that after World War II ended, despite the frantic efforts of the price controllers to call a halt to rising prices, the price level skyrocketed. As Knight comments on the 1945-48 period (controls were lifted in October of 1946), "strong inflationary pressures were felt in virtually every sector of the economy. The only sector not so seriously affected was the service sector, and this was due mainly to the fact that the bulk of consumer demand was centered on durable and nondurable goods, whose supply had been either restricted or stopped during the war." More to the point, the price of services remained somewhat less active because **services had been supplied at above-ceiling prices during the War**. It is simply too hard to police the service sector of the economy. This is why it is far preferable to be a supplier of services than a supplier of manufactured products. They leave fewer records. They are easy to barter.

Fourth comes the partial thaw. The thaw is inevitable. The long list of unanswerable questions provided by Knight must be dealt with on an ad hoc basis by the price controllers. Some prices will be adjusted, new formulas will be devised, circumstances will be honored, and some degree of price flexibility will be restored. Not much flexibility, you understand, but enough to give the planners something to do. If prices get out of hand—the bureaucratic visible hand—then another freeze may be imposed. But in any economy short of fascism, a degree of price flexibility will have to operate.

These four stages of controls provide the entrepreneur with opportunities for capital preservation. Minor upward adjustments are seldom recognized, and enforcers seldom discover them. When discovered, enforcers use a gentle touch, especially with first offenders. Small businessmen are left far more free than the regulations would indicate. Thus, the economy survives. If the controls were really enforced, the economy would be destroyed in the central population centers and seriously disrupted in the rural areas.

The Age of the Caesars

Professor Hans Sennholz warns of a coming generation of fascism and controls, the Age of the Caesars. He is convinced that the ethics of envy will be put into force by fascist controllers. His Age of the Caesars is therefore the Age of the Seizers. The public will put up with the controls so long as they think that the rich and powerful are being put through the wringer of the control system. In such a period, the energetic, productive citizen is classified with the criminals. Nixon's August 15th speech is indicative of the mentality of the controllers: "In the past 7 years, there has been an average of one international monetary crisis every year. Now who gains from these crises? Not the workingman; not the investor; not the real producers of wealth. The gainers are the international money speculators. Because they thrive on crises, they help create them." And what was the sin of these international money speculators? Why, to bet against the British pound, the Italian lira, the U.S. dollar. To ask for payment in gold, as guaranteed by the U.S. government. To hedge against inflation. To speculate against the International Monetary Fund, the intellectual creation of John Maynard Keynes. Worst of all, they had sought a profit through accurate forecasting, making the deliberate manipulations of the domestic monetary planners far more difficult, making the shearing of the average citizen more costly to the confiscators.

What was Nixon's response? He closed the gold window, thereby announcing to the world what the speculators had said for years: the U.S. dollar was an inflationary fiat currency. And what authority did he invoke to shut the gold window? None. That's right; he had no statutory authority, he had no executive order up his sleeve, he had nothing. He simply told Treasury Secretary Connally to stop making payments in gold and to float the dollar in direct violation of IMF rules. There was not even the slightest pretence at creating a sense of legality.

The public cheered.

Caesar, you may recall, was a very popular fellow. He was also smart enough not to keep any tapes. Nixon wasn't so popular with those who wanted to destroy him, although Galbraith awarded his old subordinate in the Office of Price Administration an A- for his grade in economics

("Galbraith Gives Nixon an A-minus," *Business Week*, Oct. 16, 1971). He did keep tapes. He is gone today, but the economics of Caesarism is with us still, for the ethics of Caesarism is almost universal.

CONCLUSION

Well, that's it. You now have more information on the strategy of survival under price controls than most people in the United States. There are real profit possibilities ahead for those who plan now for the unpleasant future that is all too likely. I don't know if anyone can really be better off under controls than he would have been without them, but one thing is for certain: it is better to know in advance the kind of disruptions that are coming than to drift into them unaware and unprepared. You will be better off than you would have been had you not had access to the information in this book.

To make this book most useful, I would suggest that you refer back to it when you read the headlines in the newspapers about the rising price level or the importance of strong governmental action to control rising prices. You won't remember everything in this book after a single reading. It's worth reviewing.

I hope that everyone who reads this book does begin to take some of the steps outlined inside its covers. It won't do anyone much good to have known what was going to happen if the person never took any action to act in terms of what he knew in advance. It doesn't do much good to say, "I told you so," if you're only talking to yourself.

The goal of profit should be more than the mere amassing of goods. The whole idea of storing up wealth is to be productive with it when you later need it. I would hope that every reader who takes the proper steps to improve his chances for financial and family survival will not forget the need of others in the society to survive. The division of labor is vital for the future of us all, and if some people need help to get them through the crisis, so that they can become productive once again on the far side of price controls, then those of us who have planned wisely will be in a position to help.

Another important thing to remember is that **leadership requires leisure.** If good men and women are to assert leadership on the far side of disaster, then they need assets sufficient to provide them with leisure. What we should aim at is financial survival, but survival is not mere existing; it means being productive in every area of life open to a man, given his talents.

I hope the world I have described never arrives. I hope my grim assessment never comes to fruition. But I am afraid that it will. Let us make the best of it. There are steps we can take to improve our opportunities in the future.

And never forget my motto: **It is better to be rich and healthy than it is to be poor and sick.**

BIBLIOGRAPHY

Let's state the obvious. We can't read everything. Furthermore, no one book will cover everything we need to know, even in a narrow, specialized field. Therefore, we have a responsibility to keep reading. We have to keep thinking and rethinking. There is no way that any "how to make a lot of money" book can show you how to do everything. I hope that my book has introduced you to a number of new ideas, and that these ideas will lead you to a series of personal investment strategies that will prove beneficial in retrospect. It is my hope that every reader will take on one area of specialization and make it his own personal "profit avenue." I am providing a minimal list of books that will help you to make concrete decisions about your personal investment future. This list is in no way complete. It is simply an introduction.

If you are content to have read my book, and my book alone, then you have not really understood the message of my book. If you sit on your hands now, you have made the very mistake my book was designed to warn against. Keep on pursuing knowledge. Spend some time and money to prepare yourself. Think about the various scenarios for the future, and start planning for them. The day you stop reading is the day your investment portfolio, whatever it is and however large or small it may be, is in danger. You cannot afford to park your brains. **Take time to read**. Forget about the $5 or $10 a book costs. That's peanuts. The real cost is the very valuable **time** you take to read and understand a book, not the purchase price. I have tried to find the best books in the various fields, so that you can save time searching out the ones that you need. Now you have a responsibility to buy and read the ones that you think will help you. You now have knowledge, since you have finished my book. With knowledge comes personal responsibility. However, with knowledge also comes power. Use your power profitably and responsibly.

I have given addresses and 1977 prices in cases where the books are self-published or difficult to locate. For all others, consult *Books in Print* at your local bookstore.

205

Price Controls

Mark Skousen, *Playing the Price Controls Game* (Arlington House)

The Illusion of Wage and Price Control (Fraser Institute, Vancouver, B.C.; $6)

Rent Control: A Popular Paradox (Fraser Institute, Vancouver B.C.; $3) (The Fraser Institute's address is 626 Bute St., Vancouver, B.C., V6E 3M1.)

Marshall Clinard, *The Black Market* (Patterson Smith)

Crawford Goodwin (ed.), *Exhortation and Controls* (Brookings Institution)

Nicholas Balabkins, *Germany Under Direct Controls* (Rutgers University Press)

Council on Wage & Price Stability, *Historical Working Papers on the Economic Stabilization Program, August 15, 1971 to April 30, 1974* (Government Printing Office; Order number 0-564-606, 607; $14.40)

Investing

David Smyth, *You Can Survive Any Financial Disaster* (Regnery)

David Smyth and Lawrence Stuntz, *The Speculator's Handbook* (Regnery)

Harry Browne, *You Can Profit from a Monetary Crisis* (Macmillan)

Klein & Wolman, *The Beat Inflation Strategy* (Simon & Schuster)

John Pugsley, *Common Sense Economics* (Common Sense Press, 711 W. 17th St., Suite G-6, Costa Mesa, CA 92627; $13.25)

The Manual of Inflation Hedges (Kephart Communications, 901 N. Washington Blvd., Alexandria, VA 22314; $10)

A Quick Course in Hard Money Investments (Kephart Communications; $10)

Mark Skousen, *The Sensible Man's Guide to Survival Investments* (High Street Press, P.O. Box 31058, Washington, D.C. 20031; $10)

Howard J. Ruff, *How to Prosper During the Coming Bad Years* (Times Books, $8.95)

Collectors Markets

Donald J. Hoppe, *How to Invest in Gold Coins* (Arco).

Q. David Bowers, *High Profits in Rare Coin Investments* (Bowers & Ruddy Galleries, 6922 Hollywood Blvd., Los Angeles, CA 90028; $7)

Richard Rush, *Investments You Can Live With and Enjoy* (U.S. News & World Report, 620 5th Ave., New York City, NY 10020)

Morton Shulman, *Anyone Can Make Big Money Buying Art* (Macmillan)

Money and Banking

Murray Rothbard, *What Has Government Done to Our Money?* (Pine Tree Press; $1.50) Order from Foundation for Economic Education

Andrew Dickson White, *Fiat Money Inflation in France* (Caxton)

William Rees-Mogg, *The Crisis of World Inflation* (London: Hamish Hamilton; distributed by Blackwell's, Broad Street, Oxford, England; $2.50)

Antony C. Sutton, *The War on Gold* ('76 Press, P.O. Box 2686, Seal Beach, CA 90740; $10)

Mark Skousen, *The 1978 Insider's Banking & Credit Almanac* (Kephart Communications, 901 N. Washington Blvd., Alexandria, VA 22314; $13)

Harry Browne, *Harry Browne's Complete Guide to Swiss Banks* (McGraw-Hill)

General Economics

Henry Hazlitt, *Economics in One Lesson* (McFadden)

Gary North, *An Introduction to Christian Economics* (Craig Press). First two sections.

Murray Rothbard, *Man, Economy and State* (Sheed & Ward). Chapter 11, especially.

Ludwig von Mises, *Human Action* (Regnery). Chapter 20 is crucial.

Ludwig von Mises, *The Theory of Money and Credit* (Foundation for Economic Education). The most important book of all, but academic and difficult.

All of these books in the general economics section are available from the Foundation for Economic Education, Irvington-on-Hudson, New York, 10533. The Foundation offers a very fine free monthly magazine, *The Freeman*. You should subscribe to it. Also, they publish an important book list, *Literature of Freedom*, which is available on request. **Get on their mailing list!**

Real Estate

William Nickerson, *How I Turned $1,000 into Three Million in Real Estate—In My Spare Time* (Simon & Schuster)

Al Lowry, *How You Can Become Financially Independent by Investing in Real Estate* (Simon & Schuster)

Daniel J. deBenedictis, *The Complete Real Estate Adviser* (Cornerstone)

John Kamin, *How to Make Money Fast Speculating in Distressed Property* (Forecaster, 19623 Ventura Blvd., Tarzana, CA 91356, $12)

George Bockl, *How Real Estate Fortunes Are Made* (Prentice-Hall)

George Bockl, *How to Use Leverage to Make Money in Local Real Estate* (Prentice-Hall)

All of these books recommend using extensive debt to "pyramid" a real estate empire. This works all right in a pure, straight-line inflation. We may have recessions, price controls, and other disasters along the way. Therefore, these highly "leveraged" debt pyramids should be avoided in general, although limited debt can be used for short-term speculation (under six years). Try to keep your pyramid out of debt at least once every seven years for a full year. This keeps you from risking total collapse. The trick will be in knowing when to get off the debt pyramid. The books all show how to buy and sell, how to evaluate good buys, and how to trade properties to avoid paying capital gains taxes. But use the debt pyramid with caution. Remember, no debt pyramid expands forever. Debt is a tool for rapid accumulation of "hard goods," in this case income-producing real estate property, when debt-free investing would not be possible at all. You allow inflation to pay off your debt. But rent controls, rationing, and shortages threaten all investing, so plan to get off the debt pyramid at least by 1984.

Economic Newsletters

Not everyone would normally consider subscribing to an economic newsletter. They normally cost over $50 a year, they come out a couple times a month, or maybe only once a month, and they are small. The cost per page, compared to *Time* magazine, is astronomical. Why pay it? There are several reasons. For example:

1. You want innovative new investment ideas.
2. You want unconventional economic or political information.
3. You are short of time and want to "hire" someone else to do the massive amount of reading necessary to find the relevant bits of information.
4. You want someone with your basic perspective to summarize the news.
5. You want information from someone who isn't dependent upon advertising revenue.
6. You want to learn about new products and services from someone who isn't trying to earn a commission by selling something to you. ("Never ask a barber if you need a haircut.")

To buy these services, you have to pay more per word than you do with mass-circulation, advertising revenue-dependent, overly cautious newspapers and magazines. You have to pay unconventional subscription prices in order to buy unconventional information. If you are content to base your decisions on the mass media, as interpreted by Walter Cronkite, then you probably won't subscribe to a newsletter service.

The following newsletters constitute only a tiny fraction of those available. One organization that will send you dozens of sample copies of available newsletters for very little money is this one:

Select Information Exchange
2095 Broadway
New York, NY 10023

Drop SIE a card telling of your interest in finding out about their sample copy program.

Specific Recommendations

I'm in the newletter business. It has been very good to me, so obviously I'm biased in favor of newsletters. But even if I weren't in the business, I'd subscribe to several of them. My time is way too valuable not to have a few full-time "information scroungers" working for me. **The more valuable your time is, the more you need succinct, well-researched newsletters.** A good rule to follow is never to become wholly dependent on a single newsletter's advice (yes, even my **Remnant Review**). Follow the old biblical proverb: "Where no counsel is, the people fall: but in the multitude of counsellors there is safety" (Proverbs 11:14). Most of these can be sampled by sending $3 for the latest issue. (In the case of **Remnant Review**, you already have about 20 samples, since each chapter of this book represents one issue of the newsletter. The section on automobile repair represents two issues.)

Remnant Review (15 Oakland Ave., Harrison, NY 10528; $60/22 issues). Almost everything is covered from time to time: shortages, controls, real estate, precious metals, alternative currencies, unconventional inflation hedges, rationing, etc. It does not cover the stock market, however.

The Ruff Times (P.O. Box 2000, San Ramon, CA 94583; $105/24 issues). This 8-page newsletter covers several topics each issue. It is a good one for newcomers to the "hard money" field. The toll-free hot-line is a bargain. Subscribers can call in any time for investment advice (except stock market and bond market advice).

Daily News Digest (P.O. Box 39027, Phoenix, AZ 85061; $125/52 issues). For the busy professional, this letter is indispensable. The editor culls from dozens of sources the latest news on gold, silver, energy, national defense, investment alternatives, Federal statistics, and other topics that catch the fancy of newsletter readers. You can skim this and get the highlights of the U.S. financial press. Weekly.

Personal Finance (5809 Annapolis Rd., Bladensburg, MD 20710; $36/24 issues, new subscriber's price). A very good introductory letter to alternative investments in general. Less expensive than most. An all-purpose investment letter. Highly recommended.

Common Sense Viewpoint (711 W. 17th., Suite G-6, Costa Mesa, CA 92627; $75/12 issues). A mini-book each month. Very libertarian editorial policy. It covers stocks, commodities, and interest rates each issue, plus a main investment editorial of several pages. Edited by John Pugsley.

World Money Analyst (1300 Connecticut Ave., N.W., Washington, D.C. 20036; $95/12 issues). This letter is jam-packed with analysis, plus a monthly interview in depth with an important "hard money" expert. Regular columnists cover commodities, metals, inflation, and the world economy. Lots of information for the money. Very much an "Austrian School" (Prof. Mises) oriented letter.

World Market Perspective (ERC Publishing, P.O. Box 91491, West Vancouver, B.C., Canada V7V 3P2; $96/12 issues). This is another "Austrian School" perspective newsletter. It covers one topic in depth each month. Its specialty is the precious metals. Clients of the company receive it free. They sell leveraged silver accounts through Swiss banks.

P S Letter (P.O. Box 598, Rogue River, OR 97537; $100/12 issues). For anyone who is seriously worried about economic breakdown, the *P S Letter* is indispensable. The editor, Mel Tappan, is a dedicated survivalist, and no newsletter has more accurate, more pertinent information on survival equipment and strategies. It's "far out" by today's standards; by the standards of 1984, I think it's better to aim in the same direction Tappan is shooting at.

Tax Angles (5809 Annapolis Rd., Bladensburg, MD 20710; $30/12 issues). A very useful newsletter for small businessmen. No other letter covers taxes and tax hedging better than this one.

Numisco Letter (175 W. Jackson Blvd., Suite A-640, Chicago, IL 60604; $48/12 issues). This is a good introduction to the whole field of rare coin investing. For the investor looking for a neglected "hard money" field, rare coins is just about the best.

Rosen Numismatic Advisory (P.O. Box 231, East Meadow, NY 11554; $60/12 issues). Another good advisory service for coin collectors. In this neglected area, two letters are not too many.

The Reaper (P.O. Box 39026, Phoenix, AZ 85069; $195). One of the better commodity futures newsletters. It covers more than just commodities. You need several commodity letters if you're in this highly risky investment field.

Bruce Gould on Commodities (P.O. Box 16, Seattle, WA 98111; $285/24 issues). Gould is very good. He doesn't provide tips on which commodity to buy or sell; he offers careful analysis of how the markets are going. You decide. The letter is a useful back-up to the trader's sheets that put you in and out of markets.

Precious Stones Newsletter (P.O. Box 4649, Thousand Oaks, CA 91359; $96/12 issues). For someone with a good chunk of capital to store in small, highly transportable precious stones, this letter is important.

Real Estate Investing Letter (306 Dartmouth St., Boston, MA 02116; $39/12 issues). A basic, competent letter on all aspects of the real estate markets.

Homeowner's Moneyletter (Rt. 3, Box 127, Shelbyville, IN 46176; $24/12 issues). A very good letter aimed at the homeowner. This investment is the biggest one most people own; so it pays to have a letter helping you to manage your home efficiently in terms of resale, improvements, etc. Well worth the money.

Dow Theory Letter (P.O. Box 1759, La Jolla, CA 92037; $125/26 issues). A good stock market letter from a master of the Dow Theory system. Technical analysis, with some fundamentals.

Bank Credit Analyst (Butterfield Bldg., Front St., Hamilton, Bermuda; $295/12 issues). One of the most expensive investment letters around, but very good. If you manage more than $50,000 of funds, you should subscribe to this letter.

Trilateral Observer (P.O. Box 4775, Scottsdale, AZ 85258; $60/12 issues). This newsletter monitors the activities of the Trilateral Commission. The editor, Antony Sutton, is a free market investment expert, as well as a superb researcher in the field of international affairs.

Don Bell Reports (P.O. Box 2223, Palm Beach, FL 33480; $30/26 issues). A good report on politics, economics, and bureaucratic intervention. Reasonably priced. Close watching of the Washington policy makers.

Audio Alert (108 Galewood Rd., Timonium, MD 21903; $140/12 tapes). This service provides a monthly series of interviews, 4 each tape. For busy businessmen who can use a car tape player to educate themselves while driving, this is a good service. It also includes a printed summary of the 4 interviews for handy reference.

Free Bank Newsletters

Monthly Economic Letter (Economics Dept., First National City Bank, 399 Park Ave., New York, NY 10022)

Morgan Guaranty Survey (23 Wall St., New York, NY 10015)

World Report (First National Bank of Chicago, Business and Economics Research Division, One First National Plaza, Chicago, IL 60670)

St. Louis Federal Reserve Bank

This organization publishes several sophisticated reports that are available free of charge. The research staff of this Federal Reserve Bank is more free market oriented than the others. For what it's worth. (P.O. Box 442, St. Louis, MO 63166)

U.S. Financial Data (weekly)

Monetary Trends (monthly)

National Economic Trends (monthly)

International Economic Conditions (quarterly)

Monthly Report

Magazines

Countryside (Waterloo, WI 53594; $16/18 issues)

Mother Earth News (105 Stoney Mtn. Rd., Hendersonville, NC 28739; ($12/6 issues)

Acres, USA (P.O. Box 9547, Raytown, MO 64113; $7/12 issues)

Organic Gardening & Farming (33 East Minor St., Emmaus, PA 18049; $7.85/12 issues)

Home Energy Digest (8009 34th Ave., So., Minneapolis, MN 55420; $7.95/4 issues)

Woodstove Directory (P.O. Box 4474, Manchester, NH 03108; $2.50/1 issue)

SERVICES AND PRODUCTS

Coins (survival)

Camino Coin Co.
P.O. Box 3131
San Mateo, CA 94403
(415) 341-7991

C. Rhyne & Associates
110 Cherry St., No. 202
Seattle, WA 98104
(206) 623-6900

Joel D. Coen
39 W. 55th St.
New York, NY 10019
(800) 223-0868 (U.S.A.)
(212) 246-5025 (New York)

Bramble Coins
P.O. Box 10026
Lansing, MI 48901
(800) 248-5952 (U.S.A.)

Bank of Nova Scotia
44 King St.
Toronto, Canada

Coins (rare, numismatic)

Camino Coin Co.
P.O. Box 3131
San Mateo, CA 94403
(415) 341-7991

Numisco
175 W. Jackson Blvd.
Chicago, IL 60604
(800) 621-5272

Coins (bank loans)

Deak National Bank
Main Street
Fleischmanns, NY 12430
(914) 254-5252

Food Storage

Simpler Life Foods
P.O. Box 671
Hereford, TX 79045
(806) 364-0730

Shiloh Farms
White Oak Rd.
Martindale, PA 17549
(717) 354-4936

Martens Foods
P.O. Box 5969
Tahoe City, CA 95730
(800) 824-7861 (U.S.A.)

Tools

Brookstone Catalog
127 Vose Farm Rd.
Peterborough, NH 03458

U.S. General Supply
100 General Pl.
Jericho, NY 11753

Survival Equipment

Survival, Inc.
16809 Central Ave.
Carson, CA 90746
(800) 421-2179 (U.S.A.)
(213) 631-6197 (Calif.)

Survival Counselling

Joel Skousen (West Coast)
903 State St.
Hood River,, OR 97031
(503) 386-6553

Survival Services (East Coast)
American Bureau of Economic Research
713 W. Cornwallis
Durham, NC 27707

Air Rifles

Beeman's
47 Paul Dr., Suite 25-B
San Rafael, CA 94903

Air Rifle Headquarters
P.O. Box 327
Grantsville, WV 26141

Storage Tanks

Industrial Fiberglass
3065 W. 21st St.
Salt Lake City, UT 84119
(801) 972-6658

Automotive Accessories

Frantz Oil Filter
P.O. Box 6188
Stockton, CA 95206

L.E.C. Lubricants
D.W. Adams, Inc.
13607 Braemar Dr.
Dallas, TX 75234

Insurance

David Holmes
Life Insurance Truth Society
1 Miletus Way
Cross Plains, TX 76443
(817) 725-6635

George Williams
Linscomb & Williams
5909 W. Loop, Suite 500
Houston, TX 77401
(713) 661-5000

"Penny" Mining Stocks

Sam Parks Co.
Seattle Trade Center
Suite 5109
2601 Elliott Ave.
Seattle, WA 98121
(800) 426-0598

Diamonds

Reliance Products
1900 Olympic Blvd.
Walnut Creek, CA 94596
(800) 227-1590 (U.S.A.)
(800) 642-2406 (Calif.)

American Diamond Co.
La Jolla Bank & Trust Bldg.
P.O. Box 2800
La Jolla, CA 92038
(800) 854-2288 (U.S.A.)
(714) 483-2100 (Calif.)

Financial Alternatives, Inc.
174 Currie-Hall Parkway
Kent, OH 44240
(216) 678-3791
(also colored stones)

Keogh Plans (retirement)

Lincoln Trust Co.
P.O. Box 5831
Denver, CO 80217

First Citizens Bank & Trust
P.O. Box 3028
Greenville, SC 29602

Security National Bank
1 Security Plaza
Kansas City, KS 66117

First State Bank of Oregon
1212 S.W. Main St.
Portland, OR 97207

Lafayette Bank & Trust Co.
345 State St.
Bridgeport, CT. 06604

Bank of Hickory Hills
7800 W. 95th
Hickory Hills, IL 60547

Money Market Funds

Capital Preservation Fund
459 Hamilton Ave.
Palo Alto, CA 94301
(800) 227-8380 (U.S.A.)
(800) 982-5844 (Calif.)

First Multifund for Income
32 East 57th Street
New York, NY 10022
(800) 221-7961

Directory of Money Market Funds
Hirsch Organization
Six Deer Trail
Old Tappan, NJ 07675
$1.00

INDEX*

---

*The letter "f." after a page number denotes "and page following;" "ff." denotes "and pages following."

217

ABOUT THE AUTHOR

Gary North received his Ph.D in history from the University of California, Riverside, having specialized in economic history. In 1971 he joined the senior staff of the Foundation for Economic Education (FEE) in Irvington-on-Hudson, New York. In 1973 he became the economist for the Pacific Coast Coin Exchange. He became a member of the staff of the Chalcedon Foundation in California in the summer of 1973, and he still serves in a part-time capacity for that organization. In 1976 he became research assistant for Congressman Ron Paul of Houston. (Paul lost his bid for re-election by 268 votes out of over 193,000 in November, 1976.)

He is the author of several books: *Marx's Religion of Revolution* (1968), *An Introduction to Christian Economics* (1973), *Puritan Economic Experiments* (1975), *None Dare Call It Witchcraft* (1976), and he edited a collection of essays on education, *Foundations of Christian Scholarship* (1976). His articles and reviews have appeared in over two dozen periodicals, including *The Wall Street Journal*, *Commercial & Financial Chronicle*, *Journal of Political Economy*, *National Review*, *Human Events*, *The Freeman*, *Modern Age*, *Numismatic News*, *COINage*, *Coin Mart*, *California Farmer*, *Private Practice*, *Christian Economics*, *Inflation Survival Letter*, and *The Alternative*.

Dr. North edits the bi-weekly economic report, *Remnant Review*, which is devoted to alternative investments: gold, silver, and other inflation-hedging possibilities. (It does not cover stocks and bonds.) He also edits the twice yearly scholars' periodical, *The Journal of Christian Reconstruction*.

Finally, he serves as executive director of the American Bureau of Economic Research, the publisher of *How You Can Profit from the Coming Price Controls*.

REMNANT REVIEW

You've read the book. You now have some idea of what is in store for the American economy. It's not a pretty picture. Depending on how long the controls stay on and how vigorously they are enforced, the economy is in for a long, hard battle with shortages, bottlenecks, and unnecessary costs. Once controls go on, the crisis is guaranteed.

You have information that very few Americans even suspect exists. You also have extra responsibilities. With all knowledge comes responsibility. Knowledge is power, and power must be exercised responsibly. You have to apply what you know. You have to keep up with the fast-breaking developments that relate to price controls and the shortage economy. You have to stay ahead of the pack if you to avoid being caught by the coming shortages. In short, you have to take appropriate action now, but you will have to take action in the future. There is no escape from this responsibility.

The question that now faces you is this: how to keep up the economic news that relates to price controls? Where to get the information? How to avoid the deliberate distorting of the bad news? The government and the conventional American news media are not going to be very helpful after controls are imposed.

There is one way to stay ahead of the news. That way is called *Remnant Review*. This bi-weekly newsletter comes out 22 times a year. Most of the information in this book appeared first in *Remnant Review*. I am the editor. So if you think the book makes sense, and you are convinced that the time of troubles is coming, you probably should subscribe.

Like most small circulation newsletters, mine doesn't accept advertising. It accepts no kickbacks. I write solely for the benefit of the subscribers. This power of the subscribers keeps me honest. It keeps me relevant. It forces me to keep up on what is going on. But the reader has to pay for this news, and on a cost-per-word basis, it's far more expensive than a regular magazine or mass circulation newspaper. You get information that is boiled down by someone who is alert to the effects of government-mandated price controls. Not many newspapers have the slightest idea of what controls are all about, and their readers are not kept informed. By subscribing to *Remnant Review*, you get access to early trends, plus news

HOW YOU CAN PROFIT FROM THE COMING PRICE CONTROLS

about alternative investment opportunities. I do the hard research, and you read the final results.

If you have appreciated the information presented in *How You Can Profit from the Coming Price Controls*, then you will appreciate *Remnant Review*.

Information is expensive. **The greatest mistake a person can make in economic matters is to assume that accurate, relevant information is practically free.** It is anything but free. No one knows everything in advance, but there are degrees of accuracy. The conventional press has done a poor job over the last decade in predicting such things as double-digit price inflation, price controls, shortages, the energy crisis, the rise of gold and silver, and numerous other "unconventional" topics. That's why thoughtful investors subscribe to a newsletter like *Remnant Review*.

As economic newsletters go, mine is reasonable. A lot of them cost $75, $100, even $200 a year. This one costs $60. Considering the economic disruptions that are coming, $60 isn't too much to pay to keep up with the news. If the newsletters saves you $60 a year (and it should), then you get to read the rest of the news free of charge. (Well, not quite; your time is valuable. But I keep the newsletter lively.) If you make money on the deal, as well as saving $60, then you're way ahead. (I don't cover stocks and bonds.)

Remnant Review is offered on a **money-back guarantee.** If, after receiving up to three issues, you decide you're not getting your money's worth, just ask for a 100% refund before the fourth issue is mailed. It's just that easy.

Why delay? If you do, you may forget how critical the coming months are: Procrastination is ridiculous when a crisis is brewing. Is $60 worth more to you than survival information? Write:

> Remnant Review
> 713 W. Cornwallis
> Durham, N.C. 27707

Gary North